Two for the Road

# TWO for the ROAD

## Our Love Affair with American Food

**JANE and MICHAEL STERN**

HOUGHTON MIFFLIN COMPANY

Boston    New York

First Houghton Mifflin paperback edition 2007

Visit our Web site: www.houghtonmifflinbooks.com.

*Library of Congress Cataloging-in-Publication Data*

Stern, Jane.
  Two for the road : our love affair with American food / Jane and Michael Stern.
      p. cm.
    Includes index.
    ISBN-13: 978-0-618-32963-2
    ISBN-10: 0-618-32963-3
1. Cookery, American.  2. Cookery—United States.
I. Stern, Michael, date.  II. Title.
    TX715.S84435 2006
    394.1'2097309511—dc22          2005031611
ISBN-13: 978-0-618-87268-8 (pbk.)
ISBN-10: 0-618-87268-X (pbk.)

Book design by Anne Chalmers
Text typefaces: Minion and Meta

Printed in the United States of America

MP 10 9 8 7 6 5 4 3 2 1

To Tom and Ellen Knox

# Acknowledgments

Without knowing it until fairly recently, we have been researching this book for thirty years. If it were possible to thank every person who has given us a good-eats tip or favorite recipe or who has shared advice, wisdom, and humor as we traveled around the country, these acknowledgments would be longer than the book itself. Our goals are always to find delicious food and fabulous places, but it is the people we meet along the way who make our job a joy.

Our hearts are especially filled with gratitude for those we work with every day. At *Gourmet* magazine we know we can count on Ruth Reichl, John "Doc" Willoughby, Larry Karol, James Rodewald, and Shannon Fox to be staunch allies and constant inspiration to write well, eat more, and travel fearlessly.

We started the roadfood journey many years ago alone, but today our colleagues at Roadfood.com are with us in spirit wherever we sit down to eat. How we savor the companionship, enthusiasm, and expertise of Big Steve Rushmore and Stephen Rushmore, Jr., Kristin Little, Marc Bruno, Cindy Keuchle, and Bruce Bilmes and Sue Boyle.

This book never would have materialized if not for the steadfast confidence of our editor, Rux Martin, who so often has been the compass we needed. From the beginning, Rux's presence has been relentless, maddening, cajoling, rousing, and ultimately magical. We thank her for making us better writers. We are also hugely grateful to our agent, Doe Coover, who believed in us even at times when we didn't believe in ourselves, and who has an amazing ability to make the world of publishing a pleasant place to be.

Finally, we thank Maryann Rudolph and all the nice kids and adults at Sunny Brook Farm, Ned Schankman, Priscilla Lightcap, Jackie Willing, and the Muttley Crew for ensuring that our beloved horses, dogs, and bird don't get lonely when we travel.

# Contents

# Two for the Road

# Two for the Road

Our first date was over a white clam pizza at Pepe's Pizzeria on Wooster Square in New Haven, Connecticut, and it was instantly apparent as we gazed into each other's eyes across the thin-crusted Neapolitan pie, speckled with tiny, tender clams and frosted with olive oil, that we shared a passion for garlic. Our initial lust for each other was fueled by an orgy of lobster rolls, split hot dogs, Yankee Doodle Double Dandy Doodle Burger cheeseburgers, calzones, and cannolis.

Michael had won a Woodrow Wilson Fellowship at Yale, where we had both gone to study art, so we had plenty of money to spend exploring restaurants up and down the Yankee shore. Compared to the average grad student, he was a high roller with a monthly stipend to squander. He also possessed what was, to Jane's New York City sensibility, an amazing status symbol: a car. At twenty-one, Jane had not yet learned how to drive. The car was our ticket to romance and to eating adventures.

The fellowship money was diverted from expensive textbooks and art museum field trips to fund a comparative study of the differences among pizzas as made by Pepe's, Sally's, and the Spot in the old Italian neighborhood, as well as the Greek-style pizzas at Pizza House, which was less than fifty yards from our apartment. If pizza was our major interest, we minored in fried dough at summertime fairs, clams and chowder and lobsters all along the coast, and Yorkshire pudding at Mory's, the Yalie dining club, where it was still possible to have a completely gelatinized meal, from aspic to Jell-O. Nearly every day, Michael had a choice to face: a seminar in medieval imagery in a dank basement lecture room in New Haven or a trip to the Rhode Island beaches with Jane for a shore dinner and a hot fudge sundae on ginger ice cream? Our passion for each other, and for finding things to eat, won out every time.

We were married in 1970, and a year later we got our degrees, which meant that the fellowship-subsidized grad school eating bonanza was coming to an end. It was the worst of times and the best of times. We moved to a little shack in the woods of Guilford, Connecticut, where we didn't even have a telephone. We were hiding out from life. Jane's mother and father died of cancer within a year of each other. Her stepfather disinherited her. Her two favorite cousins died, and her aunt was institutionalized. In despair, Jane made the fifteen-mile drive into New Haven three times a week to stare at the index cards in the Yale Employment Center. Michael spent his time cultivating and smoking cannabis. After tens of thousands of dollars were spent on our highfalutin educations, we realized we had little interest in pursuing what we had studied.

And so we did what generations of writers have done before us. We hit the road. The difference is that when we did so, we had no idea that we were to become writers. We just wanted to get away from everything.

We proposed a book about truck-stop dining to a young editor, who thought it was a cute idea and gave us the princely advance of $2,500. We thought we had won the lottery. But after signing the contract to write the book, we froze. Who were we to write about food, even truck-stop food? Where did we come off, telling people what was good to eat? Our shared mental image of a restaurant critic was gleaned from old movies: a patrician fellow with a silk ascot, his pinkie in the air and a sneer on his face. Somebody like Vincent Price but soured with indigestion. Restaurant critics were gourmets, and gourmets ate such grotesque things as creamed snails, sick-looking liver pâtés, cheeses that smelled like feet, and odd organs from inside unusual animals. In our mind's eye, gourmet food was joke food, like what you might be forced to ingest during a fraternity hazing. We preferred hamburgers, mashed potatoes, and apple cobbler.

The notion that we had promised our publisher to write a coast-to-coast guidebook was overwhelming. We had pretty much not gone anywhere at all. We had no knowledge of exactly where these marvelous truck stops were, scant experience writing, and no money beyond the first half of our advance.

We sat together at the kitchen table of our $99-per-month cabin trying to figure out what to do. The one-room shack where we lived might seem romantic if you saw it in the movies, but in real life it was hideously uncomfortable. After living there for nearly a year, we discovered a case of decomposing dynamite in the crawlspace above the ceiling, left behind by a 1960s radical who was a former tenant. The gas stove was so old and decrepit that it once combusted and singed Jane's eyebrows off as she checked on a roasting chicken. This home of ours was a good incentive for getting on the road.

We agreed on a plan: we would review every restaurant in America. This seemed not the slightest bit of a stretch to us. Not having traveled much, we looked at the Rand McNally map spread out on the kitchen table and could plainly see that America was a manageable place, no more than a foot and a half in length, composed of pretty pastel-colored states balanced on one another like building blocks.

Strategy well in place, we launched into part two of the plan: buying a suitable car for the journey. Just as buying a new handbag has always been Jane's favorite antidote for whatever ails her, buying a car is Michael's solution to just about any problem. Even Sigmund Freud would blush at the patent sexual symbolism of both objects, but we were too young and dumb to notice or care.

At a nearby car dealership, we met a salesman whose necktie we remember to this day, more than a quarter century later. Somehow this guy had managed to knot it absolutely flat, so that its front apron cascaded directly from his collar with no lump whatsoever, sort of like a sheet of molten polyester. As we told the salesman our needs and he touted the glories of the new '75 Chevy line, we paid far more attention to his neckwear than to vehicular statistics. When we finally stopped marveling at it and told him our budget, he became significantly less chummy, got up from his desk, and led us around to the back lot, where the less alluring and less expensive used vehicles were kept, out of sight of new-car shoppers. He pointed to a pre-owned Chevrolet Suburban. It was vomit green — the barf of someone who lived on frozen peas. Several body panels had been painted in a shop that didn't worry too much about matching the factory-original metallic color, so it had become a kind of rolling ode to all possible avocado hues, including even black (the hood). It was huge and it was ugly, something like a cross between a World War II tank and an over-the-hill Brady Bunch station wagon.

Jane grimaced at the sight of it. Michael tried to convince her that it had a rugged look, befitting the intrepid travelers we wanted to be. He lifted the hood and looked at the engine, pretending to know what he was inspecting. And just to show the salesman that we were no patsies when it came to purchasing a roadworthy vehicle, we both walked around and kicked all four tires. They didn't pop on impact, but neither did any of them appear to have a lot of tread.

One thing the car had in its favor was vast amounts of room inside. To save money in our travels, we planned to camp out in it, forgoing motel rooms.

"I'll sew curtains and we can hang them on the back windows for privacy," Jane said optimistically, never having sewn anything in her life.

"And it does have two air conditioners," Michael noted. "We won't be hot!"

By the time we wrote the check, we were convinced that this heap would be a rather deluxe residence on wheels for the next two years.

The following morning, on the way to the grocery store, the left rear tire blew. And that summer gas prices doubled. We faced the first big gas crisis in a vehicle that got approximately eight miles to the gallon.

Jane had plenty of time to sew curtains for the back windows, because five months into the research for *Roadfood*, we had not yet left Connecticut. In fact, we hadn't even left New Haven County.

Yale had trained us to be meticulous in our research, and, ever the diligent academics, we commenced work on the guidebook by picking up the local Yellow Pages and opening to "Restaurant." We began with those starting with the letter *A*. We ate at the Acropolis Diner and made notes about the good souvlaki. We went to Addie's Café, where we didn't much care for the hash browns, then on to Angela's Pizzeria, where we thought the pepperoni pie was better then the sausage, and Archie Moore's tavern, where the beer inevitably distracted us from our mission of sampling the menu.

At the end of five months we had gotten to Donat's, an overreaching French restaurant where rich professors ate, and had yet to travel more than twelve miles from home. We envisioned the millennia that stretched out before we began reviewing restaurants in, say, Kansas.

Something was wrong with our plan.

"People will not take us seriously if we haven't eaten everywhere," moaned Jane, who, like so many writers, lives in constant fear that someone will discover she doesn't know everything — or anything at all.

"Tough shit," Michael responded. Jane thought he had a point.

We sat down at the kitchen table again, scrutinized the map, and came up with a new plan.

With a Magic Marker we drew a squiggly continuous line through forty-eight states. It would take a full two years and countless tanks of gas to travel this route, but at least we would finally get on the road. We would see all the pretty pastel states and eat in every one of them.

The new plan in place, we went shopping for supplies. We loaded the cavernous green Suburban with inflatable mattresses, sleeping bags, mosquito netting, snakebite kits, and everything else two urban Jews who had never slept anywhere but in a bed figured they would need to camp out.

"*No!*" Michael railed as Jane insisted on buying tin plates, a small Coleman stove, and a stack of collapsible cutlery. "We are going to be eating in a dozen restaurants every day," he said. "The last thing we're going to want to do when we make camp is cook another meal."

Jane added a portable oxygen tank to the stash of material, because she was convinced that she would not be able to breathe in mountainous states like Colorado.

We were good to go. We spent a whole day packing the Suburban with supplies to take us across the country and through all seasons. The lumpy calico curtains Jane had sewn for the back-seat area made the car even uglier, if that was possible. We turned the skeleton key in the lock of our cabin door and drove away.

We sped west out of Connecticut over the Hudson River and into New Jersey. First stop: early lunch in a diner. Ahh yes, a New Jersey diner! What could be a more excellent start to our adventure?

Sadly, the food was mediocre; the mashed potatoes were made from a powdered mix. When we asked the waitress what kind of pie there was, she answered, "Red." Sure enough, the slice we got was sweet translucent red mucilage without even a hint of fruit. We got off the Jersey Turnpike a few exits farther south and found a place called Nature's Cupboard. It was a vegetarian restaurant run by Woodstock alumni, and it smelled more like Nature's Locker Room. We didn't bother to order, just turned around and headed south again. After three more unproductive stops at highway exit ramps, where we found rubbery chicken croquettes, a desiccated Philly cheese steak, and cardboard-crusted pizza, our enthusiasm was waning. By the time we got to Maryland, it was suppertime.

We decided to spend our first night on the road at a place called Jellystone Park, one of a national chain of campgrounds that feature a goofy image of Yogi Bear to welcome visitors. For a few bucks paid to a lady at the gatehouse, we were directed to a small plot of turf where we were told to park and set up.

The gatekeeper knew of no restaurants anywhere near the park, but she did direct us to a convenience store, where we bought ready-made ham sandwiches on white bread, bags of potato chips, and cans of soda, which we ate sitting in the front seat of our car in the store parking lot. We drove to our spot at Jellystone Park to bed down for the night.

The place was filled with families in oversized motor homes with small cars attached to the back. Their immense recreational vehicles sprouted TV antennas and had golf carts and lawn chairs lashed to the roof. Many of them were plastered with decals proclaiming their owners' membership in the Good Sam club, meaning they were certifiably nice people — good Samaritans — who would pull alongside a wounded or disabled fellow traveler to offer help. On the backs of some of the big rolling homes, the owners had their names painted in florid script, generally using the errant apostrophe so common on mailboxes everywhere: "The Smith's: Bill and Edna."

The RV community took one look at our overgrown station wagon and turned their backs on us. They may have been Good Sams to one another, but we were clearly not in their league. We didn't have a real motor home with a television and kitchen and wall-to-wall carpeting, and besides, the curtains Jane had stitched were flagrantly homemade. They hated us. We hated them.

"Don't you just know those stupid Winnebagos are going to be clogging every superhighway from here to California," Michael groused, imagining us at the end of a long line of motor homes traveling at thirty miles an hour from coast to coast, staring for weeks at the ass end of "The Smith's: Bill and Edna." It was at that moment that we vowed to travel only on back roads — a spur-of-the-moment decision that determined the path for our eating career.

The RV camp-out was the longest night of our lives. We tossed and turned on the clammy rubber air mattresses. The Suburban, which had seemed so big when it was empty, came to feel as claustrophobic as a mummy's sarcophagus. Despite the mosquito netting, which had a habit of getting tangled around our legs, we were soon swatting at bugs the size of velociraptors, and when we had to pee in the middle of the night, we were too afraid to make the trek to the Jellystone restrooms, lest a bear eat us. Despite all our snakebite kits and collapsible silverware, we had forgotten to take along a flashlight.

We left at dawn in despair and sold all the camping junk at the first pawnshop we saw. Back in our newly roomy car, we drove away from that first unpleasant night on the road with our culinary dreams dashed. We meandered south along back roads, finding nothing notable to eat. At twilight we were so tired that we pulled into the first roadside motel that didn't look as if Norman Bates was the proprietor. Entering our unit, as the motel-keeper referred to the room, we blinked in awe at the modernity of a television set and a tiled shower stall, feeling a little like Ishi, the Stone Age tribesman wandering out of the woods into civilization for the first time. We slept wonderfully, and when the sun rose in the morning, we were so happy not to be surrounded by huge, hostile motor homes, we even thought our Suburban looked rather sleek and handsome.

We pushed an eight-track Merle Haggard tape into the slot, and as Merle serenaded us with songs of workin' men, we cruised in the direction of the nearest little town on the map, at least ten miles away from the interstate.

It was a pretty south Virginia hamlet of clapboard houses with broad front porches. The rising sun cast the long shadows of ancient oak trees across tidy front lawns. An old man wearing overalls sat on a wooden chair and waved at us as we drove by his porch. We passed children riding their bikes in what we assumed was the direction of the schoolyard. We were traveling at bicycle speed ourselves, just taking in the sights.

"I smell biscuits," Michael said, leaning his head out the open window and driving where his nose led him, toward a storefront café on the main street. Outside, the pickup trucks of customers were lined up on a diagonal, along with two local police cruisers. Pansies spilled forth from the bright blue flowerboxes under the café windows.

There was not a single out-of-state license plate on the vehicles in the street except for ours.

Despite the ache of hunger, we hesitated as we stepped from our car into the street. This was the mid-1970s, and according to *Easy Rider* and *Deliverance*, it was them against us, and everyone who wasn't us was a redneck with a shotgun aimed in our direction. At this point, no one would have mistaken Michael for a local farmer. His hair grazed his shoulders and he wore wire-rimmed glasses like John Lennon's. Jane's outfit included an embroidered peasant blouse with jangling earrings. We would have gone unnoticed at any eastern college campus coffeehouse, but suddenly we were nervous about going inside.

Our growling stomachs got the better of us. On the back wall, coffee cups hung on a pegboard, each one marked with the name of the customer to whom it belonged. A dozen men in work clothes sat at a big round table right at the front of the café, drinking from their personalized mugs, looking out the window, commenting on who was driving past, and trading news. Seated at other tables, men and women chatted back and forth to each other as in a home kitchen.

As the door swung closed behind us, all conversation stopped. Every person in the café looked at us. We froze as they looked us up and down. In that long, long moment, we couldn't help but notice the thick oval plates of ham and eggs and hot biscuits in front of nearly everybody in the place. The smell of peppery cream gravy, salt-cured country ham, and fresh-brewed coffee made us dizzy with hunger. Still, we didn't dare make a move.

"There's two seats over there," a waitress called to us from behind the counter. We sat down fast on a pair of chrome-banded uphol-stered stools at a marble counter so old that it seemed to have an even row of indentations where decades of elbows had rested. Two nonper-sonalized coffee cups were placed in front of us, already filled and with a spoon plunked in each, ready to stir. Slowly the hum in the room began to increase as the breakfasters reanimated.

The waitress stood before us, order pad in hand. "We don't get too many strangers passing through here since the interstate was built," she said, apparently aware of our discomfort. "We just ain't never seen y'all before."

Minutes after we ordered, the empty counter space in front of us filled with thick partitioned plates made of unbreakable blue plastic, the big partition holding ham and eggs, the two smaller ones containing grits and stewed apples. Four hot biscuits loosely wrapped in wax paper were nestled in a plastic basket. Little dishes held pats of butter, and glass ramekins were filled with wine-dark cherry preserves. Sold in Mason jars by the cash register, they were made a few miles away. As we ate, we picked up the eight-page local newspaper that a previous counter-sitter had left behind and read all about the potluck dinner that the Baptist church was having and about the damage done to Elroy Schmidt's mailbox when the school bus accidentally backed into it. We read the frantic letter asking anyone who had seen Buck Thompson's bluetick hound to please call the sheriff.

We ate until blissfully satisfied, and as we rose to pay at the cash register, a man also walking up to pay his bill stood aside, tipped his cap, and politely allowed Jane to proceed ahead of him. His harshly lined farmer's face and sweat-darkened mesh work cap had seemed ominous when we entered, but this courtly gesture and his soft "Morning, ma'am" made us realize how off-base our fears had been.

Out in the street, three other men were staring at our license plates. "Connect-tee-cut," one of them said out loud, impressed by the jawbreaking complexity of our home state's name.

"That is some fine vehicle," another said to Michael, who repressed the urge to sell him the Suburban on the spot.

"Thanks," Michael said. "And that's one nice café you have here. Good breakfast."

"You come back soon," they said as we got in and turned the key in the ignition.

We looked at each other and smiled. The biscuits and country ham had left a glow on our taste buds, and our spirits had been warmed by the community of people we had stumbled into. We gazed at the map of the U.S.A. with the squiggly route we had drawn all over it. The long line no longer seemed like a daunting task. Now it was a wide-open door.

Hungry for more, we drove on.

# Southern Café Stewed Apples

We always liked apple pie, apple crisp, apple dumplings, and apple brown Betty, but we hadn't encountered side dishes of stewed apples until we ate in the South. The ones we had in our Virginia breakfast were a revelation, and since then we have come to appreciate fully the luxury of tender, long-cooked apples as a great companion for pig meat — country ham, pork chops, even barbecue — and especially as a sweet balance for bitter greens or tangy green tomatoes on an all-vegetable plate.

- 4 tart apples (Rome or Granny Smith), cored, peeled, and sliced into chunks no larger than 1 inch
- 1½ cups water
- ⅓ cup light brown sugar
- 2 tablespoons all-purpose flour
- ¼ teaspoon salt
- ½ teaspoon ground cinnamon

Combine all the ingredients in a medium saucepan. Stir well and cook at a low simmer for 30 to 45 minutes, stirring frequently, until the apples are tender but not falling apart. Serve warm or hot.

6 SERVINGS

# New Haven White Clam Pizza

Frank Pepe's Pizzeria Napoletana in New Haven makes white clam pizza only when tiny fresh littleneck clams from Rhode Island are available. When the supply runs out for the day, that's the end of it. Shortly after discovering this pizza, we went back to Pepe's, waited in the inevitable line for an hour, and got our booth — only to be informed that the kitchen had just run out of clams. That shortage caused us to learn to cook. Over the course of a weekend, we bought a pizza peel and stone, figured out how to stretch a bomb of dough, and made the first of what seem like several thousand white clam pizzas.

If you plan on baking more than the occasional pizza, it makes sense to do as we did and invest in a pizza stone and a baker's peel to slide the pizzas in and out. This recipe calls for both, although it is possible to use a cookie sheet (if you can tolerate less than brittle-crisp crust).

THE DOUGH

- 1   package dry yeast
- 1   teaspoon sugar
- 1   cup warm water
- 2–2¾   cups all-purpose flour
- 2   teaspoons salt
- Cornmeal

THE TOPPING

- 3   large garlic cloves
- 3   tablespoons olive oil
- 1   dozen just-shucked littleneck clams
- 1   teaspoon dried oregano
- 2   tablespoons grated Parmesan cheese

MAKE THE DOUGH: Dissolve the yeast and sugar in $1/4$ cup of the warm water in a small bowl. Stir the remaining $3/4$ cup water into 2 cups of the flour in a large bowl. Add the salt, and when the yeast is bubbly, add it, too. Stir it all together and turn the dough out onto a floured board. Let the dough rest while you clean and oil a large ceramic bowl.

Knead the dough vigorously for a full 15 minutes, adding flour if necessary to create a silky dough. Return it to the bowl and cover it with two tight layers of plastic wrap. Let it rise in a warm place until doubled in size, 2 to 3 hours.

Place a pizza stone on the bottom rack of the oven and preheat the oven to 450 degrees.

Punch down the dough and flatten it on a lightly floured board. Pounding with the heel of your hand, carefully and methodically work the dough into a circle no more than $1/4$ inch thick in the center, rising to a $1/2$-inch ring around the circumference. Sprinkle a baker's peel generously with cornmeal and put the circle of dough on it. Cover it lightly with a sheet of plastic wrap (so it doesn't dry out) and let it rest while you open the clams.

MAKE THE TOPPING: While the dough is resting, mince the garlic and let it steep in the olive oil. After the dough has rested for 10 to 12 minutes, brush on the oil and garlic, leaving the half-inch circumference untouched. Spread the clams around the pie with a dash of their own juice. Sprinkle on the oregano and cheese.

TO BAKE: Use the baker's peel to transfer the pizza to the preheated stone in the oven. (The cornmeal will act as miniature ball bearings to help it slide neatly onto the stone.)

Bake for 15 minutes, or until the crust is light brown. Remove the pizza, slice, and serve with beer or soda and plenty of napkins.

MAKES ONE 12-INCH PIZZA, 2 SERVINGS

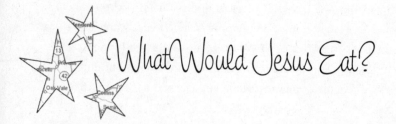

# What Would Jesus Eat?

In that first year of travel, we were dazzled by the food we found when venturing into unlikely restaurants in small towns and off two-lane highways. Soon we felt most at home when we were away from home. We grew accustomed to café patrons swiveling their heads when we entered and folks on sidewalks staring as we drove slowly past, windows down, sniffing for cinnamon buns hot from the oven. It wasn't only the two of us who didn't fit the average local profile. After our big Suburban got rear-ended by a fully loaded gravel truck on the border of North and South Carolina, our fallback transportation was a series of junky student-style cars guaranteed to raise suspicion among Detroitcentric drivers everywhere. They always seemed to break down in some place like Uncertain, Texas, or Enigma, Georgia, where the mechanics regarded a VW bug as a far-fetched exotic and we got all kinds of advice about investing in a reasonable vehicle, such as a Ford pickup.

Despite second-rate wheels, we grew to feel that the road was where we belonged. Invariably, after a few weeks of being stuck in our rented Connecticut shack, in which the Unabomber would have felt at home, we became ravenous for more local specialties and itched to see more of the country we were falling in love with.

Travel did wonders for us as a couple. As we sailed along the highways and back roads, going deeper and deeper into a mysterious America, we came to rely on each other's company and comfort. De-

16

spite frequent elbow battles for the car's armrest and endless debates about which seafood shack ladled up the best chowder, our shared discoveries became a bond of security between us in an otherwise strange world. Nowadays we carry a notebook computer and a cell phone, and *USA Today* is everywhere, so travelers feel not so far from home. But when we started, being in rural America felt like traveling the dark side of the moon. Our cheap motel rooms often had no phones, and our car's AM radio picked up nothing but static. At night, we clung to each other under thin blankets. We rubbed each other's back, we drank Jack Daniel's at midnight, we hummed the theme songs from the *Mary Tyler Moore Show* and *The Bob Newhart Show* just to feel at home. We thought about sophisticated urbane movies from the 1950s that had bright yellow Checker cabs and people in nice gray business suits.

A quarter-century ago, the American landscape was very different from what it is today. We feel 150 years old to admit that when we started hunting for roadfood, there were no Wal-Marts, no Kmarts, no Home Depots, no Targets, no Outbacks, no Olive Gardens, no Red Lobsters, and no Starbuckses. There was fast food, but it wasn't everywhere. This was a good thing.

Every place we went looked different. Today, a lot of Connecticut looks like Arizona, which looks like North Carolina, which looks like Illinois. It is possible to crisscross this country and never eat, shop, or stay in a strange place. This is not a good thing.

In the early days of hunting for roadfood, we rarely stayed in a chain motel. The chains simply did not exist in the small towns and on the back roads. More typical were mom-and-pop places, dirt cheap and with amenities to match: bathmats made of paper like a diner placemat, bars of soap about the size of a pack of matches, a small TV chained to the cinderblock wall to prevent theft. Side tables were edged with cigarette burns, bedsprings groaned, and we became masters of bedding down without allowing any skin to touch the horrible old bedspread.

We prayed that the people next door would not be killers, hookers, or truckers who left their refrigerator trucks idling all night just outside the front door. One night during our first cross-country trip, we checked into a bleak place on the road through Mineral Wells, Texas. As the sun set, we could hear the town's tough guys screeching their tires and catcalling at women up and down the main drag. We were sure we heard gunfire. We chained the door and shivered under the motel's skinny excuse for a blanket, waiting for morning and praying to get out of town alive. In one truly hideous motel in Florida, the screaming and fighting in the room next door escalated so drastically that we checked out at 11 P.M., found the first highway entrance, hit 70 mph, and drove until we reached the safety of dawn.

We were hotel virgins. We had never set foot in a Ritz-Carlton or Four Seasons. We didn't know about turndown service, chocolates on the pillow, valet parking, health clubs, or duvets made of eiderdown. Our idea of luxury was a motel that had a washer and dryer available to the public and a paper sash across the bowl of the toilet announcing that it had been sanitized for our protection.

As uncomfortable as some accommodations might have been, the nighttime dread of our low-budget travels was eclipsed by the joys we found in cheap, nonchain restaurants. Before fast food muscled its way into town, nearly every place had at least one good café. Maybe it was on the town square, and in the clean light of morning it looked scrubbed and pretty. When we started writing about such places, we had no clue as to how to find them. Gradually we developed roadfood radar. Here are some of the don'ts we learned early on:

> Don't eat at the fancy place with the biggest ad in the Yellow Pages.

➤ Don't ask the desk clerk for help.
➤ Don't believe billboards on the highway.
➤ Don't eat in a place that smells like Pine-Sol.
➤ Don't eat in a place where the waitress coughs a lot and scratches her hair with her pencil.
➤ Don't eat in a restaurant that touts itself as world-famous.
➤ Beware of any restaurant with too cute a name: Klem's Kuntry Kitchen, Ye Ol' Village Smithy, Toot 'n' Com-In.
➤ The bigger the catering facilities, the worse the food.

On the flip side, we learned to seek out any place that

➤ is open only for breakfast and lunch.
➤ serves no booze.
➤ has old ladies with hairnets working in the kitchen.
➤ has handmade pies proudly displayed in a glass case on the counter.
➤ has jukeboxes that still contain Hank Williams songs.
➤ is outfitted with Formica-topped tables with a boomerang pattern.
➤ has weird ways of ordering a meal, like a telephone connected to the kitchen or miniature order pads that customers fill out with a miniature pencil.

From the beginning we were charmed by the South. Unlike Wyoming and the big square states that loomed on the left side of the map, the South was fairly easy to get to. It was at most a three-day drive from our Connecticut home. But there was something else appealing about it. The South has a reputation for hospitality, and despite our sense of being oddballs in the culture, we felt welcome there.

Everything was wildly strange compared to the life we had known in the Northeast and Midwest. We were struck by the ubiquity of signs and billboards that welcomed everyone who passed to various churches, usually Baptist but often something strange and exciting, like African Apostolic or Snake-Handling Charismatic. Sometimes the religious advertisements were truly flabbergasting, like a huge billboard that showed teeny-weenie mortals in the shadow of a gigantic Jesus urging passersby to have "Fun in the Son" and a movable-letter sign outside a small church that warned, "I'll Be Back to Get You Soon. Love, Jesus." And what is one to make of a poster inviting one and all to an "Antiabortion and Fish-Fry Rally"?

We fantasized about going through some of those church doors on Sunday, learning the hymns and shaking hands with people in pews to the right and to the left of us. While we did not attend services, we regularly bonded with the churchgoers in our own road-foodish way. We always tried to find the café in town that served a big Sunday meal after church. It became a ritual to stake out a table with a sweeping view of the room and wait for the surge of hungry parishioners to fill up the place at noontime.

We had the most amazing such meal at the Mendenhall Hotel in Mendenhall, Mississippi, where the popular boarding-house tradition of round-table dining was invented in 1915. Each of the room's three tables was surrounded by a dozen chairs, and in the center of each was a lazy Susan on which were crowded bowls and platters of everything the kitchen cooked that day.

The morning we came across the place, Fred Morgan, the grandson of the man who built the original tables, stood at the door greeting friends and neighbors fresh from church. The crowd coming in reminded us of the Jell-O selection in a top-of-the-line cafeteria: a kaleidoscope of colored clothing, spangles, frills, and lacy poufs, men in baby-blue polyester suits with white plastic shoes, ladies with church hats as broad and fanciful as something you would see at the

Ascot races, tiny girls in lace anklets, their blond hair a mass of curls and ribbons, little boys in what look like formal white mini-tuxedos. Oh, bliss! We watched these people eat as though this were their last meal on earth. Damn the white tuxes and the floral sprigged silk frocks — they plowed into food like trenchermen. Plates of fried chicken became denuded skeletons, yeast rolls were squished down to mop the last of the giblet gravy, and shrieks about the goodness of the pecan (emphasis on the first syllable) pie rang in the air.

Frankly, we had trouble figuring out the revolving-table strategy, but the unspoken etiquette of such places requires old-timers to show newcomers how it works. One white-suited gent who looked like a skinny Colonel Sanders saw that our boarding-house reach simply wasn't quick enough to hook the fried chicken when it went past, so he advised, "When that plate you want comes your way, grab the whole thing. Help yourself, then put it back in any empty spot that circles past." We soon learned another aspect of round-table etiquette: eating slowly is impolite. After all, more parishioners are coming for Sunday supper, so it's not right to dine at a leisurely pace. Even gracious southern ladies in frilly summer dresses and polite gentlemen in seersucker jackets sat down and dug in immediately and without hesitation and continued eating and piling up their plates with more food until they were done. A corollary etiquette note: at a round-table meal, you can talk with your mouth full. Speed-eating supercharges people's appetites for conversation, and it is rare indeed for anyone to sit through lunch or dinner in silence. The most popular topic by far is food; rhapsodizing about what you're eating while you're eating it adds to the bliss of the communal dining experience.

A great cafeteria can vastly enhance the joy of Sunday supper, too. Bryce's, where the people of Texarkana have been standing in line to dine since 1931, belongs in the roadfood dictionary as the definition of *bountiful.* We discovered it the first time we drove from the Ozarks into Texas. Like others in the upper echelon of cafeteria-style restaurants, Bryce's puts desserts at the head of the line. The logic is that if the cakes and pies were at the end, there would be no room on anyone's tray for them. We were starving, so we grabbed banana pudding with a halo of meringue on top and, to keep it company, hot peach cobbler with a lattice crust. Then came salads, which again meant choosing multiple things: hunks of ice-cold coral-colored melon, tiny shards of fresh cabbage in bright cole slaw, pickly things like beets and marinated cauliflower, and then the best of all, a slew of "congealed" salads, which is southern for outrageous blocks of bright blue gelatin and fluffy pink Jell-O with pineapple chunks and red-hot candies. By the time we had passed the salads, our imbalanced meals looked like stained glass, and we had taken so much that we had to run back for supplementary trays and pull them along like a four-car freight train.

Now came the big decision, the entrée, and because it was Sunday, a huge ham and a steamship round of beef stood ready to be sliced by the stalwart-looking lady at the cutting board. Every southern buffet server knows not to crowd the meats against the side dishes, so after the meats were plated, we pointed to the broccoli casserole and stewed turnip greens and candied yams graced with itty-bitty marshmallows and spicy triangles of jalapeño cornbread and big puffy yeast rolls and green beans simmered forever with a thick ham bone, each of which was proffered in a plate of its own. We had just enough room on the secondary trays for glasses of iced sweet tea and a few margarine pats for the rolls.

Aside from how wonderful the food was, what amazed us most about such meals was their cost. For enough food to feed a small village or two Sterns, we paid $5 or $6 back in the mid-1970s. Today the bill might be $15 — not much more than you'd pay for a few Mc-Something-or-others handed to you in a paper bag.

One of the first hurdles we overcame down South was being Jewish in a culture that is so assertively Christian.

At a lunch counter in North Carolina, a waitress skidded toward us on industrial-strength rubber shoes and asked Jane, "Jewish tea?"

"What?" Jane croaked. "'Jewish tea?'" she whispered to Michael. "Do you think they have special tea set aside for Jews?"

"No," Michael explained. "She said, 'Djyou wish tea?'"

Jane was not entirely convinced.

Of course there are many southern Jews, and there have been for generations. But it took us a while to figure this out by understanding nuances of the conversations we had with locals. They would ask us in an ultrapolite way if we were "in dry goods." We had no idea why they thought this. It certainly had nothing to do with the beauty of our attire, which on the road consisted usually of blue jeans and food-stained T-shirts. It wasn't until a friend of ours, born in Mississippi, explained that a lot of Jews who went South in the nineteenth century opened clothing stores, two of the best-known being the Schwab family of Memphis and the Berlins of Charleston.

Given our cultural denseness on this matter, you can imagine that it took us a long time to work out one of the absolute rules of finding roadfood in the South: there is a direct correlation between the excellence of the food and the number of pictures of Jesus on the wall. This is true in all kinds of restaurants, but especially in barbecues, where the Lord frequently shares wall space with pictures of pigs.

Of course, pigs are not worshipped in the South, but the image of the pig in and around barbecue restaurants provides comfort, security, and joy, which dovetails with similar feelings instilled by religious belief. We felt irreverent, if not actually sinful, making note of this fact until we walked into Hannah's Bar-B-Q in Lenoir, North Carolina, one day before lunch hour and saw a waitress merrily tidying up the vast collection of pig figurines along shelves and tables throughout the restaurant. Oblivious of us as she dusted, she was exuberantly singing the soprano part of "A Mighty Fortress Is Our God," no doubt something she performed with a church choir. Among her piggy statuettes, salt-and-pepper shakers, and cookie jars were several original portraits of a crowned, cape-wearing oinker carrying a fork like a royal scepter. She later explained to us that this plump-faced hog is named Bobby-Q Pig and is the superhero mascot of Hannah's. Bobby-Q's wall space was interspersed with signs throughout the establishment reminding customers that JESUS IS LORD. When the woman noticed us behind her in the room, she turned around and smiled, walked to a counter to pick up two menus, pointed us to a table, and joined us there, never once missing a word or note of her song. She handed us the menus just when she reached the last line — "His kingdom is forever!" — her voice hitting a crescendo nearly high enough to crack the ceramic pigs on her shelves. As we opened the menus, she made us jump with the enthusiasm of her "Amen!"

As we see it, the art of smoke-cooking meat and an honest devotion to God depend on similar qualities of character. Making great barbecue is a slow and simple process that requires faith more than showboat technique. Ask the great pitmasters why their "cue" is so delicious, and few will boast of secret ingredients or unique talents. They speak humbly of their belief in a primordial process by which mundane ingredients transcend themselves and become something divine. Those who tend the smoke pit never tell you that *they* are the ones who make the magic happen. They merely facilitate it by stacking the hickory logs in the right way and tending the pork butts with care.

Our pigs-plus-Jesus theory of great barbecue crystallized at Harold's in Atlanta, a grand urban smoke pit that has built a half-century's reputation on velvet-soft sliced pork, racks of meaty ribs, and bowls of old-fashioned Brunswick stew. We were tipped off to it by an Atlanta native who said the barbecue was fantastic but warned us in dire terms to go to Harold's only during daylight hours, as it was a very scary place. Our tipster was partly correct. Harold's neighborhood, anchored by a federal penitentiary, is grim indeed. The cinderblock and brick building, with bars on every window, isn't exactly welcoming. But Harold's sign features good old southern comfort in the form of a pig wearing wire-rimmed glasses, his tongue wagging with pleasure as he sits atop a roaring flame. Curiously, pigs on signs in the South are always happy, even when the signs show them being cooked for supper.

The moment we walked into Harold's, any anxiety generated by the mean streets outside dissipated. For one thing, the wood-paneled walls were draped with all manner of earnest religious homilies, including this one above the door to the rear dining room: "God has time to listen if you have time to pray." And there was no way we could feel ignored when confronted by a staff who treated us as though we were new congregants appearing at church, their job being to bring us close to the bosom of the Lord. In this case, they wanted to make sure we were comfortable at our counter seats although more commodious tables were available. We said that we liked the counter because it afforded a view of the grate over hot coals where pork sandwiches were heated. From that moment on, both the cook and the waitress made it their business to step aside so as not to block our view of the warming food, and when Michael pulled out a camera to take pictures, the cook took extra care to make sure the pork slices on the bread were piled high and neatly.

After lunch we stepped outside and walked around back to get our car. One of Harold's pit men pushed past us wheeling a grocery store cart. The cart was heavy, filled with split logs retrieved from a shed behind the restaurant, and its wheels were wobbling out of alignment. It took a huge amount of energy to drive that cart over rough pavement from the shed to the pit inside. "Is that your secret?" we asked as the man paused to wipe his brow. "You cook the pork over hickory wood?"

He shook his head and explained that you should not cook anything directly over burning wood. Once the wood was taken inside, it would be made into charcoal, and the coals were used for cooking. "Flames are bad," he said in no uncertain terms. "The glow is good." He explained that the puffs of smoke wafting from the coals gave pork its succulence, and then he went on at great length to tell us exactly what kind of glow is needed on the coals to produce smoke with the right temperature and tang. "Yellow-gold is what you want," he said. "White-hot coal is lazy, and red will burn." In our minds we pictured a badly constructed barbecue engulfed in Hades' flames and a good one floating on a balmy cloud of hickory smoke.

After a few years of hunting for roadfood, we realized that we had begun to refer to our very favorite places as shrines, and indeed, when we set out for a favorite restaurant a thousand miles from home, we did so with all the anticipatory joy of a pilgrim on a sacred journey. We had no Bible to direct us, but we did have a few roadfood reverends on whom we could always rely for veritable sermons of where to eat and what to eat when we got there. One of these was a guy who sent us a list of a dozen or so favorite places about once every two years. The list was written in ballpoint pen on blue-lined notebook paper and included minimal description: "Carter House, Waycross, Georgia, chicken and dumplings." The notes were signed "Bill

Yankee," which we began to suspect was a nom de plume, since Mr. Yankee never included a return address or phone number and communicated precious little about who he was or why, in heaven's name, he regularly found such celestial places to eat. But as we tried his suggestions, we realized that this Bill Yankee, whoever he was, had impeccable taste and was always to be trusted. So when he sent us a note with a single suggestion on it, we paid heed. The note said, "I've eaten a lot of barbecue, but the Ridgewood Restaurant in east Tennessee is the best. In fact, if you try it and don't rate it four stars, send me your bill and I'll pay for your meal." We were on our way.

Long before GPS and Mapquest, getting lost was our lifestyle. As we drove through the east Tennessee hills on a road that twisted into a realm of primitive otherworldliness, we felt like strangers in a strange land. Through a tunnel of trees, we passed preplumbing log homes with dilapidated La-Z-Boy recliners on their front porches for the residents' relaxation. As foreign as it seemed, it wasn't scary, for every porch-sitter we drove by waved hello as if the passing of a car were a happy event. The homes showed little visible décor, but every one featured at least one quasi-religious icon: a tacked-up velvet rug of Elvis with a bead of sweat breaking on his cloudy brow, a terrycloth towel hung on the porch rail emblazoned with an inspirational portrait of NASCAR's Dale Earnhardt, a life-size plaster lawn statue of a noble German shepherd guarding the rickety wood dwelling with ears perked as if waiting to hear his master's voice. As the road narrowed to a rough path through the woods, we saw an eight-by-ten-inch sign nailed to a tree advertising a nearby workshop that specialized in church pew repadding and also sold bait for fishermen. Not too far beyond this sign in a hollow by the side of the way, we came upon the Ridgewood Barbecue. It was as close to the burning bush as we have ever been in our travels; the restaurant was rimmed with a radiant halo of sunlight beaming through a veil of smoke from the freestanding hickory pit outside.

When we walked into the restaurant, we were suddenly sightless. It was still bright outside. The Ridgewood has no picture windows and keeps the lights relatively low, like a wood-frame country church. We stood in the vestibule as our eyes adjusted to the dim light, and we must have looked like babies learning to see, our faces showing confusion, great effort, then the gradual joy of comprehension. As we saw, we also sniffed, and the aroma of smoldering green hickory was a heady incense. Tall pork-heaped sandwiches ready for the tables became visible as waitresses toted them from the kitchen. When we finally sat down and tasted the pork, it was truly a moment of ecstasy, a pig epiphany.

The Ridgewood was run by Grace Proffitt (since deceased; it is now in the hands of her son), and we are not stretching our spiritual metaphor too far to say that Mrs. Proffitt was a high priestess of barbecue. This place was her domain and had been a barbecue-lovers' destination since she first started smoking whole hams there in 1948. "Back then," she told us, "I used to drive up and down through the hollers to pick up my waitresses for work each day." And what a staff she had! Like Mrs. Proffitt, the waitstaff were all women of queenly proportions — strong, efficient, and all business. You didn't josh and joke with these pros; nor did you bend any rules. A few years later, after we had appeared on *Good Morning, America* with Mrs. Proffitt and her restaurant had earned some measure of national renown, we returned for supper. As we left at closing time — 7:30 P.M. — two of the waitresses came to the front door to lock it behind us. The restaurant's seats were still nearly full and there was a line of people waiting outside to get in. Nonetheless, the lock was turned, and we got the feeling that if one of the standees' fingers had been in the door frame when 7:30 arrived, the door would have been shut tight anyway.

It isn't only in buffets and barbecue parlors that southern cooks see themselves as sous-chefs to Jesus. Down in Lake Village, Arkansas, just west of the Mississippi River, Rhoda Adams and her husband, James, run a small roadside café famous for tamales. In fact, its formal name is Rhoda's Famous Hot Tamales, although followers know it as Miss Rhoda's place. We learned about it as we ate our way south along the Mississippi River years ago, looking for places that still made great hot tamales — a delta passion that apparently began when a mysterious Texan or Mexican started selling them on a street corner in one of the small towns decades ago. Nearly everywhere we stopped — even in places that offered excellent tamales — the word was absolute: if we wanted to taste the best tamales ever made, we should find Miss Rhoda's place.

The night before we got to Lake Village, we feasted on steak (and tamales) at Doe's Eat Place, just across the river in Greenville, so we were at Miss Rhoda's place for breakfast, about 8 A.M. We could smell tamales steaming even before we walked in. Other than Miss Rhoda and James, we were the only people there, so the four of us sat at a kitchenette table and talked about Mississippi River food over coffee, hot biscuits, fried eggs, and sizzled country ham. While she didn't have written recipes, Rhoda did let us know that she always added chicken to the beef in her tamales — "All but the gristle," she joked — thus infusing them with the stuff that gives so much soul food (and Jewish cooking) its soulfulness: chicken fat. She got up and went back to the stove to bring us a dozen piping hot ones, tied with string into bundles of three. As we untied them, unwrapped the husks, and shoveled up the unbelievably savory beef-spiced cornmeal with saltine crackers (the way it's done hereabouts), she told us that she had learned her technique by watching her aunt make tamales long ago.

But when we pressed further to find the secret of her tamales' goodness, she said it was not chicken or any other single ingredient that made the difference. She said she owed whatever talent she had to the Man above. "Glory to God!" she answered when we told her that we considered these the best tamales we had ever had. She raised her eyes heavenward and pointed to the front of the blue T-shirt she was wearing. It said, "When Praises Goes Up, Blessings Come Down."

Our first encounter with a restaurant where religion is always the special of the day was a tiny café we discovered during an early cross-country trip, when roadfood was only a notion. We were still trying to figure out if indeed there really was anything interesting about American eats. This place turned out to be incontrovertible evidence that a whole world of good food and fascinating food people was out there, ready to be chronicled.

It had been a long morning of stops in restaurants that didn't seem at all worth writing about. Anyone who has ever traveled into strange towns around the country searching for something good to eat knows the sense of frustration and despair that ensues when it seems impossible to find anything beyond the $2.99 breakfast special of eggs, toast, and potatoes and the lunch of tuna melts or preformed burger patties. Let's face it: there is a lot of boring food out there! But our radar began to beep when we saw a sign on the outskirts of a village that said CITY CAFÉ — CHRISTIAN ATMOSPHERE.

We found the place at noontime. It was surrounded by cars. One booth was open, but before we sat down, we walked to the cash register and picked up a mimeographed brochure written by the owner, Iola Burgraff. It was titled "Angels Singing to Iola" and it was headlined "Giant Angel Speaks to Rev. Burgraff Concerning Nixon, June 3, 1973." Ms. Rev. Burgraff was the cook, the owner, and a Christian visionary. She was also "in touch" with multitudes of dead people she personally had seen rising and coming into the café. It seemed that even death could not keep loyal customers away from her lemon icebox pie and red velvet cake. Near the cash register was a picture she had drawn showing Nixon standing in the palm of the Lord with an oil well spouting black gold behind him. She was so convinced that her café was sitting on the world's largest oil reserve that she and her flock of true believers had dug a hole somewhere behind the café and were waiting for it to bring forth the promised oil.

"Have you seen him?" asked a man in overalls sitting in the booth next to ours.

"Er, umm, yes," Jane answered, not certain whether the man meant Richard Nixon, the Lord Jesus, or perhaps just a busboy in the café. The man smiled and turned away, apparently satisfied.

We could smell fried chicken sizzling in iron skillets on the kitchen stoves in back, but we were also tempted by plates of baked ham with macaroni salad, snow slaw (pure white cole slaw), and corn bread that we saw on other people's tables. We consulted with our waitress, Zelda, who had the whole dining room to serve all by herself. "It's hard to get Christian help," she said, explaining why she was alone, but somehow she managed to take the time to be so friendly to us that it was almost embarrassing.

"Which should we get?" we asked. "Chicken or ham?"

She paused and seemed truly to consider our quandary, then offered this advice. "Do you know what I do when I face a question and I don't know the answer?" she said. "I reflect and I ask myself, 'What would Jesus do?' Chicken or ham? I don't know. What would Jesus eat?"

# Mary's Place Deviled Crab

Deviled crab is popular all along southern shores, and it is a specialty in South Carolina. It was there we once came across a takeout joint called Fishnet Seafoods, the proprietors of which were powerfully religious. All around their little shop, which was a former gas station, they posted signs reminding customers of Jesus' goodness and ultimate importance. Their belief was so strong that they called their deviled crab by a different name: Jesus crab. When we inquired about this dish, one of the employees told us, "It's deviled crab, but too good to be named for the devil."

Our introduction to the best deviled crab, though, was not on the Atlantic but near the Gulf Coast, in the town of Coden, Alabama, at a bare-bones little eatery named Mary's Place. Mary Hunter's menu was Creole soul food with a Mobile Bay twist, and here we learned to appreciate such Gulf Coast passions as spicy steamed crabs and West Indies salad, cool crabmeat and chopped onions in a bright vinaigrette. (Mary passed away in 1990, but the restaurant is still there, and still terrific.)

Mary once explained to us that the essential ingredient that made her deviled crab so luxurious was supermarket white bread soaked in whole milk. The deviled part comes from Tabasco sauce, and if you like it hot as Hades, you can double or triple the amount in this nonincendiary version.

- 6    slices white bread
- 1    cup whole milk
- 1    large egg
- 4    tablespoons (½ stick) butter

½   cup minced green bell pepper

1   celery rib, minced fine

1   garlic clove, minced fine

1   pound crabmeat, picked clean

1   tablespoon Dijon mustard

1   teaspoon Worcestershire sauce

10   drops Tabasco sauce

6–10   clean, empty crab shells or ovenproof ramekins

Preheat the oven to 400 degrees.

Tear the bread into pieces. Combine the milk and egg in a medium bowl and soak the bread thoroughly in this mixture.

Melt the butter in a medium skillet and sauté the pepper, celery, and garlic until they soften, 3 to 4 minutes. Remove from the heat.

Add the crabmeat to the milk-soaked bread and combine it, using your hands. Add the mustard, Worcestershire sauce, and Tabasco sauce. Add the sautéed vegetables. Mix well.

Rub olive or vegetable oil into the crab shells or ramekins. Pack the crab mixture into them. Bake for 12 to 15 minutes, until sizzling. Serve hot.

6 TO 8 SERVINGS AS AN APPETIZER

# Los Besos del Angel (Angel's Kisses)

Tucson's El Charro Café is infused with the religious spirit of the Virgin of Guadalupe. Nuestra Señora de Guadalupe is the most popular of the saints in the Southwest's pop culture. Her image appears as a picture or statue in such expected places as churches and home altars but also on silk-screened T-shirts and on the doors of low-rider cars and long-haul trucks. Her likeness can be found at political rallies and union marches.

Most images of "Lupe" show roses at her feet. The iconography dates back to the 1500s, when a man named Juan Diego saw an apparition of the Virgin Mary. Mary told Juan to go to the bishop of Mexico City, which he did, twice. But each time he was rebuffed. For his third try, the Virgin instructed him to take wild roses, which he found growing at the exact spot where she had appeared. The bishop saw that an image of the Virgin was imprinted on the cloak in which Juan had wrapped the roses.

The rose vines that creep up the outside walls of El Charro have been known to bloom mysteriously on December 12, the Virgin's feast day. On our most recent trip to the restaurant, Jane bought a pair of Mexican earrings made of recycled bottle caps decorated with sequins and the image of the Virgin, and we also came home with a bumper sticker that shows her picture and says IN GUAD WE TRUST.

These lighter-than-air meringues are an El Charro recipe that chef Carlotta Flores told us probably descends from the many Jewish settlers of Tucson, who brought their baking skills from France and Germany.

6    large egg whites, at room temperature
½    teaspoon cream of tartar
1    teaspoon almond extract
1½   cups sugar
     Fresh fruit or ice cream

Preheat the oven to 225 degrees. Line a baking sheet with brown paper or parchment. Butter and flour the paper.

Beat the egg whites and cream of tartar in a large bowl until soft peaks form. Add the almond extract. Gently beat in the sugar, mixing thoroughly but not overbeating. Place this mixture in a pastry bag and pipe 6 rounds onto the baking sheet.

Quickly place the sheet in the oven for 45 minutes, or until the meringues are dry. Cool completely. They may be stored in a dry place in an airtight container for up to a week.

Use the meringues as a bed for fresh fruit and/or ice cream.

MAKES 6 MERINGUES

# Twelve Meals a Day

When we tell people that we research roadfood by eating twelve meals a day, they think it's poetic license. But it is true. As travel became a way of life for us, we learned to start very early so we could eat a lot all day long. We woke up around 4 A.M., showered, dressed, threw the luggage into the car, and headed out to find breakfast, either alongside the road or, better still, on a town square or Main Street. The kind of place we fell in love with hits its peak at six in the morning, so we wanted to be ensconced in a good booth by that time, ready to order, to eat, and to learn about where we were in America.

For the first meal of the day, we overordered and overate, especially if the menu listed such local specialties as beignets (Creole doughnuts), migas (Tex-Mex tortilla-laced eggs), huevos rancheros, Down East blueberry muffins, Lancaster County waffles, or Tennessee ham with biscuits and red-eye gravy.

We could eat just about anyone under the table, so the first few breakfasts of the day were no problem at all. We awoke ravenous, and with healthy appetites like ours, it was nothing to polish off multiple plates of sourdough French toast in northern California or monster pancakes in Billings, Montana. In the early days of travel, we never met anyone who ate boring sensible breakfasts of Special K with skim milk. Skim milk probably wasn't available even if you asked for it. Our memory of most cafés is that just about everyone smoked cigarettes while they chatted and chewed and welcomed the break of day.

Coffee was a constant problem. We both like it dark and strong, whereas most of the people with whom we rubbed elbows liked theirs farmer-style, which means weak enough for you to drink four or five cups at breakfast as you sit with your friends and neighbors. (Needless to say, this was long before the era of Starbucks and three-dollar lattes.) Furthermore, at many of these roadfood stops, regular customers had their own personal coffee mugs, kept on pegboard hooks, which they reached for and filled the moment they walked in. We felt odd grabbing for Clem's or Elmer's mug, so we dutifully waited for the waitress to bring us house mugs, usually already brimming with coffee and outfitted with a spoon. Once that first cup had arrived, waitresses patrolled the counter and dining room with fresh pots. Refills were automatic unless you did something dramatic like turn an emptied cup upside down or place your hand over the top as she approached. The latter proved to be a dangerous tactic if the waitress was gabbing with other diners and pouring on autopilot.

So we drank weak coffee and cleaned our plates, then moved on to breakfast number two, then breakfast number three. By midmorning, when our appetites started to lag and we weren't eating everything we had ordered, we began to face the worried-waitress problem.

"You don't like your food? What's the matter, dears?"

"It's great. We're just not hungry."

"But you ordered so much." Sometimes the waitress was so upset that she went back to the kitchen to notify the cook. Then a white-haired granny would run out, looking dismayed.

Having survived upbringings with our Jewish mothers, we thought we knew guilt. Nothing had prepared us for how bad we felt trying to explain our way out of the situation. At the time, writing *Roadfood* was only an ambition; we had never published anything, and so we had no food articles or books to show as an explanation of what we were doing. The very idea of a restaurant writer would have been ludicrous to most of these people, let alone a restaurant writer concerned about flapjacks.

And so to scores of kind old ladies across America we must have appeared to be liars, fakers, or — worst of all — wastrels who thought it was perfectly all right to waltz into Madge's Café in western Nebraska and leave behind half of a three-egg omelet and all of our buttered toast. We could read their minds: "Sausage links do not grow on trees . . ." So we pushed the food around on our plates and used whatever garnishes there were to hide what we hadn't eaten.

After the third or fourth breakfast, it was generally time to make miles. Depending on how far apart towns were and how many likely roadfood places each one had, we tried to travel a few hundred miles a day. In southern Louisiana, we might not go more than fifty miles, the good-eats possibilities were so dense. In the Dakotas, five hundred miles between meals was common.

Since we spent so much time in the car, what we drove seemed very important. After destroying the vomit-green Suburban in a crash, we went through a seemingly endless series of replacements, every one of which had something wrong with it, either a fatal flaw or a huge annoyance. One car spit ice crystals through the air-conditioning vents. A convertible leaked profusely whenever it rained. One pickup truck would not start if the humidity was over 50 percent; another had an exhaust system that fed fumes into the passenger compartment, making us dizzy and faint after thirty minutes. Then there was the coupe that stank of what must have been the four-pack-a-day habit of its former owner, and a primitive four-by-four so tall and nonaerodynamic that it behaved like a mainsail in the wind. All our cars were cheap and ugly. The only one that was not was a black stick-shift 1959 Mercedes with cherry-red leather seats and a mere few hundred thousand miles on the odometer, which we got for the bargain price of $500. It had a minor problem, though; it would not start if there was any moisture in the air at all, and to get it going we had to remove the distributor cap and spray the copper contacts with roach spray — a trick taught us by the seller.

A large number of our early cars were Volkswagens, then the lowest form of four-wheel transportation. They were inexpensive to operate and easy to drive, and while frighteningly unsafe by modern standards, they did have their advantages in poor driving conditions. Once in a blizzard on Route 80 in western Pennsylvania, Jane hit the brakes on our Beetle too hard. The car did a full 360-degree spin, missed a passing semi, and wound up in the median between the east-bound and westbound lanes. We simply got out and pushed it back onto the roadbed like a toy, climbed in, and drove away.

Whatever we drove, it usually got us to lunch, which is Jane's fa-vorite meal of the day. Michael was and still is a breakfast guy, but Jane is a lady who lunches. Whenever we found ourselves at a wonderful place like the old Miller's Tea Room of Cleveland, Ohio, eating chicken à la king served in a deep-fried potato nest, Jane's eyes bright-ened. Confronted by the sight of a dozen shimmering individual Jell-O salads brought to the table on a tray so each diner could select a favorite color and combo, followed by a battered silver tray stocked with little sticky buns, cloverleaf rolls, corn-bread sticks, and blue-berry gem muffins, she would begin to moan that this was simply the best food in the United States, in the world, maybe in the universe. It was all just too good, too delicious; she wanted one of everything . . . And that is pretty much what we would consume.

Opportunity to eat a lunch like this absolutely eclipsed any feel-ings of fullness left over from breakfasts. Our stomachs were growling, for we were blessed with the best and only tool absolutely necessary for the job we set out to do: a healthy appetite.

After the first lunch, we would move on and find another, stopping in Cleveland at the Balaton for chicken paprikash and apple strudel, at Renée's for Polish pierogi, at Rick's Café for ribs, or at the Flat Iron Café for perch. By the fourth midday meal, we were beginning to unnerve waitresses again by not cleaning our plates. Sometimes we tried to avoid the whole situation and ask for the food to go, then eat what we could in the car. But Michael is a stickler for seeing the whole meal presented as it should be on a table, so unless we were having barbecue or something that seemed right and proper out of a paper bag, we sat at the table or counter and faced what the menu offered.

Michael, the documentarian, entered the restaurants loaded down like a Mexican donkey with heavyweight Rolleiflexes and Hasselblads with tripods and flash attachments to take beauty shots of the food as soon as it arrived at the table. Needless to say, this caused some commotion. People simply couldn't understand why someone would want to take a picture of a slice of pie or a cup of chowder. The idea that we might be food writers meant absolutely nothing, and the Food Network was a few decades away from being a gleam in a TV producer's eye, so Michael with his camera was usually regarded as some kind of nutcase passing through town. As he did not seem dangerous to himself or others, people generally humored him.

"Do you want to take a picture of my chicken sandwich?" someone would call out, and if the plate of food looked good, Michael would go over and snap away. This caused gales of laughter, and Jane would swivel her head to see people making the universal sign of craziness. She would benignly nod in agreement, which was much easier than trying to explain that we were attempting to write a guidebook to regional food, which would have sounded at least as crazy.

Michael, a compulsive note-taker, also spread his pads of paper and pens and notebooks all over the table as we ate. Jane, a more discreet researcher, carried a manual typewriter in the car and relied on her memory for everything. Then, back in the motel at night, she two-finger-typed her thoughts on everything she had eaten that day.

Before we got to the motel, however, there were dinners to eat. We generally tried to take a midafternoon digestive break as we sailed along after lunch, but this rarely worked out well. While we may not have stopped for too many full lunches after around 2 P.M., we constantly found pie slices that needed sampling, cheese curds to investigate, local apples from a farmstand, roasted chile sandwiches sold by the side of the road, maple candy, pepperoni rolls, salmon jerky, boiled peanuts, and countless essential snacks.

If we ever hit a wall appetite-wise, it was at dinner. We always tried to start no later than five o'clock. In most parts of rural America, this is no early-bird special; it is the time people eat. Dinner servings tend to be bigger and take longer than other meals, and since we had already had eight or nine meals that day and traveled a few hundred miles, we just didn't have the stamina for more than two or three dinners. Often nauseated, clinging tightly to our supply of Alka-Seltzer, we drove "home" to our little motel in the pines, on the highway access road, near a cornfield, alongside the railroad tracks, or behind the whorehouse. We bolted the door, turned the TV to one of the three available channels to watch primitive pro wrestling or *The Late Show,* and tried to relax. We should have looked horrible in the bathroom mirror, but we did not. Our clothes had food dribbles on them, and sometimes our eyes looked bloodshot, but it was obvious that we were as well fed as a pair of Kobe steers and as happy as two Ipswich clams.

After a year on the road, we noticed that we had begun to expand. The pair-of-pants incident was proof. When Jane's father died, in 1971, Michael inherited a favorite pair of his pants — custommade, western-style, boot-cut gabardine circa 1955, from the time Jane's family had moved to Tucson. Like Michael, Jane's father was tall and lean, and for a while the pants fit perfectly. But in the mid-1970s, in Socorro, New Mexico, at a restaurant named La Casita, where an old lady named Juanita Martinez stirred a wicked pot of bright red chili sauce on her stovetop, Michael stood up from a booth and bent over to hoist up his camera bag. We heard a resounding tearing sound. The seam had split, and in a remarkable way: the pants cleaved into two entirely separate trousers, held together only by the waistband. The rip started at the top of the fly in the front and ended at the beltline in back. Michael sent Jane to the car for a pair of jeans, then surreptitiously skulked into the bathroom to change.

Michael dumped the pants in a trash basket outside. Jane retrieved them, insisting that the pants knew on some mystical level that we were heading for Arizona, where they had originally come from, and they deserved a proper, dignified burial in their home state. A few days later, somewhere near the Painted Desert, we laid the pants to rest, using a plastic coffee cup to scoop up dry desert sand and make a plot in which they could spend eternity. Jane said some suitable words over them and we drove on.

Gaining weight was becoming a problem. Michael started to take long runs before sunrise, then again after we pulled in for the night. This turned into a source of conflict when Jane began to obsess about the fact that Michael left his wallet behind on the night table.

"How can you go out without identification?" she hissed at him when he came back from a run.

Michael stood in the motel doorway, breathing hard and sweating. "Why do I need identification?" he asked, truly perplexed. He had just spent an hour happily trotting past fields of cows chewing their cud.

Jane stopped pacing, turned, and started to answer, but found herself speechless.

"You mean so they can identify my body?" he said.

"Yes, that is exactly the reason!" Jane said. "You cannot run with no ID along roads where no one will know who you are."

"I will not carry my wallet!" Michael yelled back. We were very good at yelling at each other.

The next morning when Michael got up to run, Jane got up too, and to Michael's wild annoyance she followed him in the car at five miles an hour along the country road, shouting out the window, "At least they will have someone to identify you!"

To this, Michael raised his middle finger, and then he ran onto a path between tall rows of corn where the car couldn't go.

Michael became trim again. Part of it was the demonic exercising, part was good genetics, part was being a young man. Jane was not so lucky. Each piece of pie and cheeseburger took its toll. She gave up the tight jeans and leather pants that she had sported in college and took to wearing strange versions of clothing that allowed for comfortable expansion. One unfortunate choice was a vast pair of overalls bought at a farm store. "Oh, Christ," she said when she saw her reflection in the glass of a restaurant window. "I look like Haystacks Calhoun."

The next shopping spree was in Memphis, at Schwab's, the city's ancient department store, which still sold 1940s-style housedresses for $1.99 each. They were big shapeless shifts made of great calicos and ginghams, but they were tissue-thin, and they fell apart at the first laundromat they met. Then, as if out of the blue, an Amish dry-goods store called Gohn Brothers in Shipshewana, Indiana, proved to be

Jane's salvation. There she fell in love with Amish women's underpants: giant flesh-colored bloomers that went from knee to waist. They did not even have a size, because they were designed to look equally ridiculous on everyone. Jane ceased to care what she wore on top of the Amish underpants, finding an A-framed denim smock that served all purposes. The underpants were like road armor, and in Jane's peculiar way of processing information, they went from merely being comfortable underpants to being *lucky underpants.*

If she was wearing her lucky Amish underpants, we would find great roadfood, great motels, great flea-market junk, and great radio channels to listen to, and we would get great gas mileage. Having underpants that ruled one's life was actually a very easy scheme, because it took a lot of guesswork out of things, and thank goodness Amish products are made like iron, because Jane still has a few pairs of the original undies.

Stealth and guile became essential tools if we were to survive eating twelve meals a day. Jane scrounged or bought plastic bags to hide in her purse. The ideal size was a big one, the kind you find in a nice hotel room so you can send your clothes to the cleaner. However, since we didn't stay in nice hotels, such bags were only a distant dream. Regular plastic bags from the 7-Eleven worked fine. When we were feeling that we simply couldn't eat another bite, we waited for the waitress to turn her back, then scooped up the remains on our plates and slid them into the plastic bag, held open in Jane's waiting purse on her lap. Usually this worked well, but not with waitresses who paid close attention to what they had served us and wondered how we had managed to swallow clamshells, chicken bones, olive pits, and lobster carapaces. We smiled like a couple of ninnies, paid the bill, and left.

Despite getting out of the restaurant without suffering through an inquisition, we felt awfully guilty about just tossing good food into the trash. But what are you going to do with half a meal heaved into a plastic bag? Or even with half a meal if you ask to have it packed in a doggie bag? Who wants somebody else's sampled waffle?

On some occasions we walked out of restaurants with food without bite marks in it. One time, traveling through easternmost Tennessee, we got a couple of slabs of ribs at an excellent barbecue. We ate one, but then a few more dinners on the road from Tennessee into Virginia came between us and the other one. Late that night we arrived in Roanoke with a rack of ribs and no appetite to eat them.

We decided that before we even found a motel, we would drive along the city streets and give our prize to someone who would appreciate some of Tennessee's best barbecue. The ribs were neatly wrapped in aluminum foil — a tidy bundle that we slid inside a clean brown paper bag. What hungry person wouldn't love this gift? On a corner near the Roanoke railroad tracks we spotted three down-at-the-heels guys standing in a cluster looking uncomfortable: homeless people whose distress might well be relieved by the delicious pork we bore. We stopped the car and got out, Michael carrying the bag, Jane accompanying him as part of our beneficent procession. As we reached them, holding out the brown paper bag, we suddenly heard sirens. Flashing police lights were all around, and the road was instantly crowded with cruisers. The five of us were set upon and frisked as one of the officers grabbed the bag and emptied it onto the hood of his Crown Vic. The look on his face when he unfurled the foil was pure poison. His drug bust had turned into a rib bust, and it was only after a few hours of explaining in the Roanoke police station that we were snarlingly released to find a room for the night. That was the last time we tried to gift perfect strangers with surplus food from a day of eating on the road.

## Chivito

When we are not traveling and feel the need to eat the maximum amount of food in a single dish, we head down the road to the Olive Market for a chivito. This little restaurant and store near our home in Georgetown, Connecticut, stocks an inventory of great cheeses, olives, and olive oil, and it's where we go in the morning for strong coffee and frittatas and on weekend nights for spectacular "gaucho dinners" that reflect the Uruguayan roots of co-owner Fernando Pereyra: huge platters of grilled pork, beef, chicken, and lamb that would no doubt have made Dr. Atkins grin from ear to ear.

The most amazing item on the Olive Market menu is a lunch sandwich called the chivito. This is a flabbergasting hot Dagwood that combines the triple joy of a BLT, a cheese steak, and a ham and cheese sandwich on one bun. Fernando recommends serving the monumental creation with French fries, but when we dine at the Olive Market, we like to have it with a bag of rosemary–olive oil potato chips . . . and maybe a pitcher of sangria, too.

As for the hard roll, it is important to seek out one with character — essential as a suitable foil for all the meats — and with enough substance so it won't disintegrate under the weight of all its ingredients.

- 2   slices bacon
- 1   ¼-inch slice filet mignon
     Salt and pepper
- 1   large egg
- 1   hard roll (the Northeast's Portuguese roll, a small New Orleans muffuletta roll, or any sturdy Italian torpedo or Sheboygan, Wisconsin, bakery roll)

Mayonnaise

1   slice Black Forest ham

1   slice provolone cheese

Lettuce

2   tomato slices

1   slice onion

Fry the bacon in a hot skillet. When it is cooked, remove to drain but leave the bacon fat in the skillet.

Pound the filet mignon until it is about the size of the hard roll. Salt and pepper it on both sides, then fry it in the bacon grease. When it has cooked until pink in the center, remove it to drain. Then fry the egg, removing it when the yolk is cooked but still runny.

Meanwhile, slice the hard roll in half and toast it. Spread mayonnaise on both halves. On the bottom, place the filet mignon, followed by the ham, provolone, fried egg, bacon, lettuce, tomato, and onion.

Serve with French fries and many napkins.

MAKES 1 SANDWICH

# Hoppel Poppel

If you are looking for a really big breakfast in Wisconsin or Iowa, find a place that serves hoppel poppel. We first came across this mighty meal-in-a-skillet in Amana, Iowa, at a fine old restaurant called the Ronneburg. We assumed hoppel poppel's name was something that the proprietors' family had invented, and that perhaps the dish was somehow descended from the hearty farm kitchens of their Lutheran Separatist ancestors (who were among the founders of the Amana Colonies in the nineteenth century).

Like slumgullion or cioppino, hoppel poppel is a hodgepodge dish in which eggs are scrambled with potatoes, salami or sausage, onions, peppers, and cheese, and we soon learned that it is not unique to the Lutherans. A few trips later, we were eating our way around the Great Lakes, and one morning after a night-before of planked whitefish with haystack potatoes on the side, we went to Benjamin's Delicatessen in Milwaukee for a nice Jewish breakfast. There again was hoppel poppel, sandwiched on the menu between the corned beef omelet and the fried kreplach (meat dumpling) plate. It was listed as a Benjy's special, and customers had their choice of regular hoppel poppel, which was browned potatoes, salami, and scrambled eggs, or super hoppel poppel, which added green peppers, mushrooms, and melted cheese to the formula.

The main difference between the Amana and Milwaukee versions was the meat. At the Ronneberg, it's bacon. At Benjamin's, all-beef salami is the meat of choice. Scouring our spiral-bound cookbook collection, we have found more recipes for hoppel poppel (sometimes written "hoffel poffel"), plain and super, with bacon and/or sausage, but we have never come across an explanation of why it's called what it is. If anybody knows its genealogy, we'd love to hear about it.

8   small thin-skinned potatoes
¼   cup corn oil
6   tablespoons (¾ stick) butter
1   cup diced onion (optional)
⅔   cup sliced mushrooms
1   cup diced green bell pepper
1   cup diced all-beef salami
10  large eggs
2   tablespoons milk
2   tablespoons chopped fresh parsley
1   cup grated cheddar cheese
    Salt and pepper to taste

Boil the potatoes until just barely tender, about 15 minutes. Drain and cut them into ¼-inch-thick slices. In a large skillet over medium heat, fry the potatoes in the oil, tossing and stirring until they begin to brown. Add the butter to the skillet, then the onion (if using), mushrooms, pepper, and salami. Continue cooking and stirring until the potatoes begin to get crisp, the salami is crusty, and the vegetables are limp.

Lightly beat the eggs with the milk and parsley in a medium bowl. Pour them into the skillet over all the other ingredients. Stir occasionally. As the eggs begin to set, sprinkle on the cheese. Cover and cook, without stirring, about 6 more minutes, until the eggs are fully set but still moist. Add salt and pepper to taste.

Accompany hoppel poppel with toast or toasted bagels.

4 TO 6 SERVINGS

# The Perfect Roadfood Find

The Great Plains were a problem for us from the beginning. Being efficient sorts of people, we found it much more inviting to take a road trip to, say, northern California or the shore of Lake Michigan or Texas hill country, where virtually every turn of the road offered up a memorable place to eat and each town was just a few miles away from the last one. In such locations we could eat all day, and eat well, and gather heaps of material to write about. In the vast prairies west of Siouxland and north of the Oregon Trail, the pickin's got mighty sparse. In a long day we would drive five hundred miles and visit three crossroads communities and find perhaps one café that served a halfway decent piece of huckleberry pie — if we were lucky. Our assumption was that people of the plains might eat well at home, but their homes are simply too far apart and their communities too small to support any kind of really good restaurant, roadfood or otherwise.

North Dakota wasn't completely barren. On our first trip through, during America's bicentennial celebration in 1976, we found a swell Ukrainian place in Elgin, where the proprietors named their holubski (stuffed cabbage) "pigs in blankets" so visitors wouldn't be put off, and the Wentz Café in Napoleon served very good cream pies. But subsequent expeditions through oceans of wheat fields convinced us that the Roughrider State was one of those places where it simply was not possible for travelers to eat well unless they happened to be accomplished campfire cooks. The dearth of inviting restaurants makes it all the more remarkable that it was in North Dakota that we found the Holy Grail — our very favorite roadfood find.

*Find* is not exactly the correct word, since we did not come across it by accident. No one, not even we Sterns, just happens to drive through Havana, North Dakota. Surrounded by millions of acres of flat farmland that is easy on the eye but not particularly scenic, Havana — population 124 — isn't on the way to anywhere. We went there on purpose because of something we read. In our quest to discover excellent local eats, we take a lot of under-the-radar publications that appeal to folks for whom celebrity marriages and miracle diets are of little interest. One such magazine is the estimable *Farm & Ranch Living*, a magazine devoted to those who prize country life. To give you an idea of its editorial bent, a recent issue included stories about Goldie the Hen ("Was she a pet or a menace?"), Fergie the Tractor ("A natty little Massey-Ferguson that has survived half a century"), and aerial shots ("Crops form pretty patterns when you take pictures of them from an airplane"). The December-January 1987 issue included a story titled "Tables Are Turned at the Farmers' Inn," about how a café in Havana was saved from extinction by the townspeople. We clipped the article and held on to it for nine years, until 1996, when we finally headed off to the great western wheat belt to see the Farmers' Inn for ourselves.

Fargo was our base camp, and while it is not a gastronome's bonanza, we did fall in love with the chocolate-covered potato chips made by Carol Widman's Candy Company on 13th Avenue SW. For years we mail-ordered these excellent sweet-and-savory chips (shipped only in cool weather), and we also liked Widman's for its truly local menu of confectionery treats, which included chocolate-covered sunflower seeds and chocolate-covered wheat.

We wanted to be at the Farmers' Inn when it started serving

breakfast, so we left Fargo while it was still night. Under a sickle-shaped moon in a sky full of stars, we jigged our way southwest from the Bois de Sioux River on the two-lanes of Richland County. As we sped along the rigidly straight roads through the tallgrass prairie of the Sheyenne National Grasslands, the sun rose behind us. For as far as we could see, mist lifted from the black earth and endless rows of sunflowers coiled up to face the daybreak, their stalks casting long shadows to the west.

Although Havana is less than a hundred miles from Fargo, the drive seemed never to end. The stunning steadiness of the landscape — absolutely the same soft farm fields for mile after mile along roads that are as flat as a floor — put us into an enchanted state, with no remaining sense of real clock ticks and actual miles. Then, while barreling along Highway 32 at a pace that could have been 10 or 100 miles per hour, we saw an astonishing sight: a barn. Any manmade structure in the Never Land we had entered would have been cause for awe, but this barn featured on its side a primitive sign that read FARMERS INN ... HOME COOKED MEALS along with an idyllic painted mural of the fields that surrounded it. We turned off the highway onto a dirt road that led past the barn and soon found ourselves on the main street of Havana. There were three buildings in a row, facing the train tracks, and a dozen grain elevators on the other side of the road. The building that was not Jay's Standard Station or the post office was the Farmers' Inn.

The sun was still huge and low and red in the sky when we pulled up and parked in front of the restaurant, where a sign outside said somewhat cryptically FARMERS' INN II. Was this now a chain? We could smell coffee and the sweet, yeasty aroma of oven-hot rolls as soon as we stepped out of the car. Our entrance into the small, one-room café was what we had come to expect in such remote venues: an extremely uncomfortable moment when conversations stop and everybody in the room looks to see who has just come in.

The silence was broken. "Welcome!" called out a big pink man wearing a red apron and tending pancakes at the grill behind the counter with two spatulas, one in each hand.

A woman sitting at a table with two gents in soft, worn overalls stood up and came to the door. Without a word, she swept a hand toward her table, beckoning us to sit down and join her threesome. As we followed her, conversations at the other tables started up again, slow and quiet. It seemed to us that everyone else in the room wanted to eavesdrop and hear what we had to say for ourselves. We were correct. The arrival of strangers at the Farmers' Inn was not an everyday occurrence. Everyone in this room knew everyone else who lived within a hundred-mile radius, and we were not among them; nor could we pass as wheat farmers visiting from the Red River Valley.

As we explained that we were traveling around the country looking for good places to eat, Murdean Gulsvig, the pancake-maker, set down plates of hot flapjacks in front of us and proclaimed, "You found the best!" Looking at the pancakes, we were ready to agree. These were ravishing: plate-wide, as thin as flannel, pale beige with a faint crisp surface and a fine lace edge. When a stack of three was severed with the edge of a fork, a sourdough aroma unfurled from the triple ribbons. Their tender insides had a fetching tang that begged for a drizzle of sweet corn syrup.

It took only the slightest prodding to elicit the story of the Farmers' Inn from our three tablemates, and we were only too happy to listen as we laid waste to the farmland flapjacks in front of us. As the story unfolded, other customers gathered around, coffee cups in hand, each of them with a bit of his or her own history to add to the tale.

We learned that when Slim Miller first opened the Havana Café in 1913, Havana was a thriving community of 450 souls, sending wheat back east on the Great Northern rail line. For thirty-five years Slim's place served breakfast and the midday meal (here known as dinner) to farmers who came to town after early-morning chores, then took another break at noon. Slim sold the place in '48, after which several owners came and went. In the postwar years, many farms in southeastern North Dakota made the transition from grain to row crops; agriculture modernized and small family farms grew scarcer. As time passed, Havana's population declined, business at the restaurant dwindled, and the old café building began to crumble. Finally, in 1984, the Havana Café closed, leaving the town without a restaurant.

It was only then that the citizens realized how much the café had meant to them. They had grown accustomed to having a place in town where they could go for a cup of coffee, a piece of pie, and, most important, the company of friends. In this seemingly infinite terrain, contact with people outside the house was precious, and with the café shut, it wasn't happening. Neighbors had no place to go to meet neighbors. Jay Saunders, who ran the gas station, put a pot of coffee in his office for visitors to share. American Legionnaires opened up their hall as an informal gathering place. But neither of those well-meaning expressions of welcome provided the kind of easy come-and-go atmosphere of a small-town café, which is so conducive to a relaxed exchange of news and opinions.

Understanding that a restaurant in such a remote location had little chance of success if someone tried to operate it as a profit-making business, the Havana Community Club (which included the entire population of the town) decided to reopen the café on its own. Men pitched in and fixed up the old building as best they could, and wives volunteered to run the kitchen, agreeing to cook their specialties for neighbors, family, and friends one day a month. The Havana school had just closed (children now travel north to the bigger town of Forman for their education), so the refurbished eatery was able to get good appliances and equipment from the old school cafeteria kitchen. When the Farmers' Inn opened a few weeks before Christmas in 1984, a comical sign on the bulletin board reflected the true soul of a meeting place in the midst of a sparsely peopled landscape: THERAPY SESSION 9 A.M.–12 P.M. AND 1 P.M.–4:00 P.M. NO CHARGE.

Some days, half the population of town came in for dinner. In the bitter North Dakota winter, when temperatures drop far below zero and farmers often finish chores early, tables were occupied for hours with pinochle players. And from 6 A.M. on, the hot coffee never stopped flowing. As we heard the story of the restaurant, we watched one tall, thin farmer in a plaid shirt and hunting cap help himself to yet another cup of coffee at the coffee station. A kitchen volunteer who had taken a break from washing dishes to join us noted, "If we charged fifty cents a cup, we'd be rich!" Of course, once you bought your first cup for fifty cents, café custom allowed you to refill it all morning long.

Once the citizens of Havana realized that their cooperative effort was going to work, they determined that the old café building was hopelessly dilapidated. So they pooled their resources and built a new one, which opened in the winter of 1986. Farmers' Inn II was a utilitarian steel structure with a single spanking-clean carpeted dining room, where wood-grain Formica tables were outfitted with hand-hewn wooden napkin holders in the shape of cows, pigs, tractors, and horses — all cut and painted by a local retired elevator operator (that's a *grain* elevator, by the way — the only structure around here more than two stories tall). A bulletin board near the front door included a flier for a polka band headlined by Jimmie Jensen, the

"Swinging Swede," and a manila folder tacked up with a note on it saying, "Please Put Your Havana News in Folder." Items deposited found their way into the "Havana News" column of the *Sargent County Teller*, which included such stories as "July 1st Joe Barbknecht arrived and joined his family at the Walt Barbknecht farm." About a month after we had been in town, our visit was a lead news item in the column: "Couple from Connecticut Eat Breakfast at Farmers' Inn." The story told of how we came to town just to eat pancakes and sweet rolls and find out all about the café from the Havanans who had created it. It included a picture that Murdean took of us standing outside the restaurant, squinting into the morning sun.

As we sat and chatted, one gentleman, clearly a regular, walked in and called out to Murdean, "Two eggs, over. Over hard!"

"I know, I know," replied Murdean from his place at the griddle, where he was sharing kitchen duties that day with his wife of more than fifty years, Doris. "Throw 'em up against the wall, and if they bounce, they're hard enough, right?"

Once the over-hard eggs were cooked and delivered, Murdean turned his spatulas over to another citizen and came to join us at the table. He was a whimsical septuagenarian, a retired farmer with a few tufts of red hair combed across his scalp and a corn-fed girth, and he informed us that he was something more than just the day's cook: he served as operations director for the café, ordering supplies and overseeing the planning of each month's menu and daily cooking assignments. When he and Doris drew kitchen duty, Murdean was known for his delicious coarse-ground breakfast sausage, made from a recipe he had secured from a hog farmer north of town, as well as for his ethereal pancakes.

Shortly after we sat down, as the dining room was getting crowded and the air swirled with the wake-up smells of brewing coffee and sizzling breakfast meats, Doris toted out a pan of oven-hot caramel rolls to cool near the coffee station. These rolls, like Murdean's pancakes, were astonishingly good — the best we have ever tasted, light and fluffy, swirled with veins of caramel frosting that was sweet but teetered on the edge of tasting burned. The flavor reminded us of a perfectly scorched crust on crème brûlée, but in this case it was silky soft on the tongue. We often think back on those rolls and wonder if they really were as good as we recall. Or was their flavor ineffably improved by the warmth and inspiration of this welcoming little place in the heart of the plains?

We hung around when the breakfast crowd cleared out and watched Murdean and Doris prepare dinner. As was always the case, there was one prix fixe hot meal; that day's was to be roast pork with dressing, gravy, mashed potatoes, corn, cole slaw, and lemon pie, for $4.65. The only other things on the menu were a few sandwiches and hamburgers. Doris explained to us that they were there just in case the dinner crowd was bigger than expected and they ran out of roast pork. She and Murdean spent the morning stirring the lemon filling for the pie, boiling potatoes, tasting the stuffing to see if it was seasoned right, and watching the roast cook. They looked to us like any couple expecting company for dinner; the fact that it happened to be about four dozen people meant only that the cooking pots were bigger.

"You better mash those potatoes now, or they'll get too soft," Doris called to Murdean, who had managed to escape from the kitchen to a dining room table, where he was visiting with a couple of friends who had happened by for midmorning coffee.

Murdean shrugged with good-natured resignation as he rose and headed for the stove. "See how hard she makes me work?" he said as he passed us. Doris held the pot and poured the hot milk while

Murdean did the mashing. As he worked, he boasted, "We got a ninety-nine when the health inspector came around. It would have been one hundred, but we won't wear hairnets. Jiminy Christmas, I don't have enough hair to put a net over!"

Nearly every woman we met at the midday meal took her turn running the kitchen at least one day a month. Every one made a point of distinguishing her cooking — farm cooking — from restaurant cooking. The latter, each of them explained in her own way, is more deluxe and uses ingredients you cannot easily find when you go to town to shop in the grocery store, and, worse, most of it is stuff that their husbands wouldn't recognize. While not at all embarrassed to use canned soup for a casserole or cake mix for pineapple upside-down cake, they also showed a fine touch with slow-risen butter horn rolls and old-fashioned knefla (dumpling) soup with hand-rolled dumplings. In the summer, they made use of garden tomatoes and cucumbers in their salads, and when Harlan Clefsted returned from his winter home in Arizona, there would be pies made from the lemons he brought back from his lemon tree there. Mary Ann Fliehs was known for her talent with pies — rhubarb, sour cream, lemon meringue, and coconut cream. Marie Underberg was delighted when the menu called for roast turkey, because that was her opportunity to make a big pumpkin cake for dessert.

Dining at the Farmers' Inn was like going to a church supper every day, and not only because of the bounty and goodness of the food. We will never forget the last breakfast we had there, in the summer of 1996. The townsfolk all knew we would be leaving that morning, so they gathered a bunch of the tables together, enabling a large group of us eat caramel rolls and drink coffee together. "This is what I call a gravy and potato café," declared Harvey Peterson, whose wife, Gloria, was known for the raisin sauce she made for ham. Mr. Peterson, who farmed the land for more than fifty years, spoke of the days long, long before, when Havana had had four flourishing grocery stores, two department stores, and a twenty-piece citizens' band for promenade concerts in the winter months. He recalled how empty the town had seemed when the Havana Café closed. "Now look at what we have," he said with a measure of pride, gesturing to a dining room crowded with Havanans, including oldsters bragging to each other about grandkids' school scholarships and baseball hitting averages, young families marshaling their members for a nearby T-ball tournament, and working farmers engaged in an incredibly precise discussion about the spring wheat they raise — "the best, the highest protein" — versus white wheat, winter wheat, and soft red wheat.

"The Farmers' Inn holds our community together," Mr. Peterson concluded.

"It's like going to church on Sunday," one of the cooks said. "Except you don't have to be Lutheran to have your coffee here."

"Maybe we did save this café," another added thoughtfully. "But the way I see it, this café saved us."

Driving away from Havana, we felt more satisfied, and more exhausted, than after the best Thanksgiving supper.

We learned a few years later that the Farmers' Inn had gone under private ownership again, and while we have heard excellent reports about the food served there, we have hesitated to go back. Unlike Brigadoon, the magic little town café in Havana is a place that can't be found again.

Both of the following recipes are derived from the Farmers' Inn cookbook, a collection published by the town in 1994 to celebrate their café's tenth anniversary.

# Doris Gulsvig's Rhubarb Crunch

Doris Gulsvig, born twenty miles northwest of Havana, in Stirum, North Dakota, was a teacher in the Havana school when Murdean asked her to marry him in 1945. They settled just north of town, where they raised six children. A church organist and a 4-H leader, Doris is also known among neighbors as an excellent baker, and the rhubarb she uses in this "crunch" thrives in the cool North Dakota climate. We originally made her dish as dessert, putting a scoop of vanilla ice cream on top of each serving, and the next morning we also enjoyed it for breakfast.

| | |
|---|---|
| 6 | cups sliced rhubarb |
| ¾ | cup sugar |
| 2 | tablespoons cornstarch |
| 1 | cup water |
| ½ | teaspoon vanilla extract |
| 1 | cup all-purpose flour |
| ¾ | cup quick-cooking (not instant) oatmeal |
| 1 | cup dark brown sugar |
| 1 | teaspoon ground cinnamon |
| 8 | tablespoons (1 stick) melted butter |

Preheat the oven to 350 degrees. Grease a 9-x-13-inch baking pan.

Place the rhubarb in the pan.

Combine the sugar, cornstarch, and water in a medium saucepan. Cook, stirring, until thick and clear, about 5 minutes. Stir in the vanilla. Pour over the rhubarb.

Combine the remaining ingredients in a small bowl. Mix well

and spread evenly over the rhubarb. Bake for 45 minutes, until the rhubarb is tender. Cool in the pan and serve barely warm.

15 SERVINGS

# Mildred Brummond's Beet Cake

The flavor of this delicate chocolate cake has a beguiling earthy twist, thanks to the grated beets. Without frosting, it is an excellent coffee companion. Frosted, it becomes more festive.

- 1½ cups sugar
- 3 large eggs
- ¼ teaspoon vanilla extract
- 1 cup vegetable oil
- 1½ cups grated cooked beets
- ½ cup unsweetened cocoa
- 1¾ cups all-purpose flour
- 1½ teaspoons baking soda
- ¼ teaspoon salt
- ½ cup water

Preheat the oven to 350 degrees. Grease and flour a 9-x-13-inch cake pan.

Combine the sugar, eggs, vanilla, and oil in a large bowl. Beat well. Add the beets and cocoa. Beat again. Sift the flour, baking soda, and salt together in another bowl and stir into the batter along with the water. Pour into the prepared pan.

Bake for 35 minutes, or until a sharp knife inserted into the cake comes out clean.

Cool the cake in the pan. Top with frosting if desired.

12 TO 15 SERVINGS

# Seven-Minute Frosting

This fine, old-fashioned seven-minute frosting has been one of our favorites ever since we published it in our first cookbook, *Square Meals*, in 1984. It's sweet and simple, the perfect crown for Mildred Brummond's cake or the cake on page 111.

|     |                               |
| --- | ----------------------------- |
| 2   | egg whites                    |
| 1½  | cups sugar                    |
| 5   | tablespoons water             |
| 1½  | teaspoons light corn syrup    |
| 1   | teaspoon vanilla extract      |

Combine the egg whites, sugar, water, and corn syrup in the top of a double boiler or a medium saucepan and beat with a rotary beater until they are thoroughly mixed. Place the mixture over rapidly boiling water if using a double boiler, or place the saucepan in a larger one with boiling water to come partway up the sides. Beating constantly, cook for 7 minutes, or until the frosting stands in peaks. Remove from the heat. Add the vanilla and beat until the frosting is thick enough to spread.

MAKES ENOUGH TO FROST THE TOP AND SIDES OF A TWO-LAYER CAKE

# Four for the Road

Many people think it would be fun to travel with us. Many people are wrong. We have a road trip rhythm that works just fine for Jane and Michael Stern but would be hell to those of normal appetite and laid-back way of traveling. Drive, drive, drive; eat, eat, eat; drive some more; eat some more; eat again. Go to sleep. Wake up. Eat. Drive. Eat. Drive. Most folks would find this tiring and not the least bit fun, not to mention how annoyed we would get dragging along a person with something on the mind other than roadfood.

The first time we considered inviting a guest into our back seat was in the late 1970s. We had a literary agent whose specialty was representing books that became big-budget movie deals. At this time in cultural history, intercourse between the book business and Hollywood was thriving, and everyone wanted in on the action, despite evidence that all writers got screwed and all studio people got rich. Surely we deserved a piece of the pie of these hybrid deals, which were half jokingly called boovies and mooks: books written only to become movies, the deal done before the first page was written. Exactly how our passion for barbecued ribs and roadside America would play into the formula was a bit cloudy, but we were swept away by the tide. Of course *Roadfood* would make a brilliant movie!

We hung out with our big-time agent in her grandiose New York office. She was always talking to movie stars on the phone. It was thrilling. We learned all the lingo: pay-or-play, gross vs. net, locking in the merchandise (all those *Roadfood* action figures!).

One day over lunch at the Italian Pavilion (then the chic spot to have publishing lunch), she polished off her third glass of wine and announced, "It would be wonderful for me to get in the back seat of your car and go cross-country with you!" After a few more glasses of wine, she confided that she had a chronic bladder condition and had to pee every twenty minutes.

Looking back, we were prescient to know without a shadow of a doubt that there was no way on earth we could take this high-powered woman and her high-powered bladder on a roadfood trip. Late that afternoon, when we called her from home to tell her it wouldn't work out, she seemed to draw a blank as to what we were talking about, and she promptly got off the phone to speak to Clint or Kevin or Ted.

Then we met Bob Gottlieb, king of Knopf, emperor of publishing. *Roadfood* had been published before, but we yearned to redo it. Our first encounter was in his corner office high up in the big old Random House tower on Third Avenue and 50th Street in Manhattan. He was in the midst of his brown-bag lunch of sardines and buttermilk, at the same time giving himself a haircut while speaking on the phone to superagent Irving "Swifty" Lazar. He cut his hair without looking in the mirror and used his other hand, holding the telephone, to wave us into his office.

Bob loved the idea of roadfood. Although he made a point of letting us know that he often dined at Lutèce, he also made it clear that he really loved chicken croquettes and cupcakes. Looking around his office, we were delirious with joy. Here was the great editor of our time, the publisher of Knopf, the most prestigious house in town, with a bust of Elvis on his desk and an office cluttered with the same kind of kitsch we had at home.

All our will to remain strictly a duo melted. We invited Bob to come along to Tennessee.

We soon learned that Bob owned, was responsible for, had published, had invented, was the force behind, was the founder of everything in the world. Whenever we stopped in a bookstore, Bob would merrily prance through the aisles pointing at bestsellers and saying, "Mine . . . mine . . . mine . . . mine." Some he had ghostwritten and some he had acquired as an editor. During the early 1980s he flew to meet us in Chicago. Our plan was to drive downstate and into Iowa for a week of roadfooding and flea marketing, with Bob and his friend and publishing right hand, Martha Kaplan. That afternoon the three of us strolled along Michigan Avenue in anticipation of a rib dinner at Carson's that night in Skokie. It was a glorious spring day: deep blue sky, cool breezes off Lake Michigan, the late-day sun glinting gold off skyscrapers. Bob led the way along the Magnificent Mile and began a soliloquy about the city — its history, its cultural meaning, exactly why Chicago was so great. As we walked, he made sweeping gestures toward the skyline, as if all the city were his.

"I know, Bob — I was born and raised here," Michael noted.

Bob gave him a look. "It doesn't matter, because you do not understand Chicago the way I do," he said. And on we went to eat our ribs, which, no doubt, Bob would explain to us.

In fact, Bob had never known ribs like these, nor had he been to a restaurant like Carson's, which is a dramatically midwestern eating experience. It is not at all like the kind of hole-in-the-wall hash house that tends to draw our attention in small towns or city neighborhoods. From our faraway parking place in its large lot, Carson's looked a lot like the sort of function hall where people hold rehearsal dinners or bar mitzvahs. (There are a couple of other branches around town.) Inside, the air conditioning was on high and the lights were low. Benches at the broad, capacious booths were deep and over-stuffed. This was a place designed for the extreme comfort of big eaters as well as eaters who are big. As we waited in the bar among a crowd of dressed-up, bejeweled people whose vibrant colognes and perfumes were dizzying, we knifed into immense blocks of schmaltzy chopped liver and schmeared it onto excellent sour-crusted rye bread.

Carson's ribs are baby backs, nothing like the mighty soul-food ribs of such South Side institutions as Lem's and Leon's. Nevertheless, they left us in awe. A foot-and-a-half-long rack was sensuously sticky with a baked-on sauce that was striated red-gold as if it had been painted by an artist of the Hudson River School. The sauce's flavor was a fetching balance of hot, sweet, and smoky, just the right exclamation point for the velvety moist meat that barely clung to each bone.

Although we knew we were going to Garrett Popcorn Shop that evening for a few pounds of "Chicago Mix," a half-and-half combo of caramel corn and cheese corn, we topped off our ribs with Carson's gold brick sundaes — a Chicago favorite that is vanilla ice cream topped with a chocolate sauce dotted with bits of praline and toasted pecans. Gold brick sauce hardens as soon as it is applied to the sundae, creating a sheath of enriched chocolate that melts in your mouth to complement the ice cream.

The next morning we had plate-size, four-inch-tall baked apple pancakes at the incomparable Walker Brothers Pancake House in Wilmette, north of the city. There can be no question that these prodigious monuments of eggy batter, swirled cinnamon syrup, and soft stewed apples are the most delicious pancakes in America, and yet Bob spent much of the meal singing the praises of the Royal Canadian Pancake House back near his home in New York City. We were dubious, and in fact a later visit to the not-so-Royal Canadian back east confirmed our skepticism about the thick, doughy things they serve there. But at the time we didn't dare debate the topic with Bob. We knew we would soon be in the car and on our way into the fields and farmland of downstate Illinois.

Once we got out of the city and on the road, the dynamics shifted. In many ways, Bob and Martha were at our mercy. We made the itinerary. We picked where to eat, and we ordered the meals. It was at the White Way Café in Durant, Iowa, that we first saw Bob dumbfounded. First of all, it was five o'clock and it was dinnertime. No matter how we tried to explain this, Bob simply would not — could not — understand the fact that people in farm country eat dinner early. "I'll just have a snack, then later I will eat dinner," he said. We explained that there was no "later," and that by eight o'clock, every restaurant within a hundred miles would be closed for the night.

At five the White Way was packed. It had won the coveted Pork Producers Award for Excellence — in Iowa, the equivalent of an Oscar — and everyone for miles around knew that this was the place to go for a great meal. The cost of dinner was $5, for which you got more food than at a Thanksgiving banquet. "Order pork," Michael said, which we all did, after which the waitress directed us to the salad bar.

Only once in all the time we've known Bob have we seen him rendered speechless. That moment came just after we rose from our seats and approached the White Way salad bar. We all grabbed chilled plates at one end of the long table, but as the two of us started helping ourselves, Bob stood motionless. A look of horror spread across his face, and then he broke into gales of laughter. Nothing could have prepared any true New Yorker for salad like this. For here were Iowa-style salads, which is to say that not a shred of lettuce was to be found anywhere among the dozen-plus selections. There were three different styles of layered, multicolored Jell-O, one studded with pretzel bits, one laced with cole slaw, one made from Coca-Cola and dotted with miniature marshmallows. Then there were the composed salads: pea salad with Miracle Whip and nuggets of ham, macaroni salad with pickle bits and crumbled hard-boiled egg, carrot-raisin slaw, ambrosia of canned pineapple chunks, marshmallows, mandarin orange slices, and shredded coconut all bound in sour cream. And there were puddings: chocolate, tapioca, and vanilla. "This is dessert!" Bob cried. We shook our heads, reminding him that it was the hors d' oeuvre course and dessert would be only-in-Iowa pie. Like the rube who drinks lemon water from the finger bowl in a fancy restaurant, Bob was out of his element. But being good sports, he and Martha piled salads on their plates, and Bob insisted that we photograph him with his bizarre selection. That way, people back east would believe it when he described it to them.

The pork roast was magnificent: thick, tender slices that oozed sweet juice under the weight of a mere fork. By this point in our career we were savvy enough to have ordered dessert the moment we sat down. The White Way was famous for its sour cream raisin pie, but the kitchen made only a certain number of pies each day. Latecomers to dinner — those who arrived after six — ran the risk of going pieless unless they reserved their pieces while they could. The custom of ordering dessert even before one looked at the menu was a stumper to Bob and Martha.

On the road, we were top dogs in other ways. Some of the places we discovered looked pretty rough around the edges, and so to make sure we would all come out alive, Michael became the point man. Especially at night, it was his job to leave the car — engine running — and enter the tough-looking bar where we had heard they served a wicked-good grilled bratwurst sandwich. Michael cased the joint while Jane, Bob, and Martha waited in the car, and if he came out the door giving the thumbs-up, we all went in. If he hurried out and leaped into the driver's seat, we sped away to the next restaurant on our hit list.

No matter how compatible traveling companions may be, it is annoying to deal with their on-the-road habits. Bob and Martha hated air conditioning, even on hot summer days in the Deep South; we blasted it always. To get exercise, Martha did laps in every motel pool, water into which Jane would not have stuck a germ-phobic big toe, and Bob did a weird set of old-style calisthenics that lacked only a medicine ball and Indian clubs. Worst of all, Bob and Martha drank the Tang and ate the awful supermarket doughnuts set out as "continental breakfast" in every $16-per-night motel where we stayed. Even if we were planning to start the day at Skinhead's in Paducah, Kentucky, with exemplary southern biscuits and sausage gravy, or at the Dutch Kitchen in Frackville, Pennsylvania, with hot sticky buns or pumpkin pancakes, they wanted to sit at one of the laminated tables and take full advantage of the lame breakfast amenities.

The end of the Iowa road trip for Bob and Martha was the beginning of a long haul for us. We headed back to Chicago via the Kane County, Illinois, flea market, one of the biggest in the nation. Our appetites may have been tireless, but Bob and Martha's energy for plundering flea markets was superhuman. We packed so much of their newly acquired treasure in our car that there was barely room for the two of them in the back seat when we took them to O'Hare Airport so they could fly back to New York. We drove east with a junk store's worth of macramé owls, purple choir robes, old-time lard cans, Waring blenders, creative taxidermy, paintings, purses, and shoeboxes full of linen postcards.

One chilly winter day sometime thereafter, we were comfortably ensconced at home when we got a call from Bob. We recognized his fluty, authoritative voice immediately. "Martha and I just had chicken croquettes," he announced. "They were horrible!"

He paused dramatically, then began reading an entry to us from *Roadfood* in which we had glowingly described the croquettes in the same New Jersey diner from which he had just emerged. "You know nothing about croquettes, nor about chicken," he said. "I will find you great chicken croquettes."

The next week we got a note from Bob describing a town café in Pennsylvania where he had found worthy chicken croquettes at a price he described as "criminally low."

A little skeptical, and half hoping the croquettes he'd found would be awful, we went out of our way to visit the place. And damned if the chicken croquettes weren't some of the best we've ever had: twin pyramids of coarse-ground chicken meat mixed with sage stuffing, their insides moist, like dark meat just pulled off a bone, their crust a crunchy red-gold that cracked open and sent wisps of aromatic steam above the plate. They were blanketed with cream gravy and served with a side of mashed potatoes and homemade succotash that contained butter beans with flesh as luxurious as filet mignon.

Of course we included Bob's croquette discovery in the next edition of our book. "Ah, yes, *Roadfood*," we could hear him say. "Mine!"

# Cola Cake
## with Broiled Peanut Butter Frosting

Cola cake is rarely served in restaurants, but it is a staple at bake sales throughout the South and Midwest. We got our recipe from a cookbook published by a church group in a small town in western Iowa, and it has proven to be a favorite among even our most worldly sweet-tooth friends back home.

THE CAKE

|   |   |
|---|---|
| 2 | cups all-purpose flour |
| 2 | cups sugar |
| 16 | tablespoons (2 sticks) butter, melted |
| 2 | tablespoons unsweetened cocoa |
| 1 | cup Pepsi-Cola (with fizz) |
| ½ | cup buttermilk |
| 2 | large eggs, beaten |
| 1 | teaspoon baking soda |
| 1 | teaspoon vanilla extract |
| 1–1½ | cups miniature marshmallows |

THE FROSTING

|   |   |
|---|---|
| 6 | tablespoons (¾ stick) butter, softened |
| 1 | cup dark brown sugar |
| ⅔ | cup smooth peanut butter |
| ¼ | cup milk |
| ⅔ | cup chopped salted peanuts |

TO MAKE THE CAKE: Preheat the oven to 350 degrees. Grease and flour a 9-x-13-x-2-inch baking pan.

Combine the flour and sugar in a large bowl.

Combine the melted butter, cocoa, and Pepsi in another bowl and pour it over the flour and sugar mixture. Stir until well blended. Add the buttermilk, beaten eggs, baking soda, and vanilla. Mix well. Stir in the marshmallows. Pour into the baking pan.

Bake for 40 minutes. Remove the cake from the oven.

TO MAKE THE FROSTING: While the cake is baking, cream together the butter, sugar, and peanut butter in a mixing bowl. Beat in the milk. Fold in the nuts. Frost the cake, still in the pan, while it is barely warm.

Place the frosted cake under a broiler about 4 inches from the heat source. Broil just a few seconds, or until the frosting starts to bubble. Watch constantly and be careful not to scorch it.

Let cool for at least 30 minutes before serving.

8 TO 10 SERVINGS

# Hap Townes's Shockingly Sweet Stewed Tomatoes

One of the great joys of traveling around the country with diehard New Yorkers was the opportunity to introduce them to dishes unheard of in sophisticated city restaurants. Stewed tomatoes were a shocking revelation to culinary sophisticates for whom fresh is always better than canned. In addition to celebrating the value of canned goods, this recipe is a vivid reminder that tomatoes are in fact not vegetables but fruits.

Hap Townes was the proprietor of a small, blue-collar cafeteria that was a fixture in Nashville, Tennessee, for decades. Stewed tomatoes, a favorite side dish throughout much of the South, represent the regional cooking principle of extended-time cookery that transforms produce from something that might be elegant and simple into food that is garishly kitsch. Needless to say, it is a terrible faux pas even to think of using fresh tomatoes in this recipe. Canned and long-cooked are the keys.

- 1  28-ounce can whole tomatoes, including juice
- 8  slices white bread, well toasted
- 8  tablespoons (1 stick) butter
- 1  cup sugar

Place the tomatoes and juice in a large saucepan. Tear the toast into about 4 pieces per slice and add it to the tomatoes. Add the butter and sugar.

Simmer, uncovered, for 20 minutes, stirring occasionally, until thickened. Serve warm.

6 TO 8 SERVINGS

# I Hear America Eating

After laying waste to a hundred meals in ten days or less, we get slap-happy. The roadfood obsession becomes so pervasive that it infiltrates our dreams, like the night in a Maryland motel when Michael woke up screaming because he was being chased by a huge spiced blue crab, and it makes everything we encounter appear food-related. In our demented eyes, signs and billboards suddenly are all about eating. A movie marquee for *Dead Calm* we misread as "Dead Clam." The construction sign that says PASS BY gets misinterpreted as "Chess Pie"; MOTEL 500 FEET becomes "Morels: $5.00 Apiece." POLLED HEREFORDS gets misread as "Boiled Roadfood." It may not be pathological, but it happens with such regularity that we have to conclude that our brains have become wired to go that way at the slightest provocation. Jane once saved a catalogue from Hammacher Schlemmer because she thought it said "Hamhouses and Such."

The more we are out there, away from home, wandering along blue highways and roads so small they look like gray silk filaments on the map, the more our sight and hearing warp.

The onset of roadfood delirium first became apparent to us during one of our initial trips into the South, where we found a charming old town café in Benson, North Carolina, called Dixon's. We were perched on red leather stools at noontime, eyeballing beautiful plates of fried chicken and vegetables getting eaten by regulars sitting to our left and right.

"What will you have, hons?" the waitress asked.

"Fried chicken!" we called out in unison.

"What are those vegetables?" Michael asked, pointing to a plate coming from the kitchen that featured an especially lovely arrangement of green and orange around the gold-crusted thigh, breast, and wing.

"Yams and bald okra," the waitress answered.

"How do they make okra bald?" asked Michael, imagining someone in the kitchen shaving each fuzzy pod. He was frantically scribbling notes in his notepad about this newly discovered, strange regional specialty.

The waitress didn't know how to answer him, but Jane recognized the symptoms of roadfood mind warp and chanted, "Boiled, boiled, boiled!" until Michael crossed out *bald* in his notes.

The singular food focus that drives us on the road and causes us to see and hear everything in the context of something to eat includes a fascination with the regional accents we hear at lunch counters and local dining rooms. From the ear-bending patois of Long Island to the sugarcane sweetness of north Georgia, from the bold honk of Chicago to the musical refinement of New Mexico's mountain villages, the voices people use to talk about what they eat are as enchanting as the food itself. We love the smooth musical timbre of the Appalachians and the arcane cadence of Georgia's Sea Islands, although both of them can be so intense that the meaning of what we're hearing may escape us. As we hunt along the byways of America, we hear languages that are nominally English but far from the English we grew up on. We must admit to having long conversations with people in Acadian Louisiana and in black neighborhoods on the South Side of Chicago where, like foreigners, we understand maybe one third of what we hear. Michael, who can be a great mimic, will often instantly and entirely unconsciously adopt local accents even when the specifics of the vernacular remain a mystery. Jane, who has absolutely no talent for mimicry, valiantly tries her hand at accents, but inevitably winds up sounding like a Swedish immigrant to whom English is a challenge.

Our ears aren't tuned only to the way people speak. Beyond accents, we savor the sounds of restaurants wherever we go. Many food-savvy people have rhapsodized about the great tastes and smells and sights of a road trip, but few mention what eating sounds like. In the Carolinas, for example, the barbecue experience is every bit as aural as it is oral. When you walk into a great pit such as Carl Duke's in Orangeburg, South Carolina, the room tone is such that you might think you have entered a meditation ceremony on the verge of epiphany. Hardly anyone is talking, and there is no music at all, if music means a tune you can hum. But there is a beguiling rhythm in the air — the *thump-whack-thud* of the cleaver as the pitmaster places hickory-cooked pork shoulder on the cutting block and hacks it into shreds. It's exaggerating only a little to describe the ambience as devotional. Great barbecues inspire an attitude of reverence. And it isn't only a Carolina thing. In Texas, the very geography of a classic pit gives the room a churchlike character.

The City Market in Luling (home of Texas's annual Watermelon Thump) is a good example. It has long picnic tables up front, shared by strangers; to get a meal, you pad back and enter the room where the chopping blocks are. You face the block man the way congregants face a clergyman — hungry for sustenance. Behind him is the *sanctum sanctorum*, the pit itself, from which beef briskets and sausages are retrieved and laid upon age-rounded cutting blocks to be severed into slices. Very low, behind the crinkly sound of brisket being semi-packaged in butcher's paper for customers to carry back to tables, you might hear the faint sizzle of hot sausages ready to burst with juice.

At table, true barbecue believers have little interest in conversation. In a minor key set to the cleaver's cadence, you will hear only a faint chorus of pleasure moans, slurping, and licking. This mellow harmony will be punctuated by the periodic festive *whoosh* of quick-released carbonation as caps are twisted off bottles of Dr Peppers, Cokes, and long-necks.

In contrast to the quasi-religious hush of a great barbecue, the shriek of an all-business staff can give short-order meals their own kind of hypnotic urgency. No place has a higher energy level than the Beacon Drive-In of Spartanburg, South Carolina. While it is entirely possible to order your meal from the car window (dealing with a staff of magnificent carhops), the best way to do the Beacon is to go inside and walk through the line. It is a flabbergasting experience. Entering this place is like walking into a tornado. New customers push in behind you. The line ahead moves nearly as fast as a Marine platoon in close-order drill. From behind the counter, white-aproned waiters scream at you to hurry up and place your order. "Barbecue," you stammer. "Pork-a-plenty, sliced, with slaw and onions."

Before the last syllable is out of your mouth, J. C. Strobel, master of the serving line, is yelling your order back to an immense open kitchen, where dozens of cooks chop and fry and assemble meals in what seems like total chaos and confusion, as loud as a Detroit car factory. You breeze down the counter, beneath signs advising, J. C. SAYS IT'S FINE TO PASS IN LINE and PLACE YOUR MONEY IN HAND AND HAVE YOUR ORDER IN MIND SO WE CAN GET YOU TO THE BALL GAME ON TIME, get your presweetened iced tea (there's none sweeter), and *bam!* your order is ready, on a tray set before you. The cacophony leaves most customers speechless.

Such sounds are the reason it is impossible to replicate a road-food experience at home or even in another restaurant removed from the natural region where the meal belongs. Sure, background music can provide a good reminder of the food's place of origin — zydeco tunes for a Cajun eatery, mariachi music for a burrito joint — but all the *other* things you hear are vital, too. The joy of so many memorable restaurants includes the unique sounds of cooking, serving, ordering, and eating a meal. Even if you have the exact recipe and all the proper ingredients for a dish, it is impractical, if not impossible, to audio-clone the distinct local accent of the clientele and staff, the hiss and crackle of a bacon-crowded short-order griddle at 6 A.M., the indus-trial whir of a triple-wand milk-shake blender, or the clatter of heavy Melmac plates on a linoleum counter.

Perhaps one reason we paid so much attention to restaurant sounds when we first hit the road was that the road seemed so silent. Our scrawny AM radio gave up trying to get a signal fifty miles from New York. We had no air conditioning, so we rolled down the win-dows and listened to the hum of the tires. There were no iPods, cell phones, or CD players. We talked to each other until we were sick of talking, so when we found a place to eat that allowed us to hear the sounds of other voices, it was like water in the desert.

The road was beginning to work its magic on us. Like most stressed-out souls, we normally spend as little time as possible ex-posed to the human race. At movies, we dread people sitting near us. We hate shopping malls for their agoraphobic clatter, and although carpooling is environmentally noble, we much prefer the onanistic luxury of being alone in our own car.

But when we began traveling to faraway places with strange-sounding names, we craved talking to other people. We became social creatures. We wanted to schmooze with the locals in Truth or Conse-quences, New Mexico, and in Paris, Maine. We struck up conversa-tions wherever we could. Pulled over for speeding in Kentucky bluegrass country, we spent a half-hour bending the ear of the cop about which town had the best café for lunch. Michael would get haircuts he didn't need just for the pleasure of sitting in the barber's chair and chatting, as is customary when one's head is being clippered. It was in one such chair in eastern North Carolina that we learned all about the herring that swim upstream to spawn in the Roanoke River every spring. Junior Bond, the barber, who was shaving Michael's neck with a straight razor, explained that the herring run was such a big deal that it was the occasion for people to come from Farnyeer, which we assumed was a distant town . . . until we realized he was saying "far and near."

In restaurants, we eavesdrop shamelessly. We have listened in on two mule traders swapping tricks about making an old plug look like a racehorse. We have heard workers outside a steel mill rake their rotten boss over the coals as they knock back shots and beers. We have sat with forks poised in midair as a couple of sixteen-year-olds in an adjacent booth plan their elopement.

Best of all places to tune in to local life, we discovered, is the round table in a small-town café. There is no seating arrangement so conducive to friendly conversation as this magic place in a restaurant that is shared by singles and doubles as they come and go from before dawn until midmorning. Some folks arrive and hold court; others sit down and say almost nothing. To the timid newcomer, joining such a table can seem like an intrusion, but we've never found one where we weren't welcomed . . . or at least tolerated.

One of the best sets of round tables we found was in the small town of McComb, Mississippi: the Dinner Bell. It's closed now, but in its heyday the Dinner Bell served meals in the boarding-house style inspired by the Mendenhall Hotel. Diners were seated around huge circular tables set with sixteen places. The waitstaff brought ham and dumplings, candied yams, fried chicken, and cat head–sized biscuits from the kitchen on platters and placed them on a lazy Susan built into the center of the table. Then the fun began. Someone would reach for a piece of fried chicken from the platter, then the next guy would spin the lazy Susan to grab a piece, and pretty soon, like a carousel going full tilt, platters of food would be spinning past as happy people used fork and fingers to spear or snag what they wanted. There was never any anxiety that the food would run out, nor hostility to someone who took the two best-looking drumsticks, because the platters were filled constantly throughout the meal by the kitchen staff.

The catch-as-catch-can service naturally inspired discussion, and as we enjoyed our round-table lunch, we struck up a conversation with the fellow who ran the local filling station, who was so amazed that we lived in the far-off, exotic state of Connecticut that he offered us a free air freshener for our vehicle. A gal who worked at the town dry cleaner's promised that she could remove the fried chicken stain from Michael's tie. One pig farmer in overalls asked us if we had ham this good up north (no!) and proceeded to tell all the goofy farm jokes currently making the rounds.

Eating is not the primary purpose of sitting down at one of these tables. The real agenda is socializing. One such table that we visited at a rustic café in northern Kentucky actually had a sign hanging from the ceiling overhead designating it as THE LIARS' CLUB. It is here that café regulars exchanged news, opinions, gossip, and weather reports.

We found one of our favorite round tables while hunting great biscuits in Georgia. Every morning at Mamie's Kitchen in Conyers, east of Atlanta, you find a contingent of local residents having meals that range from a cup of black coffee to biscuits topped with pork tenderloin and gravy. From this table the regulars are paged by the staff when a call comes in on the house phone, and to this table they bring whatever's on their mind of a morning. Between seven and nine, the population of the table changes continuously as husbands and wives, coworkers, friends, and family arrive, eat, coffee up, and say goodbye until tomorrow.

Sometimes the table for six has more than a dozen people crowded around it, and they all know each other very well. But in our experience, this liars' club is not cliquish. After three days of eating our way through Mamie's biscuit menu (including salmon-patty biscuits, red link sausage biscuits, and biscuits filled with streak o' lean, the true pork-lover's breakfast meat — reminiscent of bacon, but chewier, fattier, and rimmed with hard rind), we began to do as others around us were doing: pouring coffee into half-empty cups all around the small dining room whenever we got up to fetch seconds for ourselves, then carrying our fourth or fifth cup over to the big table to share in the palaver.

Peggy Vickery, a Dolly Parton look-alike with big blond hair and spectacular makeup who starts her day with a ham biscuit and coffee, joins the group every morning before opening Peggy's Hair Fashions, her nearby beauty salon.

"We tell the husbands how to treat their wives," Peggy says.

"And we try to teach these women how to treat a man," says a fellow in overalls as he spoons into a plateful of buttered grits. "But they never pay attention!"

"We kill each other when it's election time," a jelly-biscuit eater adds.

"Mostly we talk about what we did when we were young," says an older man.

"But can't do any more," his pal adds.

"But wish we could," says another.

"Now, wait a minute," Peggy says, hushing the men and pointing to us. "These two are writing a story for a family magazine."

"But Peggy, dear," says the man to her right, gesturing with his hot biscuit around the table, at which eight people are currently gathered, "we *are* family, aren't we?"

# Mamie's Buttermilk Biscuits

Anytime you order a biscuit at Mamie's, it comes hot from the oven. Its knobby golden surface has a gentle crunch, and although the inside is fleecy, it is not fragile. This is a bun with enough substance to retain its pliant texture even as it absorbs savory red-eye gravy from the drippings of country ham, juices from a patty of country sausage, or melted butter from a heap of soft-scrambled eggs. It is substantial bedding for an open-face chicken biscuit: a broad piece of boneless, pan-fried chicken laid across a split biscuit and blanketed with gravy made from the juices in the frying skillet. It even holds up as a mitt for streak o' lean, the extra-rich bacon.

Standing in the order line, you have a clear view of the biscuit maker at work above a broad silver bowl, her arms white with flour and deep in the bowl, turning over the dough, patting it down, and turning it again. She reaches down, squeezes off one biscuit's worth, and caresses it briefly between her hands until it assumes the right roundish shape and is ready to be baked. It's hypnotic to watch the ritual, and while the biscuit maker occasionally might talk with other members of the kitchen staff, who are busy frying bacon and dishing out bowls of slow-cooked grits, she spends a lot of time in meditative silence, her hands busy but eyes unfocused as if in prayer.

The only real way to learn how to make good biscuits is to apprentice with someone who knows how. The art is less a matter of ingredients (which are generally uninteresting) than of technique, which is deceptively simple. This classic recipe for buttermilk biscuits is straightforward, but give it to five cooks and you will get five different biscuits, each with its own character. The difference primarily lies in how the dough is handled or, more exactly, how *little* the dough is handled. Generally speaking, the less kneading, the fluffier the biscuit.

2½  cups self-rising flour
    Dash of salt
½   teaspoon sugar
3   tablespoons chilled shortening
½   cup buttermilk
½   cup whole milk
2   tablespoons butter, melted

Preheat the oven to 475 degrees. Lightly grease a 14-x-16-inch baking pan.

Sift the flour, salt, and sugar together into a mixing bowl. Cut in the shortening with two knives or your fingers until the mixture is coarse. Add the buttermilk, milk, and 1 tablespoon of the butter. Mix lightly until combined, but do not overmix. Turn the mixture out onto a floured surface.

With floured hands, knead the dough two or three times. (If the biscuits are to be used for sandwiches, such as ham biscuits or other breakfast sandwiches, knead it a few extra times so they will be sturdier.)

With floured hands, pat out the dough approximately ½ inch thick. Using a floured biscuit cutter or standard-size can, cut out biscuits. Do not twist the cutter when doing this — press straight down. (You can re-knead and cut the dough scraps, but biscuits from this cutting will be tougher, more suitable for sandwiches.)

Place the biscuits on the baking pan. Bake for 10 to 12 minutes, until golden brown. Remove the biscuits from the oven and brush them with the remaining butter. Serve immediately.

MAKES 12 BISCUITS

# Hopkins House Apple Salad

During our last visit to Hopkins House, in 2003, we watched Margaret Pope and her son Mike cutting apples into chunks in the kitchen, then sat down at the lunch table to experience the salad they were preparing. We love this concoction, not only for its brazen sugar content but as culinary contraband — hail the maraschino cherry! — and also because it exemplifies the candidly sweet (and canned-ingredient) salad found at so many southern buffet tables.

    3   large Red Delicious apples, cored and cut into bite-sized pieces
    1   8-ounce can crushed pineapple in pineapple juice
   30   maraschino cherries, cut in half (contents of a 10-ounce jar, drained of juice)
    1   cup sweetened coconut flakes
   ¾   cup mayonnaise

Combine the ingredients in a bowl. Mix well. Refrigerate for 30 minutes to an hour before serving.

10 SERVINGS

# Mrs. Hopkins's Copper Pennies

The Hopkins House is no more. When we began eating there in the last years of the twentieth century, the boarders already were gone, but meal service was old-fashioned boarding-house style. Over the years, working men and women from downtown Pensacola, Florida, as well as enlisted men and brass from the city's naval base learned to depend on Mrs. Hopkins as faithfully as children depend on their parents to feed them. Among the everyday Pensacolans who regularly lined up waiting for the door to open at 11 A.M. and 5 P.M., there were usually at least a few savvy foodies from distant regions who had traveled to this grand old city mansion for the rare opportunity to savor the extravagant food and high spirits of a Deep South boarding-house feast. Eating here was like going to a church supper or a big family reunion.

Once inside the dining area, you were directed to an open seat at one of several tables with capacities that ranged from four to twelve. Unless you happened to be part of the first wave in the door, you were seated among people who were already eating and talking with each other. It was amazing how quickly even reticent newcomers joined the party. Eaters with experience were delighted to explain to neophytes that the chunky dark orange vegetable with the smoky taste was fresh rutabaga, that turnip greens were greatly improved by a spritz of hot pepper sauce, and that the smooth coconut custard attained a magical sophistication when you sprinkled it with a few drops of fresh lemon to harmonize with its sweetness.

For those of us who came from, shall we say, less sociable parts of the country, the friendliness was shocking. Instantly, you were dining with cousins and aunts and uncles and chatting about where you were headed and where you had been, and would you please pass the smothered chicken, and who took the last corn muffin?

The family feel was enhanced by the maternal propriety of the dining areas, decorated with souvenir plates that Ma Hopkins received over the years as gifts from thankful patrons. White lace curtains hung over the windows, and in the vestibule, where people waited for a seat to open up, signs told you, NO HATS WORN AT TABLE, SHIRTS AND SHOES MUST BE WORN IN DINING ROOM, and TANK TOPS, UNDERSHIRTS, AND MUSCLE SHIRTS ARE NOT PERMISSIBLE. These were Mrs. Hopkins's rules, and she was not reluctant to enforce them. "She personified your typical southern grandmother," recalled Nick Geeker, a federal circuit court judge who grew up at these tables and took lunch at the boarding house (which was near the courthouse) three or four times a week. "She was not overbearing, but you didn't want to get out of line, either. She would set you straight!"

Years ago, we convinced Mrs. Hopkins to write down her recipe for cooked carrots, which she called "copper pennies." It required some interpretation, as she was not too specific about how big "1 sack carrots" was or how long to cook anything, but we did manage to come up with this formula, a beguiling sweet-and-sour vegetable dish that has become a regular at our dinner table.

2   pounds carrots, peeled and cut into ¼-inch-thick disks
1   medium green bell pepper, seeded and cut into sliver-thin rings
1   medium red onion, cut into sliver-thin rings
1   10-ounce can tomato soup
½   cup vegetable oil
⅔   cup sugar
¾   cup cider vinegar

1   teaspoon dry mustard
1   teaspoon Worcestershire sauce
1   teaspoon salt
½   teaspoon pepper

Boil the carrots until cooked but still firm. Drain. Combine the cooked carrots with the sliced pepper and onion in a heatproof bowl.

Combine all the remaining ingredients in a saucepan. Bring to a simmer over medium heat. Remove from the heat and pour the mixture over the carrots, onion, and pepper. Stir well. Cover and refrigerate overnight. Serve cold.

8 TO 10 SERVINGS

# The Maryland Paradox

Just when we thought our roadfood sights were zeroed to minute-of-angle precision, Maryland threw us off target. We were proud to bag such scarcities as liver pudding and made-from-scratch creamed chipped beef in diners of the state's western panhandle, and we hit many good places to indulge in blue crabs, stuffed flounder, and terrapin chowder all around the Chesapeake Bay. But we hadn't a clue about how to find one of the state's most distinctive dishes, because we were blind to the restaurants that serve it.

A trucker we met at Helen's Sausage House in Smyrna, Delaware, helped us see the light. We were having lunch in Helen's Elvis Room — a section of the short-order restaurant where the walls are covered with images of the King onstage, in movies, and on television. As we plowed into sandwiches of pork chops and sausages, a little yelp came out from the floor by the feet of a big man sitting next to us at his own table over a pair of double-sausage hoagies glistening with fried green peppers and sautéed onions. The guy was a huge, human-sized whole ham, widest at the shoulders, tapering down to a virtually assless torso and topped with a neck that was significantly wider than his shaved head, which sat like a smooth round apple on top. He wore no shirt, just big faded overalls that showed shockingly hairless bare pink arms and chest. The yelp we heard was followed by a scampering sound, like that of a scared rat, running out from between the man's legs toward Jane.

The critter turned out to be not a rodent but a teacup Chihuahua, which the big guy scooped off the linoleum by gracefully leaning back in his chair and sweeping one voluminous hand down like a first baseman's mitt. After catching his dog, he looked at us with a sheepish apology on his face, then glanced toward the cash register to make sure no one behind the counter had noticed his canine companion. "Cecil!" he scolded in the most unintimidating tone possible, quieting the dog in his lap with a few shreds of bread lubricated by sausage drippings. He finished his meal and left the restaurant with Cecil tucked in the front pocket of his overalls.

Homesick for our own bullmastiffs (each of which weighed fifty times what Cecil did), we struck up a conversation in the parking lot as the man walked around his eighteen-wheeler, beating on tires with an iron to make sure none was flat. We agreed with him that Helen's sausages were the best, and the conversation went to other favorite places to eat pork along the Atlantic Coast, including Italian sausage on Federal Hill in Providence and the various kinds of barbecue in North and South Carolina. The guy was devoted to the idea of roadfood (although he most certainly had never heard of our book), and he said he liked being a trucker because of all the different things he could eat wherever he went. As we chatted, we couldn't help but notice his heavy Maryland accent — the kind that says *Bommer* for *Baltimore* and *Merlin* for *Maryland* — so we figured he would be a good person to ask for tips on where to eat stuffed ham.

We were desperate for clues. We knew that stuffed ham is unique to St. Mary's County, Maryland. And we knew that starting in the autumn, it is a centerpiece at church suppers and firemen's balls and is sold by the pound at the deli counter of grocery stores. We were intent on finding restaurants that serve it, but a couple of trips along Highway 235 south from Waldorf to St. Mary's City had disclosed not a single place to sit down and order some to eat. We had begun to wonder if stuffed ham was a historical dish that had disappeared from modern restaurant menus, like Philadelphia pepper pot or true Texas chili-parlor chili. We yearned to find it, not only because it would be a coup for *Roadfood* but because it sounded so delicious.

Stuffed ham is indeed a historic dish — it goes back to colonial times and the autumn hog slaughter, when slaves were given the less desirable parts of the pig, in this case the head. A fundamental principle of soul food is the creation of something delicious out of ignominious ingredients, and what African-American cooks did with the hog's head was stuff it with leafy autumn produce, including kale, spinach, and/or cabbage, plus a hail of spice. The combination was so good that it went up the food status ladder from head to ham and became a harvest-time tradition among tobacco growers and wealthy farmers.

The trucker beamed at our inquiry, for he had spent much of his childhood in St. Mary's County eating stuffed ham, and he reeled off the names of six different eateries that served it. They were all seasonal — stuffed-ham-eating starts at Thanksgiving and ends at Easter — and every one was a tavern.

To our jejune sensibility, this did not compute. As we then conceived it, roadfood and bar food were mutually exclusive. We were accustomed to looking for regional meals in small-town cafés and charming roadside diners. The markers were flower boxes in the windows and blue ribbons taped around the pie case, waitresses who bleated, "Y'all come back," and Sunday-supper, after-church clientele. We figured that taverns were a bad place to find good food, because most patrons' palates were too numbed to appreciate the difference between Beer Nuts and beefsteak, and the rough ambience of a barroom was hardly conducive to appreciating the niceties of local food.

We knew of only a handful of exceptions to this rule: the Anchor Bar in Buffalo, New York, where Buffalo wings were first configured; Sharkey's in Binghamton, which makes a specialty of char-cooked marinated lamb skewers called spiedies; a couple of gumbo (and beer) parlors in bayou country; and Eddie's in Great Falls, Montana, which is a supper club/liquor store that boasts of steak that "tastes just like that old Marlboro Cowboy cooked it over the campfire."

The taverns we had superficially scouted in Maryland looked like dedicated drinking places — dark, rugged, and plenty scary. They smelled more of hops than of ham, and we naturally assumed that any food they served was an afterthought. But with Cecil's master's tips in our pocket, we left Baltimore early the next morning on the long, slow road south, six booze parlors serving stuffed ham in our sights. The day before, we had girded ourselves for a few days of tavern-hopping with a visit to a restaurant less like a tavern than anything imaginable — the Women's Industrial Exchange. This beguiling downtown tearoom opened in 1880, selling handcrafts to help women in need and serving such frilly dishes as Waldorf salad and charlotte russe.

St. Mary's County, between the Potomac and Patuxent Rivers, is another world. Unconnected by bridges to Virginia or the Eastern Shore, it is on the way to nowhere — a spit of land defined by complicated coves and creeks where gulls and ospreys glide overhead and the air smells of a salty sea. As we cruised through the countryside on flat two-lane roads, we were struck by how unlike the rest of America it seemed. There were taverns everywhere, and half the towns were called St. Something-or-other, and what didn't look English looked ancient and southern, whether elegant tobacco plantation buildings or roadside produce stands manned by men and women dozing on lawn chairs.

The first stop on our list was Hills Halfway House in Mechanicsville, where a group of four men at a nearby table were covered from the tops of their heads to the soles of their workboots with fine white plaster dust from their morning's work. They complained to each other about the overload of brandy from the night before, and they forked the stuffed ham from their plates into their mouths as though it were a sure cure for a hangover. Stuffed ham is an amazing-looking dish, made of "corned" ham, each bright pink slice having been punctured by a broad kitchen knife in a dozen places and the fissures stuffed with spruce-green chopped kale and cabbage and mustard seeds. The sweet ham and bitter, peppery greens are a powerhouse combo, the kind of food you eat in small forkfuls to prevent taste-bud exhaustion. Kevin Hill, whose father owned the restaurant, told us that once the whole ham has been stuffed, it is boiled for hours wrapped in sheets of cheesecloth, and that they served so much of it that two ladies in the kitchen did nothing but stuff and boil. "Of course, the old-timers used to cook it in a pillowcase," Kevin advised us.

Hills was a friendly place, but one other stop on the list we had got back in Smyrna was not. When we walked into a ham house/crab house/saloon near St. Clement Shores, where the clientele were fishermen and construction workers, the lunch crowd at the bar made it abundantly clear that we were not welcome, and that it was in our best interests to get our damn Yankee yuppie-assed license plates out of their parking lot. When the bartender-cook noted that we were toting a camera, he cursed, "What are you, real estate people?" as a big goober from his wad of chew dribbled freely from his lower lip onto his T-shirt.

One of the best tips, and a place we most certainly never would have gone into without prior advice, was Copsey's, half of which is a seafood restaurant, the other half a combination fish market and liquor store. The restaurant is outfitted with wide-roll brown paper dispensers so that long sheets can instantly be unfurled, cut, and spread across tables for the ritual messy crab feast: heaps of spiced hard-shell blue crabs that you go at with pick and mallet and accompany with pitchers of draft beer.

Copsey's is not for tourists. It offers no beginner's lessons in how to crack a crab, and no credit cards are accepted. Ours was the only car in the oyster shell–paved parking lot with out-of-state plates; we were the only eaters not calling from table to table to talk to friends, the only customers who asked to see a menu. People come to Copsey's knowing what they want to eat, and a blackboard on the wood-paneled wall gives the market price. Here, a crab feast is not a festive-occasion meal; it just *is*.

We first stumbled into the nonrestaurant part of the operation, where we found ourselves in the midst of a heated colloquy about local politics among citizens standing around the raw-seafood case over iced trays of oysters, flounder, and crabs, knocking back whiskey shots as they gabbed. Glowing with their drinks and the thrill of a hot interchange of opinions, they asked us to join them in a round. We happily obliged, and as we drank with them, the men advised us that the day's soft-shell crabs were about as tender as jelly and the sweetest they'd had in a long time. At that we exited to the adjoining restaurant, where the liquor-store conferees soon repaired to sit around a long table, onto which were dumped baskets full of spiced steamed crabs. They continued drinking and eating and arguing while we swooned over the sensational soft-shells, gorgeously plump crab cakes, a couple of pounds of peel-it-yourself steamed shrimp (infused with the same peppery orange spice mix used on the steamed crabs), and several dozen raw oysters.

Before entering, we had noticed that just across the road from Copsey's was another place, Leonard Copsey's, a takeout restaurant and seafood market with signs on every exterior wall advertising Budweiser by the case. When we asked Dagger Copsey, one of the men we had met in the liquor store, if the other place was related to his, his face turned red and he shot back, "Not by love or money but by blood." We didn't press for more information. After all, this was a drinking person's establishment, and we did not want to kindle a barroom brawl.

# St. Mary's County Stuffed Ham

Hills Halfway House, where we finally found stuffed ham, was ultimately sold by the family that owned it to make way for a Wawa convenience store. But the former owners soon opened another place nearby in Charlotte Hall — St. Mary's Landing, which remains the only place we know to get St. Mary's County stuffed ham year-round. Still, it is not *always* available. One December night when we went for supper, Lynda, the waitress, advised us that the restaurant had run out. "Honey, I just sold the last five pounds to a customer," she said. We whined that we had driven all day from Connecticut to eat stuffed ham, and Lynda listened sympathetically. We were not the first people ever to pitch a fit because the prize dish was all gone. Then she reassured us that three large hams were being prepared that evening. Given the fact that stuffing, cooking, cooling, and cutting a St. Mary's County ham is an all-day (or all-night) procedure, Lynda suggested we eat crab cakes and spicy boiled shrimp, get a good night's sleep, and return the next morning for platters of freshly sliced stuffed ham with fried mashed potato cakes at breakfast.

"Are the hams ready?" we asked Peggy Schraff of the waitstaff dawn patrol as we eased into a well-worn upholstered booth opposite the wall-mounted TV monitor that displayed Keno numbers and a countdown to the next game. It was 7 A.M. and we were the first customers to take seats in the restaurant, but barstools in the adjoining taproom were already occupied by ladies and gentlemen having shots and beers to start their day.

"You know, you don't just heat and cut a stuffed ham!" Peggy announced with some hauteur, spotting us as tenderfeet who scarcely knew a city ham from its country cousin. We had only to inquire, and

Peggy eagerly gave us the lowdown on a culinary subject dear to her heart. "You must *shock* that ham, plunge it into ice to stop the cooking right away," she declared. "Then you refrigerate it so you can serve it cool. Believe me, that's the way you want it." Stuffed ham is almost always served cool, although the menu says, "We'll serve it warm if you ask." Peggy explained to us that heat messes up the flavor of the dish; when it's cool, you get a good, clear taste of sweet ham and the tonic greens it has been boiled with.

For home cooks, stuffed ham is a special-occasion dish that serves a lot of people. Once cooked, it keeps well in the refrigerator. And while a Maryland ham is probably most authentic, we think there is no smoked ham better than that from neighboring Virginia sold by Virginia Traditions (www.virginiatraditions.com). It is smoked over hickory and has the very dense, intensely flavored meat that pairs well with heavy greens. It is also possible to buy an already cooked smoked ham; we like the applewood smoked ham sold by Nueske's of Wisconsin best (www.nueske.com). This reduces the necessary cooking time to 45 minutes to 1 hour.

- 1   smoked ham (15 pounds)
- 2   cups finely chopped kale
- 2   cups finely shredded cabbage
- 3   cups washed and coarsely chopped spinach
- ½   cup finely chopped scallions
- 6   tablespoons (¾ stick) butter
- ½   teaspoon cayenne pepper
- ½   teaspoon pepper
- ½   teaspoon crushed red pepper flakes
- 1   teaspoon salt

Cover the ham completely with water and soak it for at least 12 hours. Change the water and bring it to a slow simmer; simmer for 1 hour. Remove the ham from the water and let it cool. Cut off any rind and all but a very thin layer of fat.

Put 2 to 3 inches of water in a large stockpot and bring to a boil. Add the kale, cabbage, and spinach and reduce the heat to a low simmer. Simmer for about 5 minutes, until the greens become limp. Drain in a colander.

In a large saucepan, sauté the scallions in the butter until they are soft. Add the cooked greens, the spices, and the salt. Stir until mixed.

Use a long, sharp knife to cut 15 to 20 deep incisions in the ham. Fill each incision with as much of the greens as you can stuff in. Wrap the ham thoroughly in a double layer of cheesecloth and sew the cloth tightly together.

Put the ham in a large pot, cover with water, and bring to a boil. Simmer until tender, 3 to 4 hours. Add water if necessary to make sure the ham is covered as it simmers.

Remove the ham from the liquid and refrigerate it, leaving the cheesecloth on for a day. Remove from the refrigerator, remove the cheesecloth, and allow the ham to come to room temperature before serving. Slice thin.

25 SERVINGS

# Crab Soup

Steamed, spiced hard-shell crabs attract enormous attention around the Chesapeake Bay, and rightfully so, for they are one of the nation's great feasts, but no eager eater ought to ignore crab soup. It is as much a passion in local crab houses as chowder is on the Oregon coast. While some creamy crab soups are as mild as a Yankee stew, most versions are based on the yin-yang of sweet crabmeat and fiery spices. This recipe for the latter kind includes plenty of vegetables, to which chili powder's heat can cling, and it will leave lips aglow. Of course, the heat depends on what kind of chili powder you use, and how much.

½ cup chopped onion
⅓ cup chopped green bell pepper
4 tablespoons (½ stick) butter
4 cups fish stock (or clam juice)
¼ cup long-grain white rice
1 large, firm tomato, peeled and diced
1 pound lump crabmeat, free of shell
1 tablespoon chili powder, or to taste
½ pound fresh okra, sliced
½ teaspoon sugar
Salt and pepper to taste

In a 2-quart pot, sauté the onion and pepper in the butter until the onion is soft. Add the fish stock and rice. Boil for 15 minutes. Add the tomato, crabmeat, chili powder, and okra. Simmer for 20 minutes, stirring occasionally. Stir in the sugar and salt and pepper. Serve hot.

4 LARGE SERVINGS

# Neighboring in Iowa

For as long as anyone can remember, nothing has changed at the Penn pharmacy soda fountain counter in Sidney, Iowa, where tradition decrees that if you visit on your birthday, you get the ice cream soda of your choice for free. We visited the place in 1990, 127 years after it opened for business and probably a few decades after any kind of remodeling had taken place. Still, there was nothing self-consciously antique about this store, which stocked all the patent medicines, knickknacks, liniments, and sundries that made pharmacies such convenient neighborhood emporiums in the decades before malls and superstores.

Every day at dinner (that's the midday meal), citizens of southwestern Iowa's farmland took their places at the twelve counter stools, booths, and three tables, which were somewhat erratically arranged among displays of stationery, school supplies, and bandages. There they ate chicken salad or ham salad sandwiches and exchanged news and, if feeling sporty, dipped long-handled spoons into expertly made ice cream sodas. Penn's sodas were served in tall, fluted glasses with billows of whipped cream piled high above the rim. Cherry, chocolate, and vanilla were the most popular flavors, but more festive varieties were available than colors in a good-sized pack of Crayola crayons.

We went to the pharmacy to join Evelyn Birkby on her seventy-first birthday. Evelyn had forgotten all about the complementary soda due her until her husband, Bob, rode into town, parked his bicycle on the sidewalk in front of the drugstore, and came in to remind her. It took Bob about thirty minutes to get from Penn's front door to Evelyn, because all twelve counter stools in between were occupied and Bob exchanged words with each of their occupants. He discussed recent torrential rains, beans and tomatoes and how they were growing, and an upcoming local rodeo. "Are your toes webbed together yet?" he asked a person who had spent the early morning wading into a flooded field to pick sweet corn before it rotted. A woman sitting nearby said that the day before she had carried all her canned goods up from the basement because she was worried about a flood.

When Bob finally got to Evelyn and brought up the subject of the free soda, she told him he could have the honor of ordering it for her. She wasn't thinking much about her birthday at that moment because she was well into a good conversation with us and with people in adjacent booths and with a couple of shoppers in the medicine aisle, as well as with some of the folks drinking coffee and eating liverwurst sandwiches on nearby stools. Everyone had something to contribute to this colloquy, and Evelyn, who had made a long career of talking on the radio, was in her glory.

What she had done for more than forty years was known in the midlands as "radio homemaking," also called "neighboring on the air." Predating cell phones and e-mail, predating television talk, even predating telephone service in southwestern Iowa, Evelyn's show on KMA radio, "Down a Country Lane," was devoted to swapping recipes, reading personal letters, reciting poems, giving advice, and speaking from the heart as freely as if she were chatting with a confidante over coffee at an oilcloth-covered kitchen table in a farmhouse.

When you drive the roads of southwestern Iowa between the east and west streams of the Nishnabotna River, past methodical rows of corn and along pastures and vales where cattle graze, you can smell just how fertile the black dirt is, and you can understand how important radio once was to the people who worked the land. The good earth inspired settlers not only to farm but to start nursery businesses that provided growing plants and trees to farmers and householders. Fifteen miles east of Sidney, the town of Shenandoah, named in 1870 by Civil War veterans who thought it resembled the lush battlefields of Virginia, was well on its way to becoming the seed and nursery capital of the world by the time KMA, which called itself "the Cornbelt Station in the Heart of the Nation," began broadcasting in 1925. Earl May, owner of Shenandoah's Earl May Seed and Nursery Company, believed that a radio station would be a good way to encourage people to buy his products, by interspersing news, music, and religious services with instructive talks about agriculture and horticulture.

Radio was a new thrill for many Americans in the twenties, but it had extraordinary value for the isolated farm families of the Midwest, for whom solitude loomed as a daily problem. Radio was a source of music and fun, information and weather reports, and it was an easy way to enjoy the pleasure of other people's company. In-person visiting was a special event that often meant putting on dress clothes and serving cakes and lemonade and gathering politely in the parlor; frequently the press of chores or bad weather made that impossible. But with a radio, women could continue their housework as they listened to a friendly voice; men working in the barn had access to weather reports and farm programs. There was another good thing about the radio: for all those settlers who had come to the American Midwest from Germany, middle Europe, and Scandinavia and yearned to speak English well, the radio's roster of well-spoken homemakers, lecturers, and announcers provided continuous daily examples of the fine art of conversation. Whether they huddled close to a homemade crystal set on a kitchen table or sat genteelly around a mahogany console in the living room, KMA's far-flung audience began to think of the signal coming out of Shenandoah as a beacon that could guide them every day.

For those who grew up around Shenandoah in the mid-twentieth century, tuning to the radio homemakers of KMA was as much a part of daily life as the morning school bell or the coming of the mailman. Dorothy Stewart, who had a dairy farm with her husband in Pawnee City, Nebraska, remembered setting aside one hour every day to listen to the homemakers. She said, "I depended on them, because I couldn't get away. I had so much work to do. They were my only steady friends. I kept a notebook by the radio until it got full of their recipes and hints, then I filled up another one." Nadine Elwers, who grew up on a Shenandoah farm, added, "We weren't allowed to disturb my mother on two occasions: when there was a cake in the oven, and when she was listening to the homemaker show. That was a time that was hers. It was sacrosanct time. She ironed. Fuel for the stove had to be gathered in advance so there would be no disturbance. There had to be paper on hand to write down all the important advice given by the radio homemakers." Norma Schaff, who had just lost five hundred acres of beans because of the rain and worried that her stalks of sweet corn were about to fall down, said that she had won prizes in county fairs using what she learned by paying attention to homemaker shows. "Now we have tractor radios, so it's easier to listen," she said, and another woman at the counter added that she always took a transistor radio outside so she could hear it when she gardened.

The craft of radio homemaking faded as the century came to a close, but we were blessed to have the chance to meet the listeners and a handful of surviving practitioners in Shenandoah. Sitting in a booth at the back of the pharmacy on her birthday, Evelyn was doing what she loved to do and did better than anyone else — neighbor, a word that is still more a verb than a noun in this part of Iowa. Reflecting the etiquette in many cafés in American small towns, people at Penn's talked from booth to booth in voices loud enough for others to hear if they were interested. A hushed, private conversation would have seemed downright rude and exclusionary, and as the subject of mock mincemeat made from green tomatoes came up for discussion, all in attendance offered accounts and opinions about the recipe. Ariel Stevens, a native Shenandoahn, recalled that her husband, who was in a wheelchair and listened to several radio homemaker shows every day, heard the recipe on the air, thought it sounded good, and wrote it down; Ariel, who happened to have plenty of green tomatoes on the vine, made some. "He ate the whole batch," she recalled. "I had to make another. I tell you, you start cooking that mincemeat and those green tomatoes smell. But don't give up."

From the next booth, a woman who said she had listened to radio homemakers since before she learned to talk set down her chicken salad sandwich and added an unembroidered rave to the conversation: "It's good!" The woman's husband, sitting next to her, swirled the last of the coffee in his cup, drank it down, and nodded enthusiastically, but wordlessly, in agreement. Another woman, browsing among school supplies, called out, "You'd never know it's not real mincemeat. It's that tasty. But you can't always make it. You need plenty of tomatoes, and they have to be really green."

Talk was suspended when Bob Birkby walked to the back of the store carrying Evelyn's birthday soda. It was presented in classic soda fountain glassware — a tall, broad-mouthed, fluted goblet, crowned with a scoop of vanilla ice cream and a swirl of whipped cream, speared by a clear plastic straw, and equipped with a long-handled spoon submerged in the cold liquid below, which was the color of pink chiffon. The soda was Evelyn's favorite flavor: strawberry. She and Bob shared it, then Evelyn went back to neighboring in her booth as people came and went and visited with her until dinner was over.

During our visit, we learned things about rural foodways that we never read in any book. About the relative worth of breads, for instance. Radio homemaker Billie Oakley recalled growing up on a nearby Nebraska farm, where her mother cooked three meals a day and always baked the family's bread from rugged whole-wheat flour. But in 1930 a miracle arrived: packaged, sliced loaves of pure white Wonder Bread. From that day on, once a week Mother went to town and the family had a special treat. Instead of the crusty hearth-baked loaves to which they were accustomed, a loaf of refined-flour Wonder Bread sat on the table. Billie was a great farmhouse cook, but she still thought of supermarket bread as something extra-special.

While we were hanging around Shenandoah, staying in the $10-per-night Tall Corn Motel (the only hostelry in town), Evelyn Birkby invited us to her home in Sidney for what she called a real Iowa dinner — a collection of some of her favorite things to cook and eat. She greeted us at the front door of her modest house on a tree-shaded street on the west side of town. A small bronze plaque next to the door proclaimed, "On this site in 1897 nothing happened." Bob came around front from the backyard garden, nibbling on some just-picked wild plums that looked like cherry tomatoes. We ate at twilight at a table on the screened sunporch attached to the kitchen in the back of the house, where we could look out at the garden, listen to a family of nesting wrens, and see the monitoring equipment Bob used to report conditions to the United States Weather Service in Des Moines — not his job, but much more important than a mere hobby. On every shelf and in every nook of the Birkbys' house something commemorated rural life: a hooked rug, a quilt, a piece of cross-stitch, a loom, a doll's house, and Mason jars with put-up preserves as well as a stock of empty jars ready to be filled and sealed. The scene was not exactly an Iowa farmstead in the raw, but neither was it disingenuous. It was an ode to the rural life the Birkbys love.

Although they had moved away from the farm, their garden yielded enough produce to fill the Mason jars every year and to keep the Birkbys in good tomatoes and sweet corn all summer. At seventy-one, Evelyn was robust and rangy. She wore her hair in a tight perm and favored the big-lensed eyeglasses so à la mode when first worn by Sophia Loren in the 1970s. As our hostess, she spoke with the same familiar intimacy she used when she neighbored on the air, taking every opportunity to enthrall us with the rural customs that enthralled her.

She prefaced the meal with a prodigiously annotated and parenthesized narration of her trip to Essex, six miles north, to a butcher who assured her that the evening's pork chops came from an Iowa pig. The chops, Evelyn explained, were what people in this area call "Iowa cut," meaning nearly two inches thick. They had an unforgettable simple succulence: hefty plateaus of pork marshaled in a baking pan bubbling with thick red syrup made from ketchup and chili sauce. Tender as pot roast, their meat pulled from the bone with only a gentle fork tug, venting wisps of sweet porcine perfume.

With the pork chops, Evelyn served corn on the cob from the Birkby garden, allotting four ears per person. On a big plate next to the bowl of corn was a tub of Promise margarine, a stick of I Can't Believe It's Not Butter, and a stick of real sweet cream butter. Also on the side were broiled tomato halves topped with seasoned bread crumbs, pickled beets, a salad dressed with X-Tra-Touch Country-Style dressing, which Evelyn had lightened with a little beaten egg white, and a rugged and satisfying loaf of hard-crusted seven-grain bread, for which Evelyn apologized: only five grains were used. To garnish the bread, in addition to the margarines and butter, Evelyn provided honey from Bob's apiary, blackberry and currant jelly, and strawberry preserves (all from his fruit). The gooseberries in the gooseberry tart at dessert were Bob's, too, but the lemon chiffon ice cream beginning to soften into a silky orb on top of each piece of tart was bought in Shenandoah — made locally from a recipe developed by two ladies in Essex.

Everything we ate that night had a story to go with it, a connection to the people and the land and the history of Shenandoah. There might be better cooks out there than Evelyn Birkby, but we have never eaten a more soul-satisfying meal.

# Virginia Miller's Elegant Pork Chops

The pork chops Evelyn Birkby served us were prepared according to a recipe from Virginia Miller, a longtime KMA listener and friend who lived in an old farmhouse outside Anderson, just west of Shenandoah, and who was locally famous, Evelyn said, as a great cook. Over the years Evelyn shared many of Virginia Miller's recipes with listeners of "Down a Country Lane." The pork chop recipe was titled "Elegant Pork Chops." Mrs. Miller found it in a farm magazine and adapted it to her own tastes by using more sugar than in the original recipe and her own ketchup (from Miller tomatoes) instead of Heinz.

### THE MARINADE

|       |                        |
|-------|------------------------|
| 2     | cups soy sauce         |
| 1     | cup water              |
| ½     | cup dark brown sugar   |
| 1     | tablespoon molasses    |
| ¾     | teaspoon salt          |

| 6–8   | thick-cut pork chops   |

### THE BAKING SAUCE

|       |                            |
|-------|----------------------------|
| ⅓     | cup water                  |
| 1¾    | cups ketchup               |
| 1½    | cups chili sauce           |
| ½     | cup light brown sugar      |
| 1     | tablespoon dry mustard     |
| 2     | tablespoons Russian salad dressing |

TO MARINATE THE PORK: Combine the marinade ingredients in a baking pan large enough to hold the pork chops in a single layer, add the meat, and marinate for several hours or overnight.

Preheat the oven to 350 degrees.

Remove the chops from their marinade and place in a 9-x-13-inch baking pan. Put the pan in the oven, uncovered.

TO MAKE THE BAKING SAUCE: Combine all the ingredients for the baking sauce in a medium saucepan and bring to a boil. After the chops have been in the oven about 10 minutes, turn them and cover them with the hot baking sauce.

Cover the pan and bake the chops for about 1 hour, until they are tender, turning them several times as they cook. Serve hot, with the sauce spooned over them.

4 SERVINGS

# Jessie Young's Radio Cake

The first of the women broadcasters at KMA to become known as a radio homemaker was Jessie Young. Jessie was hired in 1926 by Earl May, the station's owner, when she lost her position as a bank teller (the bank failed). Her primary job at KMA was to be singing, but her ability to read commercials persuasively in a down-to-earth manner convinced May that she ought to host her own daily women's program. The "Stitch and Chat Club," which was soon renamed "A Visit with Jessie Young," became the archetype of the radio homemaker show. Jessie discussed the niceties of housekeeping, including cooking and sewing, and also created an easygoing radio companion whom listeners could depend on every day.

The "Stitch and Chat Club" was distinguished by its unabridged authenticity. To underscore Jessie's folksy manner and encourage the audience to consider her an equal, the station ran a transmitting wire from KMA to her home kitchen, and on Saturdays the show featured the comings and goings of her four children and her husband, Floyd, including musical selections on the Novachord, a 1930s-era synthesizer, by son Robert and vocal duets by Jessie and Floyd. Jessie discussed how to make cloverleaf lace and the best way to skim fat from gravy, but she also mused about what she was fixing for supper that night and worried aloud about family problems. She talked about her daughter Eileen, an undernourished child whom she and Floyd had adopted, and she invited her elderly mother, Rosa Susanka, to join her at the microphone and share her maternal wisdom. Shenandoahns well remember Jessie Young's chocolate cake; the recipe was regularly requested via letter and postcard.

. THE CAKE

    1   cup sugar

    2   tablespoons butter, softened

    2   tablespoons unsweetened cocoa

  ¼   cup boiling water

    1   cup sour milk or buttermilk

 1⅓  cups all-purpose flour

    1   teaspoon baking soda

  ½   teaspoon salt

    1   teaspoon vanilla extract

THE FILLING

 1½  tablespoons unsweetened cocoa

 1½  tablespoons cornstarch

  ⅔   cup sugar

  ¾   cup water

  ½   teaspoon vanilla extract

TO MAKE THE CAKE: Grease and flour two 9-inch cake pans. Preheat the oven to 375 degrees.

Cream the sugar and butter in a large bowl. Stir the cocoa into the boiling water, then combine that with the sugar and butter. Add the remaining cake ingredients one at a time, beating well after each addition. Pour the batter into the cake pans and bake for 30 to 40 minutes, until a sharp knife inserted into the center of the layers comes out clean. Cool the layers in the pans on a cake rack.

TO MAKE THE FILLING: Mix the cocoa, cornstarch, and sugar in a heavy-bottomed saucepan. Beat in the water and cook the mixture over medium heat until it is thick and creamy. Remove from the heat, cool for 10 minutes, and stir in the vanilla.

Turn the cake layers out of the pans and spread the filling on one. Place the second layer on top. Use any desired frosting for the top, but leave the sides unfrosted.

10 TO 12 SERVINGS

 *Into the West*

It was the most breathtaking view we have ever seen through a windshield. Driving into the boundless rolling wheat fields of eastern Oregon as the setting sun glowed red and a hot September breeze rippled across the prairie, we were looking at the amber waves of grain of "America the Beautiful." The tune coming from our car's cassette deck was something else altogether, plaintive rather than uplifting. It was Hank Williams singing "Lonesome Whistle." There was nobody else on the road, no cows in the pastures, no farmhouses, no intersections — just us on the curving ribbon of highway that threaded through the wheat.

But we were not alone. In the back seat of the car was our friend and mentor in things equine, John Porto. John ran a horse barn back in Connecticut, where we boarded our two horses, K.T. and Piegan. John was a genuine Connecticut cowboy, a population that probably numbers under a hundred guys. But he was the real deal, a wiry muscleman who had rodeoed up and down the eastern circuit from Ballston Spa, New York, to the Carolinas. He raised champion Appaloosa horses, and he was a crackerjack farrier. At age sixty-five he worked all day long, every day, and appeared never to eat anything, subsisting quite nicely on Copenhagen chewing tobacco, Johnnie Walker scotch, and coffee.

For all his cowboy ways, John had never been west of the livestock auction in Waverly, Iowa, so one autumn as we prepared to head off on a major roadfood expedition to eat with cowboys, we asked him to come along. Traveling with John was like going places with Mr. Ed, for in many ways he was more horse than man. He saw everything along the long road through the eyes of a critter who sleeps and grazes in the great outdoors. Scenery we thought beautiful was hideous to him because it had none of the amenities a horse would want. The spectacular rock formations of Monument Valley? "There's no water here, no trees for shade," he complained. An enchanted rocky road through the Sangre de Cristo Mountains? "There is no place safe to plant your feet," he declared. When we hit the broad wheat fields of the northwestern plains, where fresh-cut hay was arrayed in bales out to the horizon and the air smelled of sweet grass, he sighed with bliss.

It was John's influence that made us go rodeo-crazy about fifteen years ago. We became obsessed with the buckaroo lifestyle, and suddenly it became glaringly apparent that our roadfood database needed major beefing up in the West. We wanted to eat what the cowboys ate, where they ate it. Our first foray was to the ranch country north of Santa Barbara, California, where Santa Maria–style barbecue perfumes the air.

We drove into Santa Maria on a Friday afternoon and smelled beef sizzling over flaming oak logs. White gusts of aromatic smoke were wafting across the city's broad avenues and through public parking lots, and everywhere we went we saw pit men firing up portable open cookers and martialing big chunks of tri-tip in rows on top of their grates. The meat cooked in the open air until its crust glistened black, at which point the men tending the pits forked it off the grill and sliced it thick.

People buy much of this fire-cooked meat to take home and eat in the dining room; however, plenty of the cookwagons that line the streets of north country towns will put a meal on a plate (paper) with a fork (plastic) and provide a place to eat (usually a portable picnic table a few yards from the cooker). The heavy flaps of meat have a mighty flavor, rimmed with pepper and garlic, infused with the tang of fire; the tri-tip's rosy fibers offer nice resistance to the tooth and surrender a lush river of juice. Eating beef in the open air is an established tradition in these parts. Some vendors have health department certification to serve meals; some do not. Despite the niceties of the law, no one expects authorities to come along and arrest pit men and customers caught eating illegal tri-tip. Local citizens have been enjoying their barbecue this way for too long to allow bureaucrats to tell them where they are permitted to do so.

It isn't only good food that makes these meals so dear to the people of California's ranching coast. Barbecue's appeal hereabouts derives also from its virtue. Nearly all the mobile weekend pits in Santa Maria are operated for charity's sake, which means you do good by eating well. The Atlas Soccer Club, for instance, sets up a cooker in the parking lot of Video El Aguila, where its members sell deliciously messy sandwiches of sliced tri-tip and salsa heaped onto sections of buttered French bread; the proceeds go toward uniforms and team trips. Women of the Moose (the ladies' auxiliary of the fraternal order) have an immensely popular barbecue stand in front of the Wells Fargo Bank. In the big town shopping center on Broadway, the Lions Club Valley Christian Boosters used to operate a huge pit (with tables) that got so popular it expanded into six-day-a-week service out of a nearby doughnut shop.

Santa Maria's distinctive style of cooking and serving beef goes back to the days when much of California really was cowboy country. It was customary for adjacent ranchers to join together and bring in all their cattle for a communal spring roundup. That time of year meant hard work for the cowhands, known in this part of the world as vaqueros (the Spanish word from which *buckaroo* evolved), who spent long days roping, branding, and earbobbing calves. When the work was done, ranchers and vaqueros from all outfits gathered together to celebrate their accomplishments. Naturally, they ate beef, butchered into big hunks and skewered on poles over open pits of burning oak. Tiny pinquito beans and salsa — a legacy of the Spanish and Portuguese heritage of many ranchers — were on the bill of fare from the beginning. The celebratory spirit of the barbecue has made it a natural favorite for any kind of great outdoor community feast.

While investigating Santa Maria barbecue, we pursued our rodeo career between meals by enrolling in bull-riding school. Who knows what we were thinking when we signed up for class with Gary Leffew, once the bull-riding champion of the world and now the man who taught young up-and-comers how to stay aboard a bucking, writhing, snot-slinging, fire-breathing, two-ton bovine for eight seconds. When we arrived at his Santa Maria ranch one morning for the first class and saw our fellow students, we realized that we had truly lost our minds. We were in our mid-forties, in only fair shape, and not exactly fearless when it came to physical danger. Our ten classmates were all under twenty years old, had zero percent body fat, and were afraid of nothing. They included twin American Indian girls who sat together silently on the arena fence and chewed and spat tobacco and a rugged sixteen-year-old boy, emancipated from his parents, who had broken his arm coming off a saddle bronc in an amateur rodeo two weeks before but had convinced a doctor to make him a special cast so he could still ride roughstock while the bones healed.

Cowboys are known for their taciturn behavior, but even Gary

Leffew, who described himself as "150 pounds of twisted steel and sex appeal," laughed out loud when the two of us joined his class. We stayed for three days and became fast friends with Gary and several of our classmates, but the bottom line is that we never once set ass on bull. Not even on Tiny, the immense black beast who was the beginner's ride because his bucks were relatively gentle. Close up, Tiny was, to us, a monster. If we had attempted to ride him, we have little doubt, we would have been known from that time on as Jane and Michael Stern, the quadriplegic food writers.

At the end of each day, the bull-riding students who hadn't been carted off to the hospital or who didn't need to stay at the ranch icing an aching crotch repaired to the small town of Nipomo and a boisterous restaurant/tavern named Jocko's. Here we found the lesser-known kind of California cuisine that we had come to love — Santa Maria barbecue. Locals don't think of it as exemplary regional cuisine; to them, Jocko's is just their favorite steakhouse, known for cuts of beef that are shockingly thick. Indeed, one *Roadfood* reader wrote to suggest that Jocko's must be the place that bad vegetarians go when they die, for in this place, red meat is the only food that matters. Jocko's cooks its steaks the Santa Maria way, over an oak log on an open pit, and serves them in the traditional manner, with pinquito beans and salsa.

There's often a wait for a table, so our drill every night was to arrive in a motorcade of overcrowded cars and pickups along with the fledgling bull riders. We all hung out at the bar, knocking back shots and beers while reminiscing about that exciting moment earlier in the day when one of Gary's sharp-horned Brahma bulls (pronounced rodeo-style, as *Braymer*) threw one of the kids into the sky so high that when he hit the dirt, he could only crawl toward the edge of the arena, just barely escaping the dreaded "ivory enema." While palavering over such fun, we inhaled secondhand smoked-meat perfume until our appetites raged for beef of our own.

As much as for the meal itself, we loved Jocko's for the company and the roadhouse atmosphere, which is absolutely nothing like that of a fancy, formal, big-city steakhouse. Surrounded by taxidermied game-animal heads on the wall, customers come here to have a wonderful time and to celebrate the joy of eating beef. The dress code is Wranglers, boots, and a Stetson or farm cap. Jane, ever the fashion maven, learned by observation that the correct way to wear blue jeans is "stacked" — skintight but with the inseam way too long and arranged from the knees down in tiny accordionlike folds.

In the midst of our rodeo mania in the 1990s, we met Jim Shoulders. Jim is the Babe Ruth of rodeo but is even more distinguished in his field than the Bambino, for the number of world champion belt buckles he won in the 1950s and 1960s for bronc and bull riding has still never been equaled or even approached. When he retired, he kept up his public image by being the celebrity rodeo face in Miller Lite beer commercials, along with a Brahma bull he had trained to be ridden as nicely as a saddle horse. After some jiggling around with an introduction provided to Jim by the Professional Rodeo Cowboys Association, we were invited to breakfast with him and his wife, Sharron, in their home town of Henryetta, Oklahoma.

Before we sat down at the cozy kitchen table, and after a short tour of what appeared to be dozens of trophy saddles, belt buckles, and the head of one of Jim's favorite bulls, stuffed and hung on the wall, the Shoulderses enthusiastically told us about the breed of cattle they were raising at their ranch, called Salorn. Salorn, a composite breed of five eighths French Salers and three eighths Texas Longhorns, is aimed at the modern, nutrition-minded beef eater, whose outlook demands low-fat meals. Jim explained that Longhorn stock makes for a hardy, adaptable breed, while the Salorn meat is especially lean, the way the tough cattle that went up the Chisholm Trail used to be.

Sharron, who was still as gorgeous as a rodeo queen, announced, "That's what we'll be having for breakfast." We wondered if at that moment she could see our faces fall with disappointment. The night before we all had gone out for grand, extremely well marbled sirloins at Oklahoma City's premier beef palace, Cattlemen's, in the old stockyards district. We had preceded the steak orgy with a platter of deep-fried testicles, known as Rocky Mountain oysters, as luscious as sweetbreads, and had plenty of fried potatoes alongside the main course. We were in no mood to start next morning with a slab of stringy, too-lean, no-juice health beef. Our crankiness about the goody-two-shoes meat was exacerbated because quite frankly, we were disillusioned that our hero, Jim Shoulders, would go over to the other side and submit himself to wimpy low-fat beef.

Not to worry. Sharron took four filets of this oh-so-virtuous beef, dunked them in egg wash, dipped them in seasoned flour, repeated the process again, and slid them into a broad cast-iron skillet full of bubbling hot lard. In doing so, she transformed the leanest cuts of cow she could find into the most opulent dish beef can be: chicken-fried steak. When the steaks came out of the pan, she made thick gravy using pan drippings and a sludge of flour and water. With piles of buttermilk biscuits hot from the oven and plenty of butter and jelly to stuff into the biscuits' steamy insides, this was the most delicious diet meal we ever ate.

Our love of rodeo took us to some of the best of the West — to Cheyenne, Wyoming; Twin Falls and Pocatello, Idaho; Window Rock, Arizona; and Wahoo, Nebraska — but we are obliged to say that the food at these events, as well as in the towns that held them, was seldom anything to remember fondly. In fact, the week we spent in Cheyenne for the huge, glorious, thrilling Frontier Days Rodeo was a roadfood nightmare. There was nothing to eat. Nothing. The one decent place in town, a ramshackle barbecue parlor, had closed the year before, and all that was left anywhere for miles around was fast food. Our choice each meal was Whoppers or Big Macs, Taco Bell burritos or Domino's pizza. Or the ancient desiccated wieners that roll on metal dowels under heat lamps for who knows how long at the 7-Eleven. For a day or two, this was bearable. But after a while it was as hellish as a diet of airplane food, and we finally resorted to supermarket meals of fruit, cheese, and crackers.

As bad as the food was, drinking at rodeos was always excellent. No matter what size the town or city, there was at least one bar that was the known place to go for the rodeo crowd, and each night it spilled over with hunky contestants still wearing numbers on their backs, some nursing fresh injuries, as well as hordes of seductive "buckle bunnies" — young girl rodeo camp followers (named because they always set their sights on the cowboys who have won gold championship buckles). The raging hormones of both sexes, combined with plenty of whiskey shots and beers and the thrill of the day's dangers and glory, gave these bars an intoxicating energy that made every night into the ultimate rodeo cast party. Even though we hadn't earned any gold buckles (except maybe one for chutzpah in showing up at Gary Leffew's) and were only on the outermost fringe of the rodeo, we were fully caught up in the spirit of devilment.

Of all the places we drank at the top-flight rodeos of the West, none was as much fun as the Let 'Er Buck Room, under the grandstand of the Pendleton Round-Up rodeo grounds in Pendleton, Oregon, where we went with our friend John Porto to see the annual fall rodeo — one of the biggest and best there is. After bedding down at a dude ranch outside town the first night, we headed straight to the Let 'Er Buck Room the next morning, about three hours before the rodeo began.

From the time it opens until late at night, every day during the wild and woolly roundup, the windowless bar is packed. For $2.50 we bought a token, necessary to circumvent the area's liquor laws, which apparently forbid direct sale of alcohol. We bought pocketfuls and commenced to drink. And we are not talking about sarsaparillas or frozen daiquiris, and not even about schooners of beer. The Let 'Er Buck menu is simple: hard liquor. Cups are plastic, and there are no coasters, because there is no place to put down a drink. The room has no tables, no chairs, and no TV. There is, however, plenty of décor. "Let 'Er Buck," which is what bronc twisters call out when they are ready to ride a wild one, has been the motto of the roundup since the beginning, and the Let 'Er Buck Room is outfitted with memorabilia from the rodeo: display cases of beaded vests and gauntlets made by Nez Perce Indian participants in the early days, big pictures of horses bucking and steers being wrestled to the ground, a bull's head mounted on the wall, a fine old pair of woolly chaps worn by a contestant many years ago.

For rodeo aficionados, the collection of souvenirs would be fascinating —if it were possible to look at the stuff. Most of the time, none of it is visible because the Let 'Er Buck Room is so crowded. You could pass out from drinking, and still be standing upright. By midmorning, all we could see was a churning sea of high-crowned cowboy hats, with a deliriously happy person under every one. Here were professional cowpunchers and dudes who wanted to look like them, grizzled rodeo veterans and baby-faced rookies, world champions and losers in bandages, gentleman ranchers and fluffy blond buckle bunnies in denim and diamonds, full-dress Indians in buckskin and white men with black eyes and dried blood around their noses. At one point the room was so packed that some of the buckle bunnies started climbing aboard the cowboys' shoulders and peeling off their blouses, thus enjoying relatively fresh air and freeing floor space for others. At this stage of the morning cocktail hour, it was too congested to get to the bar, though that didn't matter much because we, like everyone around us, were rip-snorting drunk already. Signs posted everywhere warned revelers to KEEP YOUR CLOTHES ON, in a vain attempt to discourage the women from baring their breasts. However, we witnessed no cowboys complaining.

We stumbled out of the Let 'Er Buck Room, blinded by the sun and desperately in need of something to eat. Most of the food on the roundup grounds is fair fodder: hamburgers, hot dogs, sausages and assorted barbecues, Indian fry bread, popcorn, cotton candy, and lemonade and flagons of red beer. We had never heard of red beer, a curious cocktail made by combining beer and tomato juice. "It's the best for hangovers," one local waitress advised us. "The guy who invented it long ago wanted another drink but knew he ought to have tomato juice." We grew to like this stuff during a week in Pendleton, finding it rather healthy.

The best eats at the rodeo grounds were at a mobile chuckwagon called Mario Zubiria's Basque Bar-BQ. At the time, Mr. Zubiria didn't have a restaurant, but he was well known around Pendleton as a caterer, and the robust food he made was a culinary reflection of the spice Basques contributed to buckaroo culture west of the Rockies. Over a big mobile cooker that rode on whitewalled tires, Zubiria and his men charcoal-grilled lamb chunks and chops, beef, and foot-long chorizo sausages, sending mouthwatering smoke signals rising above the arena. The lamb chunks were chewy and tangy, served in a cardboard boat with charcoal-grilled onions, green peppers, and mush-rooms. The hefty chorizo sausage, ground in Boise, Idaho, had an alarming red hue and was peppery but not very hot. Its crisp skin en-closed coarsely ground, well-garlicked pork, and although it was available on a stick for easy eating, we enjoyed it Mario's alternate way: wrapped in a loaf of French bread and smothered with grilled onions.

At night, when the rodeo was over, we wandered over to Pendleton's Main Street, which is blocked to motorized traffic dur-ing roundup to make room for a bazaar of saddle carvers and spur makers, boot vendors, clog dancers, trick ropers, a mounted cowboy band, and the Indian beauty pageant. Here, just behind the Williams Sheep Farm Sausage Wagon, we found Cimmiyotti's, which has been Pendleton's favorite steakhouse since 1959. Dark and clubby, with red flocked wallpaper and a long mirrored bar underneath crystal chandeliers in the front dining room, it is a civilized restau-rant but in no way snooty. It is deluxe in ways reminiscent of many years ago, when beefsteak was the undisputed king of the American dinner menu and Italian food with zesty red sauce was a little bit ex-otic. The affluent ambience is shot through with heaps of local color, including pictures on the wall of famous chiefs of local tribes, rodeo champions, and one stern-looking judge on horseback. Cim-miyotti's menu is bound in thick leather, hand-tooled by a nearby saddle maker. A bulletin board for customers' business cards fea-tures offers of the services of a quarterhorse stud, a slaughterhouse that takes the worry out of dead-animal disposal, and an enthusias-tic plea to cattle ranchers to consider raising "the other red meat," ostrich.

Ensconced in a posh black leatherette booth, we thought it only right to accompany cocktails with onion rings. They were brought to the table with a bottle of ketchup, and they were beautiful in an old-fashioned way: big, gnarled circles with their crust just barely clinging to the thick veins of warm onion within. They were slick and thoroughly naughty, and they made our fingers glisten as we plucked them from their basket. A dinner salad, in a little wooden bowl, was mostly iceberg lettuce, topped with sweet red vinaigrette: the *bec fin* would abhor it.

Here too beef was what really mattered at mealtime, and Cimmiyotti's served us some fine-looking steaks, listed on the menu under the heading "From the Feed Lot." There were big New York strips and tiny lady-sized tenderloins, thick filets mignon, chopped steaks and hamburgers, and even *moderne* teriyaki steaks. The specialty of the house was rib eye, a beef-lover's cut that is not overly tenderized and not ostentatiously thick. It was a cow-country steak with character and some "chaw" to it, as opposed to the plush, fork-tender steaks served in expense-account steakhouses. It had a charred flavor, but not so much as to overwhelm the essential savor of the meat, which ran with juice when you sliced off a hunk. Naturally, potato was served with steak; ordered baked, it came accompanied by a three-bowl silver server holding chives, sour cream, and an immense globe of butter.

Curiosity demanded that we try some of Cimmiyotti's Italian specialties, and they were indeed curious, mostly because we had almost forgotten about guileless Italian-American fare such as this. Here was spaghetti from an age of culinary innocence, before one worried about such niceties as Florentine fritto misto and the risottos of Lombardy. Soft white noodles were topped with chunky, oregano-flavored red sauce and showers of grated Parmesan cheese. It was a meal that was pleasantly benign and delightfully easy to eat: comfort food! Cimmiyotti's lasagna was similar, but more complicated because it had a bit of crunch (onions) and spice (sausage) and was made with three stout cheeses. Italian specialties also included cannelloni, manicotti, ravioli, and fettucine Alfredo, each served with glistening logs of toasted bread that had only the subtlest aura of garlic.

We should note parenthetically that one of the great discoveries of our western eating campaigns was the old-fashioned hyphenated foreign food in the cities and towns of the heartland. Other than Italian, the most common such cuisine is Chinese-American, as served at the amazing Pekin Noodle Parlor in Butte, Montana, above China Alley, which was once the heart of the (now defunct) Chinatown. We just happened to spot the small sign for Pekin while sitting at an outdoor table across the way at Pork Chop John's, where Montana's renowned pork chop sandwich was invented many decades ago. The orange neon CHOP SUEY sign flickered on at precisely 5 P.M. and the restaurant door was unlocked. We headed up an eerie, bare flight of stairs lit by a single Chinese lantern and found ourselves facing a lounge for cocktails (the local favorite is a "ditch" — Montanese for whiskey and water) and a row of tables for four in a dozen curtained cubicles on either side of a center aisle. We chose the latter and, after studying a menu that included deluxe cheeseburgers as well as egg foo yong, placed an order. Seated in our private dining vault, we heard the waitress's trolley rumbling along the woodplank floors of the restaurant's center aisle, the booth curtain was whisked aside, and behold! Here was a vista of foreign food the likes of which most devotees of Asian cookery forgot about forty years ago. Our chop suey and chow mein were mild, thick, and harmless; fried shrimp came girdled by a pad of breading and served on leaves of lettuce with French fried potatoes on the side; sweet-and-sour ribs dripped pineapple-flavored syrup; and the house's far from al dente noodles came in a shimmering clear broth with scallions chopped on top. The whole experience of eating here was a strange vision of Chinese America, or American Chinese, straight out of D. W. Griffith's *Broken Blossoms*.

One night at the Pendleton Round-Up, looking for more steak served with maximum cowboy atmosphere, we drove a half-hour north of the city to the Washington State line and a town with a name that sounds like an accounting firm: Milton-Freewater. A short detour off the main road led to an endearing discovery called the Oasis. It is a sprawling eatery/tavern/casino that is to modern restaurants what an old pickup truck is to late-model cars: ramshackle and rugged but endearingly soulful. Art on the walls, much of it displayed with pricetags attached, includes portraits of John Wayne and Chief Joseph; in a lounge at the far end are video poker machines and blackjack tables; another dining room is outfitted with handsome chrome-banded black Formica dinette sets. We knew we would like it as soon as we were seated in a room that provided a good view into the bar. There, perched on stools, were three large *X*'s in a row: suspenders on the broad backs of three gents in cowboy hats and pointy-toed boots, having drinks and shooting the breeze.

"How-do?" asked one, tipping his hat in our direction.

"Doing fine," said we as our meat arrived. The sirloins, branded with a neat field of crosshatch char marks on the surface, were slabs of juice and flavor with agreeable tooth resistance, a pleasure to chew. We did not avail ourselves of the opportunity to get our steak free. If you order a seventy-two-ounce sirloin and eat it all, with potato and salad, within an hour, it's on the house. We were happy to pay for a couple of normal-sized sirloins and a mesa of prime rib that was well over an inch thick, fleshy, and laden with natural gravy, all consumed without a time limit.

The best food at the rodeo wasn't actually in the town of Pendleton, and it wasn't served in a restaurant. It was at the Bar M dude ranch, where we stayed. About a half-hour east of town in the Blue Mountains, wildflowers blanket the slopes and the air smells of ponderosa pines. We shared a cabin in the woods with our friend John, and that entitled us to eat in the main lodge. Three times a day, a dinner bell clanged to signal mealtime, and as we walked in from the cabin, we relished guessing what the meal was by the smell that drew us from the woods. It is amazing how keen your nose can be when you concentrate on sniffing the differences between chicken and dumplings, stuffed pork chops, and meat loaf and potatoes. In a big dining room at long, unclothed tables that all ranch guests shared, we passed the serving platters and practiced our boarding-house reach while various members of the Baker family, who have run the ranch since the 1930s, regaled us with tall tales of bobcats and bears they had seen along the trails.

Nothing luxurious was dished out on the El Rancho pattern china, unless, like us, you consider barbecued salmon or fresh-caught trout a luxury. Home cooking was the rule: hot biscuits or cinnamon rolls to accompany morning bacon and eggs, freshly shucked corn on the cob at supper, and always bowls of red raspberry jam made from the Bakers' berry bushes just outside. One night during roundup, Mrs. Baker explained that the sliced fresh tomatoes we were eating had been bought in town at the market. They were thick and radiant with the flavor of autumn sunshine, but she felt it necessary to apologize because they weren't from her garden.

Late in the evening at the Bar M, after the last day of the Pendleton Round-Up, we strolled by moonlight along the path back to our cabin by the lake. After a meal of ham and potatoes and warm yeast rolls with jam and lemon meringue pie for dessert, we gazed up at a sky full of stars, listening to owls hoot and pine tops whisper in the breeze. It sure was different from the pandemonium of the roundup and the anything-goes insanity of the Let 'Er Buck Room. But for us, the allure of the West has a lot to do with that particular combination of ingredients: devil-may-care bravado and the divine serenity of a clear mountain night.

# Chicken-Fried Steak

If you can get half-inch-thick slices of Salorn tenderloin for this recipe, you will come close to duplicating the breakfast we had with Jim and Sharron Shoulders. Round steak is traditional, as are cube steaks (already tenderized), but even filet mignon will work. History suggests that this was a Texas cook's way to tame an ornery cut of steak, one too tough to simply fry.

6   ½-inch-thick cuts of round steak, about 4 inches in diameter
2   large eggs, beaten
1   12-ounce can evaporated milk
1   cup all-purpose flour mixed with 2 teaspoons pepper and 1 teaspoon salt
    Lard or vegetable oil for frying
¾   cup milk mixed with ¼ cup beef stock
    Salt and pepper to taste

Sandwich each steak between pieces of wax paper and beat it for 2 or 3 minutes with a blunt instrument. (An old-time heavy glass Coke bottle is traditional, but we would not encourage using easily breakable glass.) Place the steaks in a baking pan big enough to hold them in a single layer.

Combine the eggs and evaporated milk and thoroughly soak the steaks in the mixture.

Place the seasoned flour on a plate and dredge each steak in it, coating the steaks thoroughly. Do not discard the flour.

Put enough lard or oil in a deep skillet so it is more than ½ inch deep. Heat it to 360 degrees, or until a bread cube sizzles in it.

Dip the floured steaks back into the egg and milk mixture, then use a long set of tongs to ease each of them into the hot oil. Stand back when you do this; the oil will splatter. Do not crowd the steaks in the skillet.

Cook each steak for about 8 minutes, or until it is golden brown on the bottom. Turn, and cook the other side for about 6 more minutes, or until well browned.

Remove the steaks from the oil with tongs or a slotted spoon and drain them on paper towels.

Pour off all but 2 or 3 tablespoons of the oil in the skillet. Return the skillet to the heat and sprinkle 2 tablespoons of the seasoned flour over the hot oil, stirring constantly for a full minute, scraping the bottom of the skillet as you stir.

Gradually add the milk and beef stock mixture, stirring constantly. Continue cooking and stirring until the gravy is thick. Add salt and pepper.

Serve the steak and gravy with mashed potatoes and biscuits.

6 SERVINGS

# Red Beer

Beer is always the main ingredient in red beer. Tomato juice plays second fiddle. But the exact ratio can vary from an effervescent five to one, in which the beer is merely flavored, to a two-to-one mix as fruity as a drink in a health-food juice bar. The precise proportions probably ought to be adjusted to fit the body of the beer as well as the taste of the imbiber. The best red beers we had in Pendleton were made from whatever brew the bar had on tap mixed three to one with canned tomato juice (and served in large translucent plastic cups, so you can see the color). No garnishes are ever used, nor did we see anyone add pepper or Tabasco sauce, as for a Bloody Mary. However, we very much enjoyed the suggestion of a waitress at Pendleton's Circle S Barbecue, who told us that she liked to make her red beer spicier by using V8 juice.

Red beer is frequently served with the morning meal (the term *brunch* is unknown in Pendleton).

½  cup tomato juice
12  ounces beer

Pour the tomato juice into a 16-ounce cup. Gently pour in the beer, stirring just enough to mix but taking care not to stir out all the beer's bubbles.

1 SERVING

# Bringing It All Back Home

Any twenty-first-century food fan looking for Appalachian jellies, Mesilla Valley peppers, hill country brisket, White Mountain maple syrup, or Amish country popcorn can find it on the Internet and order some to be delivered to the front door within twenty-four hours. However, there was a time when we who feel that life is not worth living without such exotic back-roads treasures had to work a little harder to obtain them. The only way to get what we needed was to go to the source, pile the booty into the trunk of our car, and drive it home. We were extremely proud of our trophies, but securing them was often a wild ride fraught with danger.

The average roadfood place had no idea how to pack things for carryout, let alone for a long haul. The vilest example of this is a barbecue shack whose name is lost in the fog of time but whose sauce we remember all too well. This establishment was a dump of the first order, located on an Arkansas back road that dipped and curved through a forest. It was a shack scarcely bigger than an outhouse, open only if the weather was good, having no indoor seats and a pit out back sided by a pile of hickory logs. We stopped and ate and especially loved the sauce. It was a dark, opaque red and ferociously spiced with flecks of pepper. "Would it be possible to get some of your sauce to take home?" Jane asked the pitmaster. He pondered her request for a while, then nodded. We were delighted.

The old guy got up from his outdoor green Naugahyde recliner and slowly walked to a huge pile of garbage about ten yards behind the pit. It was a heap of all sorts of junk: car tires, parts of a washing machine, broken toys, worn roof shingles, and a useless lawn mower or two. The pitmaster rummaged around the edge of the awful mound and finally came up with an empty Jack Daniel's bottle. He walked the bottle back to the pit, put a funnel in its neck, and ladled in a fifth of hot sauce. "Sorry, I've got no top," he politely explained, wrapping the bottle's mouth with a scrap of aluminum foil he found somewhere near his cutting block. "Buck-fifty," he said, handing it to us with a smile.

This had been some delicious sauce, and while the thought occurred to us that perhaps the residual alcohol in the unwashed bottle might kill any germs, we drove down the road and did the right thing: chucked it into the first dumpster we passed.

Sanitation issues aside, transporting what we bought was the big problem. A lot of it did not travel well. Witness the notorious iced-tea saga. We had stopped in the Beacon Drive-Inn of Spartanburg, South Carolina, for pork-a-plenty plates. On the side, of course, we had sweet tea. The Beacon boasts that it makes more sweet tea than any other restaurant on earth, and it's served in huge tankards over a crushed glacier of ice. It is painfully cold and as sweet as cotton candy. There is nothing better on the side of a pork plate on a hot summer day.

With the salubrious powers of this tea in mind, Jane was thinking a week ahead, when we were planning to be heading toward California and crossing the Mojave Desert. The portable oxygen tank we always carried with us would not be enough for this trip. Flaunting tales of her childhood in the Sonoran Desert outside Tucson, she lectured Michael on just how easy it is to turn into a pile of bleached bones under the unforgiving western sun. Her solution: buy six gallons of iced tea, which the Beacon sold in the kind of thin plastic jug that milk comes in. We lined up the six jugs on the floor in front of the back seat, carefully covered them with blankets, and drove on.

Days later, as we drew close to the desert, Michael commented on the number of flies that swarmed into our car every time we opened the door to get out for a hamburger or a bowl of chili. We swatted and swatted, but as the temperature rose, the swarms grew. One hot afternoon at the edge of the desert, we stopped for gas. Jane got out and reached down to pull out a gallon of the precious tea. Moving aside the blankets, she saw six jugs all tilted on their sides. The jugs were bone-dry, and the tea that had leaked into the car's rug had mostly evaporated, leaving a syrupy, sticky residue all over the floor. Clouds of flies buzzed, and we could smell the sweet, dizzying aroma of a rug beginning to ferment.

Using every swear word in his formidable vocabulary, Michael clawed at the carpeting and tried to flush it with water from the service station's hose. Jane broke into gales of hysterical laughter, which made Michael rage even louder. Over the next several months, the fermentation smell diminished, but no matter how we washed and shampooed the rug, it did not go away completely.

The iced-tea disaster did not stop us from filling our car on every trip with spiedie marinade from upstate New York, Slap Yo' Mama fried chicken seasoning from Cajun country, pink Dorothy Lynch salad dressing from Nebraska, tins of King Leo Peppermint Sticks from Nashville, Mormon scone mix from Utah, Yoder family popcorn from Indiana, salmon jerky from the coast of Oregon, any number of no-name ground chile peppers from New Mexico, and great barbecue sauce from Kansas City, St. Louis, Chicago, North Carolina, South Carolina, Tennessee, Arkansas, and Kentucky.

Of all the trophies we've driven home with, none is as grand as a country ham. First of all, it is bomb-proof and indestructible, having already survived a long, grueling curing process. Wild and forceful though it may be, country ham is among the most tenderly nurtured of foods. Its muscular, salty punch leads your tongue toward a complex piquancy. Like veined cheese, sourdough bread, and vintage wine, great country ham awakens that special fascination taste buds have for flavors that teeter on the refined side of rot.

It is a regional specialty of small and medium-sized producers throughout the South between the Ozarks and Virginia's Dismal Swamp. Traditionally, the making of a country ham begins in the fall. The hind leg of a freshly butchered hog is rubbed with salt and sometimes sugar or pepper, as well as sodium nitrate or nitrite to improve color and to resist spoilage. The curing "green ham" absorbs its spice rub in a cool, dark storage area over a course of about four weeks, during which time it weeps moisture. After a month of losing water weight, the ham is washed, strung up in a net bag, and aged for several more months — a period that concludes with a phase known as the summer sweat. Walk into any ham house at this point of the cure and you are bowled over by a horrid smell of moldering flesh. In fact, this is the time when it is easy for a ham to go bad and spoil instead of cure. An experienced ham man finds out the condition of each ham by plunging a pick into its core, removing it, and sniffing.

During the summer sweat, a hanging ham develops a veil of mold, it sheds more weight, its flesh tightens, and its flavor grows ever more profound. Traditional producers age hams for a minimum of six months, and some will keep a few special ones hung up for years. To connoisseurs, the older the ham, the finer its character.

As a ham hangs through the winter and into spring, some ham houses waft hickory or other hardwood smoke into the aging barn. Originally, this was a practical solution for the fly problem in lowland areas. Today, the insinuation of sweet wood flavor from the smoke-house is a fundamental part of many hams' character, although high-land hams, cured in the cooler mountain regions, are seldom smoked.

Since passage of the Wholesome Meat Act of 1967, ham produc-ers who sell their product to the public must be inspected by the U.S. Department of Agriculture, which requires them to maintain sanitary standards akin to those of an operating theater. But if you want a peek at the old-fashioned way of doing things, head north out of Hot Springs, Arkansas, to St. Joe, where Coursey's Smoked Meats main-tains the old dirt-floored log cabin by the side of the road where Paula Hale's grandfather began smoking hams over fifty years ago. "He hung each ham from a nail in the wall and wrapped it in a dry-goods box," Mrs. Hale told us. Today the cabin is only a reminder of days gone by, but government regulation has not tarnished the vintage charm of the store behind the cabin. Mrs. Hale clued us in to the value of a good ham hock, which should never be thrown away once the ham has been eaten: it makes the perfect pot companion for long-cooked greens or beans.

The first country ham we bought weighed twenty pounds and stank like a corpse. We took it home from North Carolina in the back of the car. Its fetid aroma saturated the vehicle, which smelled like ham until the day we junked it.

We invited six friends for a dinner of ham, biscuits, and cherry cobbler, but we hadn't considered that we needed to do something with the ham other than unwrap it and cut it into slices, just as we would with a blubbery, bubble-gum-pink one bought in a can at the supermarket.

While the process isn't complicated, preparing a whole country ham takes time, muscle, and a washtub big enough for bathing an in-fant. First you need to soak the ham in water overnight, changing the water once or twice. Then you need to wash and scrub it to remove the mold. Once you've done all that, you cover the ham with water again and simmer it for several hours, after which you trim some of the outside fat (reserving that to make red-eye gravy). Then you bake the whole ham, glazing it if you want, or slice and fry it.

But we were ham virgins and knew none of this. So just as the guests began arriving, we slit the burlap sack and put the meat on a platter. It was revolting. It looked petrified — it was rock-hard and covered with moss-green fuzz. We tried scrubbing it with towels to remove some of the mold, then took the electric knife we had gotten for our wedding (along with a fondue set and a teak ice bucket) and started to carve. Having eaten proper country ham in restaurants, we knew it should be sliced parchment-thin, but the slabs we cut were chunky and inelegant. When the knife groaned and slowed, we tore off big hunks. The result: a platter of meat that left our guests speechless. As we set it on the dinner table, they looked at us as if we were cannibals serving them something we had buried years ago in the backyard and dug up that afternoon.

"Here's how you do it," Michael proclaimed, taking one of our rather dense biscuits and pulling it into halves. He put a chunk of ham inside, added a dollop of peach preserves we had brought home from Tennessee, then took a bite and masticated hard. Tears welled up in his eyes. The sting of salt made him salivate like Pavlov's dog. "It's supposed to be really rank and salty," he advised the guests, trying to diffuse the intensity by swallowing a large spoonful of sweet preserves.

The guests did the best they could. It was as if we had served them sheep's eyes or monkey brains — a true test of being a good sport. But the ick factor was at orange alert, and we could see pieces of ham being smuggled into napkins and hidden on plates under biscuits.

"Oh, my God," Jane said as we went to bed. Her waist was ringed with a bright red rash. We were soon on our way to the local hospital emergency room, where Jane had a conversation with a resident who told her that she could not die from ingesting uncooked country ham.

"It's nerves," Michael told her for the hundred-millionth time. Back home, equipped with rash cream and a Valium prescription, Jane opened the garbage can and surveyed the remains of the ham.

"Do you think we should take a sample back to the hospital?" she asked.

"Let's go to bed," Michael said. In the morning, the garbage man came and the ham was gone, as was the rash. As were our friends, who never called again.

# Sweet Tea

Having learned about the perils of transporting tea in the car, we needed to find out how to make our own at home. This recipe comes from the Blue Willow Inn, a great mansion east of Atlanta that is known for its groaning-board, all-you-can-eat meals.

Completely different from the hot, sugarless tea that northerners know, sweet tea is best drunk from a tall, wide-mouthed glass with clear fresh ice cubes or heaps of crushed ice. Lots and lots of ice. And of course a big pitcher for refills, as needed. If you wish, you can be fancy and squeeze a little lemon in the tea or add a sprig of mint, but really, any addition is gilding the lily. One important rule for making it is to use regular supermarket tea, not fancy gourmet tea. Another rule is to make it sweeter than you think it should be. Indeed, the motto at the Blue Willow Inn is to serve tea "strong and just a little too sweet."

According to the Blue Willow's proprietor, Louis Van Dyke, grandmothers and mothers of the South serve sweetened iced tea at every meal. In the old South, children were not allowed to drink iced tea until they were twelve years old. They drank milk, water, or lemonade. Soft drinks were never allowed at the dinner table.

Many are the hot summer days when we have gulped multiple glasses of this tea, realizing that this and only this is the beverage that God meant parched throats to drink. It quenches thirst, replenishes verve and vitality, and stimulates your appetite for a nice hot supper.

  1   gallon water
4–5  family-size tea bags (each one is enough for a quart of tea), or
      12–15 regular-size tea bags

3   cups sugar, at least
     Lemon slices, for garnish (optional)
     Sprigs of mint, for garnish (optional)

Bring the water to a boil in a large pot. Turn off the heat and add
the tea bags. Cover and steep for 12 to 15 minutes. For stronger tea, let
it steep longer, up to 20 minutes. Add the sugar, stirring vigorously
until dissolved. Allow to cool and pour over ice. Garnish as desired.

**16 SERVINGS**

# Country Corn Cakes

Other than buttermilk biscuits and red-eye gravy, country ham's best companion is a corn cake. Known throughout the mid-South as corn bread, it is a batter-based circle of steamy starchiness that is griddle-cooked just like a morning pancake. It serves as a wonderful sop for pushing through gravy of any kind. Most southern cooks use White Lily self-rising flour and self-rising cornmeal, but if you can't get them, it's almost as easy to use baking powder and baking soda, as in this recipe.

| | |
|---|---|
| 1 | cup white cornmeal |
| 1 | cup all-purpose white flour |
| 2 | teaspoons baking powder |
| ¼ | teaspoon salt |
| ¼ | teaspoon baking soda |
| 1½ | cups buttermilk |
| 2 | large eggs |
| 2 | tablespoons sugar |
| 3 | tablespoons corn oil |
| | Butter for frying and serving |

Mix together the cornmeal, flour, baking powder, and salt in a large bowl.

In a separate bowl, add the baking soda to the buttermilk, then beat in the eggs, sugar, and corn oil. Add the wet ingredients to the dry and stir until they are just mixed.

Melt a couple of tablespoons of butter in a heavy skillet over medium-high heat.

Pour about ⅓ cup of the batter into the hot skillet to make each

4-inch-diameter cake. Cook each cake until it is light brown on its underside, 1 to 2 minutes, then flip it and cook it for a half minute more. Add butter to the skillet as you cook more cakes. Serve them immediately, with a pat of butter for each.

MAKES 8 TO 10 CORN CAKES

# The Invisible Northeast

At about the same time that we were putting together the first edition of *Roadfood*, we were researching strange local attractions all around the country for another guidebook, *Amazing America*. They ranged from the Lizzie Borden Museum in Fall River, Massachusetts, to an exact replica of England's Stonehenge in Washington State. While strolling along Wisconsin Street in Cawker City, Kansas, we stopped to ask a man sitting on a bench if there was anything unusual to see in his town. He scratched his chin, shrugged his shoulders, and said he couldn't think of a thing. As we thanked him and prepared to walk on, we happened to look up. There, behind him in a large, otherwise empty lot, was the world's largest ball of twine: 17,554 pounds of string, 7 million feet long, all rolled up into a ball with a 40-foot circumference.

And so it was that after tasting all sorts of regional specialties in other states, from turtle soup in southern Indiana to olallieberry pie in California, we came back to our home in Connecticut with no idea what made it an interesting place to eat.

Granted, Connecticut is a little odd. Halfway between Boston and New York, it ranges from ultimate preppy to Indian casino. Being the birthplace of the Wiffle Ball, the Frisbee, and mosquito screens and the home of the first nut factory and bolt shop is an admirable thing, but these are not the makings of a firm and clear identity.

Consider if you will the fact that license plates are emblazoned with the words "The Constitution State" but that the constitution referred to is not America's, as in "We the people...," but a document called "The Fundamental Orders," written in 1639 and based on a sermon by the Reverend Thomas Hooker. Connecticut is also known as the Nutmeg State, which sounds quaint until you learn that no one in Connecticut ever grew nutmegs and that the name comes from colonial times, when nutmegs were costly and wily Yankees whittled fake wooden ones to sell to unsuspecting travelers as the real thing. Then there is the matter of Connecticut's own outlaw motorcycle gang. Other states boast the Hell's Angels, the Pagans, and Satan's Slaves; our guys' leathers flaunt the name the Charter Oaks, after a famous tree that contained a hole in which colonists hid their charter to keep it safe.

Now think of our main industry. Texas has ranching, Iowa has farming, northern California has wine, and Connecticut is the cradle of ... insurance.

And so we sat together in our car and decided that there was nothing to eat in Connecticut of any regional value. Of course, while we were trying to deal with this dilemma, we were driving to Jimmie's of Savin Rock for butter-dripping hot lobster rolls, we were virtually inhaling Pepe's white clam pizza in New Haven, and we regularly bought the wonderful and unusual chicken pies (with no vegetables at all) that were sold from dozens of chicken farms all around our house. We also wolfed down great cinnamon cake doughnuts from Phillip's in Woodbury and spectacular deep-fried weenies with ferocious secret-recipe hot sauce at Blackie's in Cheshire.

Just like the man in Cawker City who sat in front of the big ball of string, we had a blind spot for our state, and even worse, for the entire region of New England, which we had saved for last to explore. We sat with pencils tapping on yellow legal pads, trying to think about what exactly made New England different from all the other places we had been from sea to sea.

"Well," Michael thought out loud, "at least people around here are very . . . rude!"

It was a start.

Being a son of the Midwest, Michael had grown up expecting the openhanded welcome of the farm states' residents. We had dallied long enough in the South to enjoy the sugar-coated way we were worried and fussed over by waitresses from Louisville to the Lowcountry. The bright sunny California smiles we encountered still beamed over all the great West Coast food we had found from San Diego to the Oregon line. And New York City people, who are generally considered awfully curt, in fact never shut up, bending your ear with their loquacious version of how the world should work.

*Rude* was perhaps not the right word to describe Connecticut's character. It was more terse. "Like the Whitlock brothers," Michael said. The Whitlock Brothers were five old Yankee book dealers to whom we had sold our remaindered and unwanted books for many years. Approximately twenty-five years after we first set foot in Whitlock's Book Barn in Woodbridge, one of the brothers looked up from the pile of books we brought him and said, "Nice selection." We were so stunned by the relatively outgoing nature of his remark that we could not form an answer.

How does this Yankee terseness play out culinarily? There is no better place to start defining it than at Durgin-Park in Boston. Few places are as overtly brusque, and no place we know is so purely Beantown in character. It is over 150 years old and still serves such delightfully dowdy meals as fish cakes and spaghetti, and in the autumn, mince pie. You will be seated at a communal table, alongside strangers who are likely midway through their dinners and who will pay no attention to you as you join them at the table. Lighting is harsh, the room sounds like a school gymnasium at halftime, and the waitresses are famously gruff. The average waitress here looks like she can bench-press 300 pounds and throw you through a window if you piss her off. Nobody gets celebrity treatment, and you'd better know what you want when the waitress comes around, because these crusty birds will scold you if you're slow. They serve meals efficiently, but with all the charm of a hockey player. And the food itself, slapped onto plates in the kitchen, comes in portions suitable for Elmer the Elephant. With all this said, Durgin-Park remains one of our favorite restaurants in the whole country, and one of the very few places that serves perfect regional food even though it is also visited by lots of tourists.

One time at Durgin-Park we sat down alongside a couple from Alabama who were tasting New England fare for the first time. They asked what Indian pudding was. We described the steaming cornmeal gruel sweetened with molasses, and these good folks, whose idea of a proper dessert was fluffy coconut layer cake and divinity fudge, thought we were joking. Cereal for dessert seemed as weird to them as Eskimos eating blubber. But they were brave, and they ordered a dish. The pasty autumn-colored samp arrived hot, with vanilla ice cream melting on top. Their first taste was tentative, but they quickly discovered how to spoon up some ice cream with the pudding for a confluence of smooth sweet cream and spicy grain. "It's good," the man declared, still not fully convinced, "like sugared grits."

New England cookery will probably never get trendy, like Cajun or Tex-Mex, because its fundamental values of parsimony and plainness have no razzle-dazzle. It is hard to imagine someone like Emeril saying, "We are going to take this boiled dinner up a notch . . . *bam!* " But for those of us who prize gastronomic rituals that are an intrinsic part of one's culture, the Northeast is in fact a bonanza. Consider

Moody's Diner of Waldoboro, Maine, a beacon of square meals and excellent slices of pie since Percy Moody opened it in the early 1930s. There, over many years of exploring coastal food, we have sat in hard-backed wood booths feasting on blueberry muffins, meat loaf and mashed potatoes, hot turkey sandwiches, chowders, stews, and soups, red flannel hash, and baked beans with brown bread. On a recent trip up the coast in search of classic diners, we asked Alvah Moody, Percy's son, what he thought the best dish on the menu was. He answered without hesitation: "Tripe."

Organ-soft and juicy, tripe isn't unique to New England (cooked with the puffy hominy called posole, it is a long-established hangover cure in the Southwest); but a lot of old-timers of the region consider these marinated, deep-fried ribbons of cow stomach their soul food. Alvah recalled that several years ago Moody's tripe supplier went belly-up and it was off the menu for six months. "All of our regulars complained. They depend on us, and they come from Portland and Augusta to eat tripe because no one else makes it anymore."

We decided we needed to try some, but our waitress, Cheryl Durkee, looked up from her order pad with an expression of genuine horror when we told her we wanted a plate of it for lunch. "Are you sure?" she asked. "You're not from around here. I don't think it's for you."

"Alvah said it's great," we replied, to which she rolled her eyes in disbelief.

Cheryl finally allowed us to order the tripe, but she had to have the last word: "To me, tripe is a sour sponge soaked in vinegar and deep-fried."

Such frankness, while not unique to New England, is very much part of the experience of dining here.

But what about our little Connecticut? Another state nickname is Land of Steady Habits, and at the café counter or table this translates to meals that are far from the cutting edge. The great dishes here are not quite as dour as Maine's or Vermont's, but that's just fine. The "normal food" can be spectacular.

For example, Connecticut is one of the great hot dog capitals of America, and please remember that Michael is from Chicago and Jane from New York City, so we really do know a thing or two about hot dogs. One of the first great weenies we found close to home was something we learned about from Martha Stewart. One day she started rhapsodizing to us about a place called Rawley's in Fairfield, where the dogs are deep-fried until they are ready to burst, then rolled around on a griddle until they develop a crunchy skin, after which they are bunned under a heap of crisp bacon, onions, mustard, and relish. These are indeed A Good Thing, and it has always given us great pleasure to picture Martha leaving the pristine grounds of her house and sitting on a stool at the dumpy shack that is Rawley's, scarfing down hot dogs. As a measure of the state's high hot dog consciousness, consider a place for which we have been beating the drum for years: Super Duper Weenie, also of Fairfield, where chef and owner Gary Zemola goes to the max to ensure hot dog excellence by doing such things as pickling his own cucumbers to make his own relish to top hot dogs that are specially made for him by a local butcher.

Another asset Connecticut shares with the rest of New England is superior ice cream. Northeasterners eat nearly twice as much per capita as people in any other region. Rare is the Yankee Main Street without at least one parlor boasting sodas, shakes, and sundaes. In this part of the world, an accomplished ice cream maker is as highly regarded as a barbecue pitmaster in North Carolina or a blue-ribbon pie chef in Iowa. Fans of indigenous brands are zealous: simply say the name Round Top or Shain's (of Maine), Wentworth's, Mr. Shane,

Dr. Mike's, Big Dipper, or Timothy's (of Connecticut), or Herrell's, Toscanini's, or Brigham's (of Massachusetts) and you will set appetites agrowl.

Passion aside, New England stakes claim to several great moments in ice cream history, including the ingenious twenty-eight-flavor concept of Howard Johnson, who started in 1925 at a drugstore counter in Wollaston, Massachusetts. After HoJo's, many entrepreneurs found success selling ice cream in New England, from the Blake brothers, who opened their first Friendly's shop in Springfield, Massachusetts, in 1935, to Ben Cohen and Jerry Greenfield, who rode the tides of ice cream ardor to pop-culture fame (and fortune) with the super-rich, crazy-flavored stuff they began hand-cranking in 1978 in a defunct gas station near the University of Vermont in Burlington.

Our own personal favorite ice cream story (and favorite ice cream) is that of a humble Connecticut stand called the Ridgefield Ice Cream Shop. Proprietor Felix Lechner used to be a Carvel franchisee, and his shop looks like a Carvel stand. But many years ago, Felix decided he could do better. He bought the place and all the ice cream–making equipment and worked on creating a product he calls "custard without the egg." Elsewhere, the Carvel formula changed for the worse; the ice cream grew lighter and thin-flavored because of equipment that created a higher overrun — that is, pumped it full of air. But Felix was going the other way. Using vintage silver machines that he maintains with parts salvaged from old Carvel stands that go out of business, he creates an amazingly simple soft-serve ice cream that is smooth and deep-flavored, robust enough to mound up impossibly high on a cone and dense enough to grasp a thick coating of chocolate sprinkles or a shell of quick-dry dip-top. Because this place is so near our home, we estimate that we stop for a chocolate cone well over a hundred times a year, virtually every day we are not on the road throughout the summer.

We had lived in the southwestern part of the state for twenty-five years and made our living hunting exotic food all around the nation before we discovered a specialty unique to central Connecticut, the steamed cheeseburger. Invented in the 1920s, when people believed that steamed food was better for you than fried, it is literally unknown beyond a small circle of less than a dozen restaurants around the town of Meriden, where it began. It is a very strange variation on a common theme. The meat is cooked in a small tray inside a metal steam cabinet alongside a tray of cheddar cheese. After a few minutes in the cabinet, the meat is oozing juice and the cheddar is as soft as pudding. The two are combined on a hard roll with lettuce and tomato.

You'll find none better than at Ted's, which has set the steamed-cheeseburger gold standard since Ted Duberek opened it in 1959. It is a tiny diner with deliciously reprobate blue-plate ambience and a row of six booths along the wall. The choice seats are at the counter, where you have a view of big sticks of cheddar cheese waiting to be steamed and a pan full of fresh ground beef. Here Ted's son and successor, Paul Duberek, tends his vintage metal cook box looking like some Mephistophelean *cuisinier*, enveloped in great clouds of steam as he hoists hunks of beef onto buns and spoons gobs of molten cheese onto the beef. Accidental tourists are rare at Ted's, where most patrons have such predictable eating habits that Paul already knows whether they eat one or two burgers per sitting (the only choice you need to make, other than what to drink). Perhaps that is why Paul is especially happy when newcomers enter. They are his opportunity to expound upon a favorite subject: the history, lore, and aesthetics of the steamed cheeseburger.

In fact, it was eating at Ted's that made us think, *Holy cow, Connecticut is a hugely important treasury of hamburgers*. There is credible evidence that the burger was invented in New Haven, at Louis' Lunch, where you can still go and get one served on toast as it has always been, because hamburger buns didn't exist when it was created, in 1895. The hamburgers are cooked in metal armatures inside ancient vertical ovens that allow the grease to drip away (a design that predates the George Foreman Grill by almost a hundred years). The result is a pillowy, moist patty with a crusty edge. Ken Lassen, grandson of founder Louis and now a very senior citizen himself, happened to drop by one day in the summer of 2005 to watch his progeny cook burgers, and we got into a conversation with him about what makes these hamburgers so good. He assured us with a straight face that when he was a young man, he developed a formula for grinding different cuts in exact proportion to replicate beef from the good old prehormone days of full-flavored, range-fed longhorn cattle.

One more good argument for our home state's burger primacy: Shady Glen of Manchester. Here are the most dramatic cheeseburgers you will ever experience. Each one starts as a simple patty of beef slapped down on a high-temperature electric grill. It is flipped and then blanketed with four square slices of cheese, arranged so that only one quarter to one third of each slice rests atop the hamburger. The remainder extends beyond the circumference of the meat and melts down onto the surface of the grill. At the exact moment the grilling cheese begins to transform from molten to crisp, the cook uses a spatula to disengage it from the grill and curl it above the meat like some wondrous burgerflower — still slightly pliable, but rising up in certain symmetry. The petals of cheese, which may be topped with condiments and are crowned by a bun, are crunchy at their tip but chewy where they blend into the soft parts that adhere to the hamburger.

"This is not about flipping hamburgers," explained William J. Hoch, Sr., Shady Glen's executive manager, when we watched the creative process one day. "It requires an education to make a cheeseburger as we do. You must train your eyes to know when the cheese is ready, and you need a sure and steady hand to curl it." Mr. Hoch, who is as serious about cheeseburgers as Jean-Georges Vongerichten is about extracted vegetable juices, knows whereof he speaks. He is second cousin to John Reig, whose wife, Bernice, invented the mind-blowing cheeseburger over fifty years ago. In 1948 the Reigs opened an ice cream parlor to celebrate the richness of the product from their dairy farm, but they wanted something for the menu that would attract customers in the winter months. After three years of experimentation, Bernice perfected the creation that would become Shady Glen's signature, even more than its excellent ice cream.

Is a cheeseburger exotic or unique to the Northeast? Not exactly, and it certainly is nothing too special for most people who eat at Shady Glen or Louis' Lunch or Ted's, where it is everyday food. But the fact is that anyone traveling to Connecticut in search of a meal they won't find anywhere else on earth needs to visit these three places. And we are a little red-faced to confess that it took us years to know that.

# Indian Pudding

Dark brown, with an incalculable specific gravity, Indian pudding is monumental. It smells like burned corn and tastes ancient, conjuring visions of stark Pilgrim feeds. Unlike glamorous desserts, it will never be considered sinful or decadent or creative. No one will ever market Squanto-in-a-Bowl or All-New, Lite Hot 'n' Gritty Dessert Food Product, and we doubt we will ever see it as a Ben & Jerry's flavor. This dark brown duff defies the march of progress and the wheedling of inventive chefs. It will always be hopelessly dowdy, treasured all the more by partisans for its august character.

Although all recipes for Indian pudding are fairly similar, no version is as good as Durgin-Park's. Tommy Ryan, Durgin-Park's chef for more than forty years, suspected the difference may have something to do with the vessels in which it's cooked — unchanged for decades. One time in the early 1980s, while doing a comparison tasting of Indian puddings from Rhode Island to Maine, we arrived at Faneuil Hall just as the Durgin-Park food stand was closing, meaning we had to go into the restaurant proper to beg an order to go. Much to the chagrin of the impatient waitresses standing behind us to pay their customers' checks (at Durgin-Park, diners pay the waitress, who is responsible for paying the house), the man at the register hunted up a container (a half-gallon jar) and slopped it full of the hot dark goo — so full it overflowed down the sides, onto his and then our hands, onto our pants, onto the seat of our car, into the elevator of the Ritz-Carlton Hotel, where we were staying, and finally onto the Ritz's white linen tablecloth, which arrived under the vanilla ice cream we ordered from room service. Vanilla ice cream is the essential topping for warm Indian pudding.

Note that the baking time is 5 to 7 hours.

| | |
|---|---|
| 3 | cups milk |
| ¼ | cup molasses |
| 2 | tablespoons sugar |
| 2 | tablespoons butter, melted |
| ¼ | teaspoon salt |
| ⅛ | teaspoon baking powder |
| 1 | large egg, beaten |
| ½ | cup yellow cornmeal |

Preheat the oven to 425 degrees and grease a 1-quart ovenproof casserole.

Mix together 1½ cups of the milk with the molasses, sugar, butter, salt, baking powder, egg, and cornmeal in a large bowl. Pour the mixture into the casserole and bake until it boils, 20 to 25 minutes.

Heat the remaining 1½ cups of milk and stir it in. Lower the oven temperature to 300 degrees and bake for 5 to 7 hours. Serve warm.

4 TO 6 SERVINGS

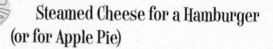

# Steamed Cheese for a Hamburger
# (or for Apple Pie)

Our friend Brian O'Rourke of O'Rourke's Diner in Middletown, Connecticut (not far from Meriden), has an old-fashioned steam cabinet for making steamed cheeseburgers or, equally wonderful, steamed cheddar cheese that is soft and smooth and eminently suitable topping a wedge of apple pie. Brian told us that we didn't really have to buy a steam cabinet to get the same results. He said that all we needed was a large skillet, a metal colander with feet, a big heatproof bowl, and a clean, empty 6½-ounce tuna can.

Put about 1 inch of water in the skillet and place it on the stove over medium heat. Position the colander above the water. Put 4 to 6 ounces of sharp Vermont cheddar cheese in the tuna can, and when the water begins to boil, put the tuna can in the colander. Then cover the colander with the big heatproof bowl, turned upside down, trapping the steam inside. In minutes the cheese will melt. Then all you have to do is spoon it onto a hamburger, a hard roll, or a piece of apple pie.

NOTE: It is possible to cook the meat in the makeshift steam box if you want to be a classicist. Put a half-inch-thick patty of raw lean ground beef in another clean tuna can and steam the burger and the cheese at the same time.

3 TO 4 SERVINGS

# The Inedible Complex

We have eaten 72,427 meals since we first started looking for road-food. On the road two hundred days a year, twelve meals a day for thirty years: that equals 72,000. And we hereby add 427 more from a special Hall of Infamy known previously only to us. These are meals so disgusting that after looking at them, smelling them, and sometimes even ingesting them, we seriously consider changing to an adventure-free career that would allow us to sit in a cubicle, eat meals from a vending machine, and never have to face such awful stuff again.

Yes, we love being professional eaters, and the joy of finding delicious meals is unsurpassed, but there is a dark underbelly to hunting roadfood. The simple truth is that the world is full of really bad places to eat. Our work would be a breeze if every restaurant we found was a crisp-curtained little nook run by a sanitary old lady whose muffins were gems and whose roast turkey dinners outshone Thanksgiving. But it is not so. And if it were so, nobody would need us to find the good places; we'd be out of a job in which we sometimes feel like scientific guinea pigs or, worse, culinary canaries in a mineshaft clouded with burned Crisco fumes.

As we have experienced it, the roadfood ratio is something like this. Out of the twelve meals we eat in a normal day, two or three are good enough to write about and eight or nine are unremarkable. But on occasion one of them is downright frightening or dangerous, or both. Sometimes a terrible meal is, in its own way, impossible to forget.

Repulsive roadfood falls into two distinct categories. The first is something that is cooked poorly: the omelet in Oklahoma that the chef sizzled in his pan for a solid quarter-hour, until it was as chewy as a radial tire; the "blackened" mystery fish in Michigan that came sheathed in a crust of burned salt; the Texas chili that was equal parts fat, gristle, and cayenne pepper. Such crimes against the palate rightfully can be called mistakes. Blunders. Bloopers. Boners.

But then there is a whole other class of hideous fare, which is a perfect rendition of what it is supposed to be. It is vile, but not because an error has been made. It is repellent because the very concept of the dish affronts the taste buds.

Of course, whose taste buds it affronts is the million-dollar question. We had a brilliant lesson in gastronomic relativity one day in Elko, Nevada, while dining at a casino steakhouse with a western singer who, like us, had come to town for Elko's annual Cowboy Poetry Gathering.

"Dis-*gust*-ing!" pronounced the balladeer as he popped a testicle into his mouth, chewed, and swallowed. After a long swig from a mug of draft beer, he looked across the table at us and declared, "I can't believe people eat them!" He then grabbed another deep-fried hunk of gonad and gobbled it with easy glee. "You have to be crazy to eat a clam!" he concluded, finishing the last of the prairie oyster hors d'oeuvre just as our steaks arrived.

The singer from Idaho, who wore a black, broad-brimmed bull rider's Stetson wherever he went, including to his dinner with us, was reacting to Michael's comment that the balls reminded him a bit of fried clams. We explained that where we live, fried clams are common, even more of a passion than fried testicles out West. He shuddered with revulsion at the idea of clam-eating and sliced into his bloody T-bone.

Whether you find testicles or clams too awful to consider eating or you like one or both of them, some local specialties are bound to make you want to gag. The brain sandwich so popular in St. Louis taverns? The euphemistically named "puddin'" made of pig innards in eastern Pennsylvania? Smelly ramps in West Virginia? Lutefisk in Minnesota?

We try to keep an open mind and an open mouth, but we have to confess that some dishes are, at least to us, as appealing as ipecac. The perfect example is an order of chitlins steamed in vinegar that we got at a little café down in Brunswick County, Virginia.

Before we describe the horror of this dish, it is only fair to fill you in on our culinary preferences. Michael is easy — he eats everything, or at least he will try anything once. He is a guy who loves steak tartare and raw oysters and will happily order cow lungs and kishke (stuffed intestines). For the first twenty-one years of her life, Jane, though, pretty much ate six things: bread, butter, cake, turkey (white meat), Necco wafers, and cheese. On a sleepover date at a girlfriend's house in the seventh grade, she was so distraught that the family dinner was served with a white sauce — an exotic substance she had never seen before — and that the salad had dressing on it that she cried hysterically until the evil people put her in a cab and sent her back home to her parents' apartment. When we met at Yale, Jane had never eaten pizza with anything on it but cheese.

As we traveled, Jane's taste in food broadened greatly. She became smitten with hot red chili and clam chowder and Indian pudding. But she is still far from omnivorous. She has maintained a lifelong phobia for an entire food group: condiments. No ketchup, no mayonnaise, no pickles, no relish, no mustard is allowed on, in, or near anything she is to eat. Her idea of hell is Thousand Island dressing, because it is made of three dreaded condiments, pickles, mayonnaise, and ketchup, and if anyone suggests that a barbecue sauce she likes might be a first cousin to ketchup, she denies there is any resemblance between the two.

Therefore, Michael is in charge of eating and writing about strange foods — foods that are strange to us, anyway. Which brings us back to chitlins steamed in vinegar. Chitlins — formally chitterlings — are pigs' intestines. A beloved soul food, they need to be cleaned well and they are usually prepared by deep-frying. They can be a bit rubbery, but basically anything deep-fried is tasty. While in southern Virginia hunting the meaty gallimaufry called Brunswick stew, we saw a little place by the side of the road that won us over immediately with a hand-rendered sign on the outside wall that showed a plate of chitlins with aromatic wisps of flavor drifting all around it. We walked inside and immediately realized that this was a restaurant with a one-item menu. The kitchen made chitlins and nothing but chitlins. No macaroni and cheese, no corn bread, no barbecue, not even sweet tea to drink. Customers who ate there brought their own side dishes and beverages, but it was apparent from the menu posted on the wall, which listed different-sized orders up to ten pounds, that a lot of business was takeout.

It was getting dark, and we had miles to cover before bedding down, so rather than sit at a table we ordered sixteen ounces to go. The man who ran the place was buzzing around the kitchen stove behind his counter, and in due time handed us a large Styrofoam "clamshell" with our portion inside. "Y'all ever eat chitlins before?" he asked.

Michael honestly replied, "Yes."

The man then said, "In these parts we don't fry them. We steam them in vinegar." We paid for ours, carried the container out to the car, and drove away.

After less than a mile, it occurred to both of us simultaneously that the inside of our car smelled like a public toilet.

"Oh, my God!" Jane cried. "What is that stench?"

We rolled down the windows, and as Michael continued to drive ever faster along the two-lane back road, Jane opened the clamshell container resting on her lap. Tubes of pale rubbery flesh swam in an acidic broth. The only way to explain the stink is to say that chitlins steamed in vinegar smell like feces marinated in urine. Maybe the chitlins had not been properly cleaned. Who knows? At that point, we were in no mood to discuss the fine points of their preparation. Michael floored the gas pedal, reached over to grab the clamshell, and sent the whole meal sailing out the window to splat in the middle of the road behind us.

Few things make us madder than seeing someone carelessly toss garbage out the window of a car. At home Jane spends a great deal of free time picking up tossed litter on our country road, muttering as she stuffs it into a Hefty bag. But honestly, the smell of chitlins steamed in vinegar was such that it made us crazy with disgust. As we sped away — windows open, air conditioning on high — we wondered if the local wildlife would eat the steaming heap of foul food or run away from it like a naughty puppy running from a shoe sprayed with Bitter Apple. Having a fair grasp of ecology, we knew that the Styrofoam clamshell would probably outlast the Earth, but there was no way we would go back and put it in the car.

Another time, on a blazing hot summer day, we stopped at a Chinese joint in St. Louis. The restaurant had no air conditioning, so the front door was propped. After the waiter took our orders, Jane glanced up and noticed that it was held ajar by an uncooked chicken. We ran for our lives.

We don't consider ourselves squeamish or overly fastidious. It's okay if cooks and servers aren't swathed in hairnets and rubber food-service gloves. When barbecue master Arthur Bryant was alive, we used to make pilgrimages to his place in Kansas City for magnificent brisket sandwiches bathed in the world's best sauce, and the sandwich man's coup de grâce didn't bother us a bit: when he finished constructing the big, messy thing, he mashed down the top with his hand, leaving distinct prints in the top slice of spongy white bread.

A cast-iron stomach has kept Michael remarkably immune to even the most nauseating food, whereas Jane, the picky one, holds the honor of getting the sickest. It happened in Los Angeles, where we were being escorted around town by our publisher's representative and her husband. He greeted us by saying, "The two of you write about the tourist traps." We took the bait and followed him from one dive to another in areas featured in the news for drive-by shootings. Michael ate burritos filled with mystery meat and depth-charge salsas. Jane ordered a large portion of unrefrigerated flan and polished it off, right down to the last spoonful.

The revenge of the flan began about twelve hours later in a nice hotel. Her stomachache came on with the speed and power of a tsunami, and pretty soon she was crawling along the floor announcing that she was dead (despite Michael's carefully reasoned argument that the dead don't complain). Finally convinced that this wasn't a case of hypochondria, Michael called the front desk and asked for the hotel doctor.

The doctor was cordial and said it was a good thing we were flying back to New York the next day, because Jane would not be feeling up to snuff for a while. Then he gave her a vial of five pills, each about the size of a quail egg, so she could have a "comfortable" plane trip home. By the time we headed for the airport, Jane was feeling no pain. The problem was that she was unable to walk. Her eyes were glassy, and she could not mumble a coherent phrase. An airline employee with a wheelchair scooped her up and deposited her in a plane seat, where she sat for the six-hour flight looking like an exhibition in Madame Tussaud's wax museum.

We admit that we (read Michael) do like to order strange foods on the road. We (read Michael) have eaten testicles of all kinds, from rooster fries to big slabs of bovine gonads. We (read Michael) have eaten cactus paddles, assorted tongues, bottom-feeding fish, rattlesnake, bison, corn fungus, scrapple, goetta (Cincinnati's pig offal hash), and more. When it comes to pig, both of us prefer eating high on the hog — bacon, pork chops, hams, and shoulders — but there is a whole branch of soul-food cookery devoted to lesser parts of the porkers' anatomy.

For reasons we cannot explain, St. Louis soul-food restaurants seem to make a specialty of these odd parts. Take the snoot sandwich at C&K Barbecue. For years we savored C&K's rib tips and chopped pork. Then we finally drew up the courage to try the snoot. As you might surmise, snoot is a snout, and we ordered ours with a comic-book image of what it was going to look like: one giant pink pig proboscis served between two slices of bread. It turned out to be nothing of the sort, and while snoot won't make our list of favorite foods, we rather liked it. The meat was shaved and cut into long ribbons, baked and deep-fried, served with good sauce on a bun. Not bad, not bad at all.

We should have stopped there, but successful snoot eating gave us courage. We assumed that like the snoot, the meat in the pig-ear sandwich would be chopped up, fried, and sauced. Wrong. What arrived at our table was two slices of white bread with an intact ear between them. It had been boiled, but otherwise looked as though it had just been cut off the head with scissors. We (read Michael) took a bite. It was amazingly tender, fatty-flavored, and not at all gristly. Not terrible-tasting . . . and yet the sandwich with the crisp bite mark inflicted on the triangular ear was a stomach-turning vision. That was not only the first but the last ear we (read Michael) ever ate.

During a trip through the Mississippi Delta, we stopped in Clarksdale, home of the blues. Roger Stolle, proprietor of Cat Head Delta Blues and Folk Art, told us to be sure to check out a place called Hicks' for its world-class tamales. Hicks' dining room was closed that day, but taped to the drive-up window was an eight-and-a-half-by-eleven-inch sheet of paper on which the day's special was written in felt-tip marker: "Hog Maws 16 oz. $3.69." We debated for a moment. Jane was sure maws were part of the mouth (which she inferred from the expression "shut your maw"); Michael believed they came from the far other end of the animal. When it was our turn, Jane asked, "Is this maw you are serving a mouth or a rectum?" The woman stared, aghast at our ignorance. Finally she recovered and explained that maws were part of the pig's stomach.

Who could resist? We ordered a pint to go with our tamales and drove south on Highway 49. With Michael at the wheel, Jane opened the cardboard container. The aroma coming from it was foul. Pieces of maw wallowed in a funky broth, the knobs of pinkish white flesh poking above the surface.

"Are you going to have some?" Jane asked. She held the container under Michael's nose like a grade-schooler daring a classmate to eat boogers.

Michael swerved toward a small factory by the side of the road, where he had spotted a dumpster. There he heaved the horrific maws "en brodo" before driving on.

That night for dinner we went to Lusco's in Greenwood, where we feasted on porterhouse steak and French-fried potatoes. Back in the hotel room, we dug into a bag of Raisinets and ate a stack of Nabisco Sugar Wafers. It doesn't get better than that.

# Sautéed Fresh Calf's Liver

Many otherwise adventurous eaters put calf's liver on their short list of inedible dishes. We are not among them. To celebrate our fortieth birthdays, we took our friends Ippy and Neal Patterson to New York's Four Seasons restaurant, where we all feasted on liver and onions, creamed spinach, and massive quantities of good Champagne.

As delicious as Four Seasons liver is, our favorite place to eat the dish is the Dorset Inn of Dorset, Vermont. Chef Sissy Hicks's calf's liver is simply the best in the world, and, astonishingly, it is the favorite meal on the dinner menu. Sissy explains its popularity by saying, "No two people in a family like calf's liver, so it is rarely cooked at home." Thus, when liver lovers dine at the inn, it is their opportunity to indulge.

- 4 strips bacon
- 8 tablespoons vegetable oil or butter
- 2 white onions, sliced
- 2 6-ounce calf's livers
  Salt and pepper to taste
  All-purpose flour for dredging

Cook the bacon in a large skillet or in the oven until crisp, and set aside to drain on paper towels.

Heat 2 tablespoons of the oil or butter in the skillet over medium heat. Sauté the onions until golden brown and set them aside.

Heat the remaining 6 tablespoons oil or butter in a medium sauté pan. Season the livers with salt and pepper and dredge them in the flour.

When the pan is hot, shake the flour from the livers and place the livers in the pan. When browned on one side, quickly turn with tongs and brown the other side. This takes about 5 minutes total (both sides) for rare, 1 to 2 minutes more per side if desired well done. Serve immediately with the onions and bacon.

2 TO 3 SERVINGS

# Mama Lo's Broccoli Casserole

Like liver, broccoli is a food that some people loathe. While we are not among them, we love the way Mama Lo's recipe for broccoli casserole transforms the healthful stalk of veggie vitamins into a dish that is rich, luxurious, and not the least bit annoyingly nutritious.

We also love this dish because it reminds us of one of our all-time favorite roadfood cafés. Mama Lo's of Gainesville, Florida, is gone now, but for years it was a soul-food beacon for students and townies, blacks and whites, single workmen on lunch break and whole families who came to indulge in Mama's deliriously flavorful suppers. The plain, whitewashed building was tiny, with only a handful of seats and a single pool table for recreation. Because Mama hand-wrote the menu every morning based on what she found in the market, only three or four copies of it were written each day. They got passed around the dining room until, by the end of lunch hour, they were as limp as cooked cabbage.

As is typical of the best southern cafés, the roster of side dishes was a joy just to read, and whether you accompanied your pork chop and dressing with fried corn and baked apple ring or collards and mac 'n' cheese, each item arrived at the table in its own separate little dish. Among the best of them was this casserole, the recipe for which Mama Lo was kind enough to share with us. It has since become a staple side dish in our household.

Butter
5   slices white bread, torn into bite-size pieces
1   bunch broccoli (1½–2 pounds)
3   large eggs

¼   cup milk
4   tablespoons (½ stick) butter, melted
1   cup grated cheddar cheese
3   tablespoons sugar
1   teaspoon salt

Preheat the oven to 350 degrees. Butter an 8-inch square Pyrex baking dish.

Cover the bottom of the dish generously with the torn bread. Cut the broccoli (florets and tops of stems) into bite-sized pieces and lay them on top of the bread.

Mix together all the remaining ingredients in a medium bowl. Pour them over the broccoli and bread. Cover with aluminum foil.

Bake for 35 minutes, until the cheese is thoroughly melted and the top is browned. Serve warm.

6 SERVINGS

# Reading Menus

We are often asked if we always agree on everything and always get along. Right, sure we do. In the thirty-five years we have been married, we have never had a fight, not even a disagreement.

In fact, it is small wonder that we have not killed each other at some point during our many years on the road. When we drive somewhere together, we feel a lot like two astronauts in a space capsule where personal space is at a minimum. Although we don't have to drink Tang and pee in our space suits, the enforced closeness can be hard. We once traveled cross-country in a little Subaru, and by the time we reached California, our upper arms were black and blue from punches accidentally thrown when one of our elbows drifted beyond its allotted space.

Besides cramped quarters, another bone of contention is maps. Jane simply cannot read one. She has no sense of north, south, east, and west. If there were such a thing as map dyslexia, she would be the poster child. Just as men pride themselves on never having to stop and ask directions, Jane pretends she knows what she is doing when she reads a map. She squints at the well-thumbed Rand McNally and theatrically drags a finger along highways and mutters to herself. We won't go into details about the number of accidental hundred-mile detours taken as Michael snoozed and Jane, at the wheel, glanced at the open map on the dashboard and confused I-80 with the Pennsylvania Turnpike or I-90 with I-94 northwest of Milwaukee. The night she headed west out of New Hampshire, bound for Maine, has become family legend.

Jane's driving has also always been a sore spot. She drives like someone's half-blind, demented aunt. Forty-five miles per hour is a blazing speed for her, and creeping along in the far right lane, tapping the brakes every few seconds, is the way she likes to motor. Behind the wheel she is scared of snow, ice, teenagers in cars, four-lane highways, rental cars that don't feel like her own, passing trucks, and night. She is afraid of animals in the road, of the ring of her cell phone, of anything that might cause a distraction. What she isn't afraid of is police cars. Jane has never in her life gotten a traffic ticket, but she has probably caused many other drivers to be pulled over because they whipped around her and sped ahead in frustration.

Michael, in contrast, goes everywhere as if he were in a NASCAR race. Early one morning in Iowa during the 1980s, we decided it would be nice to get back to Connecticut that same night. Having convinced ourselves that our car was a second home and needed to be as comfortable as a living room, we had broken the bank to buy a huge black Mercedes-Benz designed for cruising the autobahn. After about eighteen hours in the car, we were somewhere near Buffalo, New York, and it was after midnight. Michael pulled over to the side of the road when he saw three police cruisers blocking the lanes up ahead and waving at our car to stop.

"Sir, do you know you were driving one hundred and eighteen miles an hour?" one of them asked as he walked to our open car window.

Truly, Michael had no idea. The Benz was that smooth and the road was empty, and he was in a trance from nonstop driving. Apparently we had zoomed past several police officers by the side of the road and they had radioed ahead for a roadblock.

"Step out of the car," the trooper said. "Both of you."

We opened the front doors of the car and fell onto the pavement. Our legs had long ago gone numb from sitting for hours. We lay like upended turtles at the side of the road, waving our flippers in the air. The cops started laughing so hard that they finally let us go with a warning if we promised never, ever to drive in New York State again.

Despite being the writerly unit known as janeandmichaelstern, we are very different people. Jane loves to shop. Michael abhors it. Jane is from the East. Michael is midwestern. Jane is average height and broad. Michael is tall and lanky. But there are a few things about which we are totally in sync. Two that come to mind are dogs and menus. We love any bulldog-style dog. As for menus, we adore them.

We like menus the way bibliophiles like books. We enjoy touching them and looking at them — even smelling them if they've spent time in a smokehouse café or a chocolatier's showroom. We like to see how they're printed or handwritten, what typeface and what sorts of images (if any) a restaurant chooses to signify itself on paper — or leatherette, or plastic laminate. We especially like the feel of well-used menus, ones with gravy stains and barbecue-sauce fingerprints in the corner, or those painstakingly inked on blue-lined notebook paper that get passed around the dining room, the way they were at Mrs. Forde's Coffee Shop in Laurinburg, North Carolina, where the prix fixe lunch (in 1977) cost seventy-five cents.

Some menus that we have encountered are real works of art, or at least folk art, like the branded saddle-leather binders at Cimmiyotti's in Pendleton, Oregon. We have read menus painted on wine bottles, menus burned into thick planks of wood, menus smaller than a single business card or bigger than the codices of Leonardo da Vinci, menus painstakingly inscribed with calligraphic script or scrawled in chalk on bulletin boards, menus perfumed by vintage mimeograph inks, and menus shaped like oyster shells, T-bones, and the state of Idaho.

Ages ago, when we were befriended by James Beard, he took us for lunch at New York City's Lutèce, a place we had never visited on our own. Seated in the garden room at the big round table in the center, we were approached by its chef and owner, the legendary André Soltner. He and Jim Beard were old friends, and in fact Beard used to give cooking classes in the upper floors of the brownstone where the restaurant was located. Out of respect and because this is what great chefs do, M. Soltner waved away the waiter with the menus: he would make special dishes for us, not on the menu. We smiled, but we felt gypped. To be honest, we don't even remember what he made. It was good and French and very refined, with a white sauce and some green grapes, but we were still sulking because we hadn't seen the menu.

Every menu, even the most intrinsically boring one, is valuable, at least as cultural anthropology. But some are sheer joy. What foodie can resist a smile at the menu of the Cherry Hut in Beulah, Michigan? It is perfectly round and red, to evoke the signature creation of the 1920s-era roadside snack shack, cherry pie. The broad Happy Face on its cover is the face of Cheery Jerry, the Cherry-Pie-Faced Boy. (When the Cherry Hut opened, the pies were made with the boy's face etched into the top crust, the eyes and mouth serving as vents. But at some point early on it was decided that the runny filling made the pies look too much like the boy's orifices were hemorrhaging blood, so the face was abandoned in favor of normal slits.)

We love reading menus, and not only for the purpose of selecting something to eat. Some of our happiest times have been spent hanging out at the archives of Johnson & Wales University in Providence, Rhode Island, reading their collection of vintage menus that tell of dishes no longer made and prices so low they are impossible to believe. We adore ones from the turn of the twentieth century, which list such lost loves as limburger cheese and tapioca pudding. We relish menus from the 1950s, "continental" ones that are awash with culinary overkill, and the magnum opera from Trader Vic's and the Forum of the Twelve Caesars, where the point seems to be that you are not merely eating food, but partaking in a gastronomic epic directed by Cecil B. DeMille. A tattered old menu we found pasted in a scrapbook in a secondhand store in Maine tells about a long-gone Yankee inn that offered fried cods' tongues as a starter for a Sunday supper of boiled brisket with boiled turnips on the side and green apple cake for dessert. The price for the meal was thirty-five cents, a nickel extra to top things off with a pack of Fatimas or an imported cigar. The other side of the menu features a breakfast lineup of such *outré* items as milk toast, cream toast, porridge, rashers of bacon, and — gulp! — steamed vinegar tripe.

Probably our favorite subcategory of vintage menu reading is the potato list. Even the most accommodating modern restaurants seldom offer more than two or three kinds of spud — mashed, baked, French fried — but it is not uncommon to find decades-old steakhouse menus that list potatoes a dozen different ways, many of which are now all but lost from cooks' repertoires: Lyonnaise, Duchesse, Delmonico, Chantilly, Martinique, creamed, and croquettes. And it's not just potatoes you find offered in cornucopian bounty. A 1920s menu from Boston's Durgin-Park has a directory of twenty-three vegetable side dishes to accompany scrod or prime rib: new cabbage, spinach, sliced new onions, boiled onions, fried onions, carrots, new green peas, string beans, lettuce, green corn (single ear), shell beans, succotash, turnips, Harvard beets, stewed tomatoes, cole slaw (listed on one menu as "cold slaw"), fried sweet potatoes, griddled sweet potatoes, and a boiled sweet potato, plus four kinds of white potatoes.

Such a vast choice of vegetables will not be shocking to the devotee of modern southern lunchrooms, where long lists of side dishes continue to prevail. But the strange thing about so many southern restaurants with veritable shopping lists of market-fresh produce available for midday "supper" is that their menus are as taciturn as a Wyoming cowpoke. For example, when you see an item on the posted menu in the Belle Meade Buffet Cafeteria in Nashville, Tennessee, that reads simply "butter beans," do not for a minute assume that these are merely plain limas dumped from a can into a pot and heated up. In any self-respecting Dixie eatery, the cooking of butter beans is an art, and those two simple words on a menu usually imply slow simmering in a broth of ham bone and/or fatback, the vivid piggy flavor of which seeps into the flesh of the legume to make it as rich as bacon itself.

The extreme expression of plain menus/lavish food is the genre of restaurant known throughout the mid-South as "meat-and-threes." A meat-and-three eatery is one in which the day's lunch options are written on a blackboard or printed up that morning and include a choice of two or three meats and a dozen to two dozen different side dishes. A standard lunch in such a place would be a serving of fried chicken or country steak with fried okra, creamed corn, and stewed apples (plus, of course, a bread basket with hot corn bread and/or yeast rolls, sweet iced tea on the side, then coconut pie for dessert). The restaurants are known as meat-and-threes not only because that is what they serve, but because that is the bare-bones language used on their permanent menu (to which the daily-printed vegetable list is clipped). It's none too appetizing to read, unless you know the wondrous world of food choices these austere listings imply:

    Meat & 3 vegs: $4.95
    Meat & 2 vegs: $3.95
    4 vegs: $4.50

At the far opposite end of the spectrum was the late-twentieth-century fashion for painstakingly enumerating everything there was to know about a meal's provenance, either on a written menu or via waiters' recitations. A plate of steak and potatoes, for example, might be listed on the menu in novella form as "Tiger River Ranch free-range longhorn/Hereford prime dry-aged strip from the heart of the loin of a rogue maverick bovine dispatched by a Winchester 94 lever-action repeating rifle with burl walnut pistol-grip stock, button magazine, and Lyman tang sight, caliber .30-30 soft-nose 170-grain projectile, and butchered at Filbert & Sons using bone-handled Damascus steel blades on old-growth cutting boards, served with Owayhee Range Yukon Golds boiled in Dead Sea saltwater perfumed with juniper essence, then mashed in top-cream butter retrieved and churned by the Babcock family's twin adolescent milkmaid daughters." Although somewhat abated now, this exasperating ritual of offering too much information continues as a policy in upscale restaurants, where the goal is to assure diners that they are getting the best possible provender.

This is not to say we don't appreciate a good measure of enthusiasm on a menu. At Dyer's of Memphis, the "Original World Famous Burger" (since 1912) is described as a "100% all beef patty . . . Always on a Genuine Wonder Bread bun." On the menu of the long-gone Chez Helene of New Orleans, chef Austin Leslie listed everything he cooked without elaboration — filet of trout Marguery, red beans and rice, Creole shrimp — but in the true spirit of Creole excess, he couldn't resist adding adjectives to the headings for each category of food: "Delicious Vegetables," "Refreshing Beverages," "Inviting Appetizers," "Tasty Sandwiches," and "Delightful Desserts." Bill Zuber's Dugout in the Amana Colonies has a menu that promises pork sausages "fried to that 'just right' juiciness," "ham cured to perfection and expertly prepared to release that hidden flavor," and chicken with "taste tempting tenderness."

Sometimes the menu writer's passion is not about the flavor of the food but about the experience of seeing or holding it. Nick's Kitchen of Huntington, Indiana, serves a tenderloin sandwich so wide that the menu exuberantly challenges customers, "Bet You Need Both Hands!" And although it isn't food-specific, we appreciate the good tidings above the list of entrées at Charleston, West Virginia's Southern Kitchen: "Eating Out Gives Life a Lift."

A two-page plastic menu that appears to have come off an assembly line at some Menu Central printing plant, with soulless four-color mug shots of club sandwiches and chef's salads, does little to stir our appetites or interest. However, the multiple-page menus of some aspiring modern diners cannot help but inspire awe — if not appetite. We are talking about laminated volumes as thick as a city's telephone directory, wider and taller than Ten Commandments tablets, with literally hundreds of available dishes, from "The Bagel Board" and "The Omelet Empire" through "Broilings," "International Fare," and "The Sandwich Subdivision" to "Decadent Desserts" and a whole chapter devoted to after-dinner drinks and specialty coffees made with jellybean-flavored liqueurs.

Closer to our hearts are those menus that are created by hand, on paper, a chalkboard, or a movable-letter sign above the counter. Here the chef — or the menu creator, who is often a different person — has the opportunity to express favor and passion regarding what there is to eat. Even without underlines, exclamation marks, extra-large capital letters, hearts, and happy faces drawn next to favorite dishes, individually made menus give meals lots of personality.

Usually that personality is charming, maybe a little saccharine or too folksy, but sometimes it is — how shall we say it? — downright combative. Doc's, an estimable steakhouse we visited many years ago in Wichita, Kansas, has a menu so pugnacious that we stole it to keep as a souvenir. It is emblazoned all over the cover with what the management calls "Ground Rules":

➤  NO Split Orders (Defined as more than one person, adults or children, sharing the same meal. If the customer proceeds to split the meal there will be an 85¢ charge and no plate furnished.)
➤  NO Personal Checks
➤  NO Credit Cards
➤  Extra Charge for Extras
➤  Only Certain Substitutions are Permitted

Doc's personality is further expressed on the inside of the fold-open menu, which is divided into halves. One page happily headlines "OUR MOST COMPLETE MEALS." At the top of the opposite page is the somewhat contemptuous heading "MEAGER MEALS FOR THE MEAGER APPETITE."

For us, handmade menus are especially dear for their malapropisms. Over the years, we've held on to these:

The Nebraska restaurant that touted *Broiled Stake*
A beef palace in northern California that promised *Steak Cooked to Your Likeness*
The menu typed on an old typewriter that replaced *e* with *o* and *g* with *p*, creating the intriguing dish *Doop-Friod Oppplant*
The swanky restaurant that promised *All Meals Presented with Continental Services*

An overly creative menu for which the writer dreamed up a
   fresh name for the kitchen's surf 'n' turf platter: *Rudder 'N'
   Udder*

*Roast Leg of Lamp*

*Roast Tom Chicken with Gilbert Gravy*

*Sweat and Sour Shrimp*

*Poo Boy Sandwich*

*Oven Fried Children*

*Sliced Cold Cats and Titti-Frutti Ice Cream*

*Hungarian Ghoulash*

*Spaghetti with Clamps*

*Moo Shu Pork with Four Creeps*

*Escargots de Snail*

"We cater to prim Donnas"

(Parenthetically, we need to salute a great corollary of menu
reading, which is order writing. This is the lovely practice of giving
customers order pads and letting them write down or circle their own
order after perusing the menu. When you've filled it out, a waitress
comes along and looks it over to make sure you did it right. She then
whisks it away to the kitchen and returns with the items you listed.
This is a tearoom thing, mostly — still practiced at Mary Mac's in Atlanta, Satsuma in Nashville, and the Little Tea Shop in Memphis —
and it can be especially comforting if you're in a piggy mood and
want to order, say, three pieces of pie. With this system, you don't have
to say out loud, "I'll have pecan, apple, and banana cream pie" for
people at neighboring tables to hear. You choice of foods is a private
matter between you, your waitress, and your conscience.)

   Some of the most fascinating menus are the ones that don't exist.
Not on paper, anyway. We are referring to the tradition of waiters
reciting the menu rather than diners reading it. This is common in

steakhouses, where the list of available dishes is limited to different cuts of beef plus a token fish or two. The joy of dining at the old Lusco's, a luxurious and highly eccentric grocery store/steakhouse in Greenwood, Mississippi, included the experience of sitting in a private, curtained, back-room booth, into which the waiter made a stage entrance by parting the curtain and virtually singing the menu. We recall hearing about "pompano like a pearl of the deep blue ocean" and "steak tender as a mother's love."

Some places take the one-on-one ritual of an oral menu a step further by actually showing different cuts of beef to customers, in the way a shoe salesman might bring out several different pairs for a customer to scrutinize. At Doe's Eat Place, another spectacularly good Mississippi steakhouse, in Greenville, you used to tell the waitress what kind and size of steak you were interested in eating — say, a T-bone, maybe a couple of pounds — and she would go to the meat locker and return to the table with a tray of various cuts that she felt might fill the bill.

It can be fun to have the menu declaimed and demonstrated, but it does eliminate the great fundamental pleasure of menu reading. With a written menu, you enjoy it at the speed you like. You can zero in on what you want; you can linger over different kinds of pancakes; you can read and reread the parts in which the pork chops are described. Having a menu recited, with no printed version to study on your own, is like listening to an author read a passage from a book. No doubt there is something special and privileged-seeming about it, but the rhythm is set by someone else. You lose the slow, sensuous pleasure of imagining what each dish will be like and the caressing thoughts of various meals, experienced in your own mind at your own pace.

# Mrs. Bonner's Sweet Potato Pie

Mrs. Bonner's Café was a restaurant without a written menu. Mrs. Bonner went shopping every morning and cooked what looked good at the market, and when customers walked in and found a booth, she would size them up and decide what they ought to eat. It took her a while to figure out the two of us, but after looking hard through her thick glasses, she pointed an arthritic finger at Jane and declared, "You look like chicken and dumplings." The finger then swung to Michael. "And you are smoked mullet." That's what we ate that day, and both dishes were excellent. Apparently we both also looked like sweet potato pie, and Mrs. Bonner was pleased to share the recipe with us after we cleaned our plates.

- 8  tablespoons (1 stick) butter, softened
- 1  cup sugar
- 2  large eggs, beaten
- 2  cups mashed sweet potatoes (if using canned, don't use the ones packed in syrup)
- ½  cup evaporated milk
- 1  teaspoon vanilla extract
- ¼  teaspoon salt
- 1  unbaked 9-inch pie shell

Preheat the oven to 375 degrees.

Cream the butter and sugar together in a large bowl with an electric mixer. Beat in the eggs. Beat in the sweet potatoes, then the milk, vanilla, and salt. Mix well.

Pour into the pie shell and bake for 40 minutes, until dark red-gold. Cool and serve at room temperature.

6 TO 8 SERVINGS

# Leona Yarbrough's Rice Custard Pudding

The menu at Leona Yarbrough's place in Kansas City was printed every day. It was an unadorned tearoom roster of such edible niceties as turkey divan, freshly made egg salad on freshly baked whole-wheat bread, and lattice-top apple pie. Just down the street from the old Wolferman's English Muffin place, Leona's was a favorite lunch spot among Kansas Citians of all kinds, including a large crowd of blue-hairs who came for the chicken noodle soup or a well-composed salad.

Leona's desserts included excellent fruit pies and cobblers, but it was the puddings that won our hearts. Our favorite was rice custard pudding, a layered version of the diner classic.

-  2   cups water
- ½   cup long-grain white rice
- ½   teaspoon salt
- ¼   cup raisins
-  4   large eggs, beaten until frothy
- ¾   cup sugar
- ½   teaspoon vanilla extract
-  2   cups milk
-      Grated nutmeg to taste

Bring the water to a boil in a medium saucepan and add the rice and salt. Cook, uncovered, without stirring, over very low heat until the water is gone, about 45 minutes. Remove the rice from the heat, cover, and let it steam for 5 minutes. Stir in the raisins.

Preheat the oven to 350 degrees.

In a large bowl, whisk together the eggs, sugar, and vanilla until they are well blended. Whisk in the milk.

Generously butter an 8-x-6-inch glass or ceramic baking dish. Spread the rice mixture on the bottom and pour the custard carefully over the top. Sprinkle with the nutmeg.

Set the baking dish in a larger pan and pour boiling water carefully around it to come halfway up the sides. Bake for 35 to 40 minutes, until the custard is just set. Remove the pudding from its water bath and let it cool. Serve slightly warm or at room temperature.

6 SERVINGS

# Surviving the Night

A year in a villa in the South of France is nice, but it doesn't compare to a week in a motel in southern Ohio. A few years ago, to hone our senses for an honest *goût de terroir*, we set up residence for a week in a chain motel in a commercial area just off I-75 outside Dayton.

Here, on a street called Prestige Place, we were positioned directly across from the Mall of Dayton and surrounded on all sides by eight-lane shopping roads, with every national retailer and food franchise represented. Our room overlooked the stem of the Montgomery County water tower and the open-all-night Cub Food Mart, and in the hallway just inside Entrance #5, near which we always found a good space for our rented Grand Am, we walked right into a small hospitality niche. Most of the week the greeting area was empty, but as we carried in our luggage, we came upon a table of crudités (carrot sticks and celery stalks) drifting in icewater below a sign handwritten in blue permanent marker on a piece of cardboard taped to the wall: WELCOME — COMPETENT PERSON TRAINING. Surely the welcome was not meant for us, but we had to wonder whether this was a seminar for people who were already competent or for those who yearned to be. It didn't say competent at what.

Our primary purpose in making camp across from the Mall of Dayton was to eat at the city's Pine Club restaurant. We were tipped off to it by ex-Cincinnatian John Catt, who had written to describe "phenomenal steaks in a no-nonsense old world Naugahyde-laden room — kind of a Gene and Georgetti's run by, well, people from Ohio!" Chicago's Gene and Georgetti's is one of the greatest of all steakhouses, so Catt's tip was intriguing. His note concluded, "For my money, there is no better steak in the USA, and believe me, I've done the research."

The Pine Club doesn't open until four (for cocktails) and doesn't start serving food until five, so we spent our days driving north of the city into the farmland around Urbana and West Liberty. We marveled at the Crystal Sea and the Devil's Tea Table (formations of stalactites and helactites) in the Ohio Caverns; we toured Mac-A-Cheek and Mac-O-Chee, two late-nineteenth-century Gothic-style castles filled with sublime woodwork and surrounded by waves of cornfields; and we came upon a stupendously good macaroni salad at the Liberty Gathering Place. The salad was creamy with a pickle zip, dotted with hunks of hard-cooked egg and a few crunchy shreds of carrot, and the noodles themselves were cooked just beyond al dente but not too soft. This was blue-ribbon, church-supper, Independence-Day-picnic fabulous! Understand that macaroni salad usually is not a dish to which we pay much attention — how could it be other than mediocre? — but this stuff, served in a town lunchroom as a side dish to ham loaf with escalloped corn, was a bowl of revelation.

It was still daylight when we arrived at the Pine Club, and upon entering, we became suddenly blind. This is the darkest restaurant you can imagine, darker than a movie theater showing a sunny-day matinee. It was so impossible to see that the hostess literally led us to a booth by holding Michael's hand while Michael held Jane's, as if we were sightless people without dog or cane. Even an hour later, after our eyes had adjusted to the *camera obscura*, we were shadow people across the table from each other, and the primary gathering points of light in the room were the radiant manhattans, martinis, and cosmos in their stemmed glasses being carried on trays from the bar to booths, trailing the alluring perfumes of gin, vermouth, and blended whiskey.

The bar is at the center of the Pine Club, spanning two small dining rooms, with stools all around to accommodate people waiting for a table. Because there is always a wait, the bar dwellers are an unlikely mix of serious drinkers with shooters and beer, church ladies sipping rock 'n' rye, and youngsters burbling through their straws on Shirley Temples and Roy Rogerses. A big, good bar is one of the essential elements of a heartland supper club.

Supper clubs are a very specific style of restaurant, and usually a good bet in the Midwest when you are looking for a substantial evening meal and cocktails to go with it. What else defines one? Basically, a supper club is a place where supper is honed to essentials, and the Pine Club is a perfect example. It has no party rooms, no daily specials, no lunch, no soup, and no dessert. Credit cards are not accepted, nor are reservations. Open weekdays until midnight (one A.M. on Friday and Saturday), the Pine Club is simple and predictable, known for sirloins, filets mignon, and porterhouses that are cut and aged on the premises and broiled by Majid Arabia, only the second chef to work the broiler in the past thirty years. As good as the deluxe cuts are, what wowed us the most was the Pine Club's chopped steak, made from a mix of sirloin and filet mignon. We ordered one medium-rare; inside its crust was meat pink toward the edge and velvety red at its soft center — essence of beef, as intoxicating as steak tartare but with the added pleasure of warm, dripping juices.

Other than such drinkable confections as Golden Cadillacs, Grasshoppers, and a house special that combined crème de cacao and crème de noyaux, there is no dessert at the Pine Club. That's fine, because the best strategy for anyone with a sweet tooth in southern Ohio is to save it for a road trip beyond Dayton. An hour east, in West Jefferson, is an extremely humble café called Henry's, a dilapidated former gas station on the old National Road, where cook Shelley Kelly makes butterscotch pie that is the stuff of dreams. An hour south, in Cincinnati, is Graeter's ice cream (best in the Midwest?) as well as Putz's Creamy Whip, a picnic-table drive-in where lovely turtle sundaes are constructed in clear plastic cups. Upon a foundation of caramel sauce is piled a swirl of ivory-smooth custard, and the custard is crowned with chocolate syrup, whipped cream, chopped nuts, and a cherry. Putz's has been a dessert destination in Cincinnati since 1938 and is so well liked that the street on which it can be found is now formally named Putz Place.

Although the roadfood finds in the area were great, it was depressing to live for a week in our $49-per-night room. But compared to many places we have stayed while hunting good meals, the accommodations on Prestige Place were heavenly. In our experience, nothing about traveling is more hideous than a night in a really bad motel. And believe us when we tell you we have seen our share, especially in the early years of motoring around the country. Motels, like coffee, have gotten much better than they used to be.

It was no accident that Alfred Hitchcock made the Bates Motel a key element of his scary movie *Psycho*. Most people who have found themselves driving a back road late at night, desperate to find a bed, know the sick, sinking feeling of pulling into a place where unknown danger awaits.

Holiday Inn used to promote its motels with the catchphrase promise, "No Surprises." This was a brilliant strategy, for it is the surprises in sleazy motels that are the stuff of nightmares. We cite the following:

- The motel in Las Vegas with a fresh stain — not a food stain — on the bedspread
- The hotel in Milwaukee with the used sanitary napkin on the floor near the bed
- The place in Cody, Wyoming, that a guidebook described as a "quaint inn," where the couple in the room next to us copulated in bed with their door wide open so all passersby could appreciate them
- The hotel in Charleston, South Carolina, where the curious pattern in the wallpaper turned out to be an armada of crawling insects
- The motel in Kansas where our room was directly below that of a camouflage-outfitted paramilitary maniac who drank vodka and screamed all night long about killing everyone and letting God sort them out
- The motel outside Blacksburg, Virginia, where the doorknob fell off, locking us in our second-story room; the desk clerk was apparently gone for the night and didn't answer the phone for hours
- The allegedly charming New Orleans guesthouse that had velvet curtains rather than walls separating one "room" from another

With such dangers in mind, we learned to heed early warning signs:

- The worse the curtains, the stinkier the motel. Rubber-backed curtains are a sure deal-breaker — they are repositories of decades of cigarette smoke, cheap perfume, and odors too awful to identify.
- No shag rugs! Years ago, after a dinner that included way too

much bourbon, Michael decided to attach the extreme closeup lens and strobe light to his camera and went on a giddy "photo safari," taking pictures of flora and fauna trapped deep in the pile of the harvest-gold rug in our motel. The images were so appalling that when we got home, he forswore all alcohol for six months. Jane forswore shag rugs.

➤ Don't stay in a room where the TV is chained to the wall — unless your goal is to transition into a minimum-security prison.

➤ Scout out other motel guests before registering. Avoid staying near anyone attending a convention (except perhaps deaf-mute nuns), wedding celebrants, and sports-crazed parents attending their children's Little League playoffs.

➤ Upon entering any room, remove the bedspread, preferably using tongs or rubber gloves. God knows how many naked bottoms it has hosted.

➤ Avoid motels with weekly residential rates. Trust us, you won't like your neighbors. Nor will you enjoy being around when their parole officers come looking for them.

Misleading names of motels can be a real problem. Generally, it is good policy to stay at the motel or hotel that bears the name of or some relationship to the big deal in town. The Hershey Inn in Pennsylvania, the Opryland Hotel in Nashville, the Ethan Allen Inn in Danbury, Connecticut — all are lovely. The logic is that because they are attached to famous brand names with reputations to protect, you can be fairly sure of reasonable comfort and safety. But we have learned the hard way that this is not necessarily true. A while ago we were cruising around North Carolina and it was time to pull in for the night. We saw a listing somewhere for an inn that had the same name as one of the famous high-end traditional furniture makers of the area. We envisioned wing chairs, Chesterfield sofas, and mahogany side tables. When we finally found the place, it took us exactly one second to make a U-turn and drive away as fast as possible. It was not an inn as we know it, and it had no connection to the furniture maker. It was Rubber Curtain City, it featured weekly residential rates, and its tenants sat in lawn chairs drinking tall-boy Colt 45s outside their rooms, where the doors were open so you could see their unmade beds and boxes of crackers, underwear, and rumpled towels strewn around.

On rare occasions, really good surprises occur at otherwise dubious motels, and in our experience these all have to do with something to eat. In the late 1970s, when we discovered the Loveless Café and Motel outside Nashville, the motel part of the operation was closed. It was a fleabag-looking place, definitely not where we would ever choose to stay. But the southern food in its café was (and still is) legendary, and rightfully so.

We had heard that when it had opened in the 1950s, the café half of the operation was the domain of Annie Loveless, but her husband, Lon, surname to the contrary, designed the sleeping units for lovers' illicit rendezvous with garage doors next to each room so guests could park their cars out of sight. We got into a conversation with Donna McCabe, who had taken over the place in 1973, and she thought we would find it interesting to peek into a couple of the rooms. Even as we approached the row of units to the side of the motel, our noses told us of trouble ahead. Accommodations at the former no-tell motel were being used as makeshift ham houses. One hundred curing hams were hanging in a single queen-sized room (still containing its box spring and mattress, nightstand, and dresser). The stench was indescribable. It took us a good fifteen minutes to recover and return to the red-checked tables of the Loveless dining room for an utterly delicious ham dinner, served with hot buttermilk biscuits and made-that-morning peach and blackberry preserves.

We never looked inside a room at the Edisto Motel in Edisto, South Carolina. We went there for a table in the knotty-pine-paneled dining room to eat royally well. Opened by Zelma and Lanier Hickman in 1947, the inauspicious roadside establishment had nothing extraordinary on its menu, just plain and simple seafood, cooked the way people around Edisto have enjoyed it for decades: deep-fried. (At one time, Edisto's menu warned "No broiled food!")

Almost as soon as we pulled out our dinette chairs to sit at a table, Zelma joined us, order pad in hand. "We have nice fresh oysters from Lemon Island, just a few miles down the road," she crooned. Oysters, shrimp, flounder, and scallops, as well as moist, zesty deviled crabs, were the specialties of the house, served with salad or a fine cole slaw. The shrimp were irresistible, especially in the fall, when they were plumper and tastier every day until the first frost sometime late in November. An order of nothing but shrimp consisted of perhaps four or five dozen, each a good mouthful veiled in a luxurious crust that was the divine complement to their firm, sweet flesh.

The Lemon Island oysters were perfect, too. Each one was a bit bigger than a mouthful, and there were so many to an order that the plate below them was invisible. Amazingly, if you polished off this mountain of fried food, not a drop of oil remained on the plate below. Were the oysters fresh? One of these hot-from-the-fry-kettle morsels of ocean goodness was as close to a just-opened oyster on the half shell as a cooked one can possibly be, with the addition of a savory meltaway crust.

When the Edisto Motel closed for good in 1998, Lowcountry cuisine was poorer for its loss.

# Drunkard's Soup

We have never stayed in a Basque hotel, but when traveling along Interstate 80 through Nevada and California or I-84 through Idaho, these places are some of the best opportunities to eat well. About a century ago, Basque shepherds from the Pyrenees immigrated to the West, where the grazing land was ideal for sheep. These mountain men lived solitary lives for months, but when they went to town to sell their stock, they needed a place to stay and to eat. So began the Basque hotels of Elko, Winnemucca, Mountain Home, and Reno, and a tradition of serving huge, hearty meals suitable for very hungry people. Many were and still are served boarding-house style. There is always lots of red wine and loaves of hard-crusted bread, and virtually every course (and there are many) is infused with garlic.

One such dish is known as *moscor zalda*, meaning drunkard's soup, for its alleged ability to restore health to someone suffering a hangover. Frankly, we have found its powerhouse garlic kick somewhat daunting on those mornings when we are feeling indisposed as a result of the night before. But when we're sober, it's a glorious and truly salubrious dish.

    6   garlic cloves, thinly sliced
    ½   cup olive oil
    ½   loaf day-old French bread, cut into large square croutons
    4   cups chicken stock
    4   large eggs, lightly beaten
    ¼   cup chopped fresh parsley
        Salt to taste

In a heavy-bottomed pot, sauté the garlic in the oil over medium heat until it begins to soften. Add the bread squares, stirring to coat them with the oil. Cook, tossing the bread until it is light brown and crisp. Remove the bread with a slotted spoon and reserve.

Add the chicken stock to the pot. Bring it to a boil, then reduce the heat and simmer for 5 minutes. Stir in the eggs vigorously so they get stringy. Remove from the heat and stir in the parsley. Add salt. Pour the soup into individual bowls and garnish with the reserved garlic croutons.

4 LARGE SERVINGS

# Mrs. Bromley's Apricot Nut Bread

Back in the time of the trail drives north out of Texas into New Mexico, Colorado, and Kansas, cowboys called Clarendon, Texas, the Saints' Roost, because they knew that when they got to town they had to be on good behavior. They were expected to take a bath, comb their hair, and not cuss, and if they measured up, they were welcome at the tables of the town's boarding houses, which were famous for their big meals.

When we first hit the road, we found a legacy of that tradition of good eating: Mrs. Bromley's Boarding House. In this Victorian home, meals were served not only to boarders but to passersby lucky enough to know about it. All who shared this privilege remember two things about Mrs. Bromley's table: the selection of warm breads, rolls, and biscuits and the strawberry shortcake for dessert. Mrs. Bromley, who learned to cook on a wood-burning stove, shared with us her recipe for apricot nut bread.

| | |
|---|---|
| 1 | cup chopped dried apricots |
| 1 | tablespoon hot water |
| 2½ | cups sifted all-purpose flour (sift before measuring) |
| 1 | cup sugar |
| ¼ | teaspoon salt |
| ¼ | teaspoon baking powder |
| ¼ | teaspoon baking soda |
| 2 | large eggs, lightly beaten |
| 1 | cup buttermilk |
| ¼ | cup apricot nectar |
| 3 | tablespoons butter, melted |
| 1 | cup chopped walnuts |

Preheat the oven to 350 degrees. Grease a 9-x-5-inch loaf pan.

Soak the apricots in the hot water.

Sift the flour, sugar, salt, baking powder, and baking soda into a large bowl.

Mix the eggs, buttermilk, apricot nectar, and melted butter in another bowl. Add the wet ingredients to the dry and mix with an electric mixer. Stir in the apricot and nuts. Pour into the loaf pan.

Bake for 60 to 75 minutes, or until a cake tester comes out clean.

Cool on a rack. Run a knife around the sides of the loaf and invert; remove the pan and turn right side up. Serve.

MAKES 1 LOAF

# Where Appetites Know No Bounds

Not to drop names, but we're proud to say we have been to nearly all of the really big state fairs — Iowa, Minnesota, Texas, New Mexico, and Massachusetts' Big E, to list a few. We admit that each summer, when we attend our first, we walk through the admission gate with mild apprehension that modern life will have wiped the slate clean — that this year, in place of the familiar things we love to see, there will be a fat-free robo-pig, a single-use disposable quilt, and sweet corn genetically mutated to have all the flavor of tofu. But so far, so good. America's state fairs, large and small, remain bastions of popular culture in all its glory, grandiosity, innocent charm, and unabashed vulgarity. State fairs are the home of the biggest and the best, the prettiest and the loudest, the most resourceful and the most bizarre.

The point of each one is to reflect the character of the state's population, so while every state fair is different in that sense, they do share one big fat common denominator: a state fair is an opportunity to eat large. Even people of parsimonious eating habits at other times of the year tend to get into the hearty spirit when state-fair time rolls around. Those who make it a habit to eat enthusiastically whenever possible stroll onto a state fairgrounds packing a caliber of appetite that would be unheard of in any other situation. This is one time and one place where it is right and proper to binge. The insatiable omnivore can spend days laying waste to buckets full of fried cheese curds and dunce cap–sized sugar cones loaded with ice cream, cinnamon rolls as big as a bulldog's head and jalapeño corn dogs that double as yardsticks, gizmo and guinea sandwiches (heroes), Brother Bubba Basilica's barbecue-on-a-bun, and turkey legs the size of Texas.

Logic says that if you eat food the size of Texas, you too will soon be Texas-sized. And it is true: you see really, really big people at state fairs. These are folk so strapping that they make us feel like Keith Richards and Lara Flynn Boyle by comparison. Wear a size 18 dress? Hey, Slim, right this way to the petite section!

We came to appreciate fairgoers' magnitude the first time we visited the Iowa State Fair. It is held in the big city of Des Moines, but it attracts millions of people from small towns all over the state. Our attire was jeans and T-shirts, which was perfectly appropriate. The best outfit for fairgoing is a good set of overalls, preferably made by OshKosh B'Gosh, Big Smith, or Carhartt. These are good because they do not cinch your waist and therefore offer no impediment to serious eating. Overalls, or, as it sounds in much of the Midwest, *overhauls*, can hang insouciantly by one strap and leave you plenty of room for packing it in.

Our assignment in Des Moines included not only the state fair but also visiting a restaurant in town, and as evening approached, we had a flash that maybe we ought not to appear in dirty T-shirts and food-caked jeans. A call confirmed that men were indeed required to "dress for dinner." We raced to Des Moines' fanciest department store for some emergency clothing. Michael is six foot two and not scrawny, but jacket after jacket, shirt after shirt, hung limply on his frame, fluttering like a tent. "Are you in town for the fair?" the salesman asked. When we nodded, he took a second look at our dirty T-shirts and asked if we were hog farmers. We took his surmise as a compliment.

State fairs are vast. You walk and walk, and after a while your head is spinning with visions of blue-ribbon carrots and Cub Scouts crafts projects and butter sculptures displayed in cold rooms so they do not melt. After dark, when the carnie lights go on and teenagers start making out in the shadows, the midway games of chance get rolling, and for us, the chance to win some crummy doll or stuffed toy too ugly to exist is irresistible. Michael gets especially competitive at the shooting gallery. He is a crack shot, but the plush toy seems always just beyond reach. One year at the New Mexico State Fair he blasted a whole array of pop-up and cut-out animals into oblivion, but the booth operator withheld the prize. A small crowd formed to see what might have become a shootout with a gallery rifle attached by a wire to the stand. "I hit every one," Michael insisted, and Jane, always eager to embellish a story, told the booth owner that Michael was a member of a visiting police SWAT team. Only then did the hideous soft yellow Tweety Bird doll get delivered into our waiting hands. Like Sheriff Buford Pusser, we walked away tall. We had cleaned the midway of a crooked bad guy, and we had a Tweety Bird to prove it.

All that walking and shooting works up a mighty appetite, which is a good thing. The problem is deciding exactly what to eat from among the dizzying number of choices.

Culinarily speaking, each fair has a single dish or style of dish for which eaters know it best. Corn dogs are the thing in Texas, where the modern corn dog was invented in 1938. (Brothers Neil and Carl Fletcher had seen a street vendor in Dallas selling sausages that had been coated in corn batter and baked in molds resembling ears of corn; they reconfigured the idea on a stick and deep-fried it.) The corn dog is a subject about which we claim the authority of experience. Having spent thirty years on a Diogenesian quest to find an honestly good one and yet being almost always disappointed by mushy batter or flaccid frank, we consider those served forth at the Texas fair a platonic ideal. Their crust is crisp, the corn coating is flavorful, and the hot dog has snap. Then again, we're willing to admit that maybe their goodness is due in some part to the fact that they are the quintessential fair fare: basically junk food, but representing most of the food pyramid (meat, grain, oil, and even vegetable if you count the cornmeal as a vegetable derivative).

At the Big E in Springfield, Massachusetts, fried dough is the thing to eat; and while it may not have the most appetizing name for a snack, this Yankee favorite can be delicious. It is vaguely similar to a Pennsylvania funnel cake. Fresh from the fry kettle and served on a paper plate, fried dough is best when it is dished out too hot to handle. It comes either sweet or savory, topped with sugar or tomato sauce. A regional cognate of fried dough is the Southwest's Indian taco, but while it is possible to eat fried dough on the stroll, Indian tacos, as served at the New Mexico State Fair in Albuquerque, are knife-and-fork food and need to be eaten sitting at a picnic table. The flat rounds of fried bread are topped like pizzas with chili, lettuce, tomato, and cheese. Think open-face taco, and think spilling, dripping mess.

While the Minnesota fair is best known for all the things on sticks you can eat there, we are most impressed by the French fries. Nowhere have we eaten better ones. Several different food booths sell them all around the fairgrounds, in sizes that range from a modest thirty-two-ounce container to an eighty-eight-ounce bucket. It is hard to say exactly why these fries taste so swell. Perhaps it's the ambience: children screaming with glee on the midway rides, the appetizing smells of hot corn dogs and pork-chops-on-a-stick drifting through the air, the sheer joy of being at a huge state fair, where nutritional priggishness holds no sway. Or perhaps their goodness comes from how utterly fresh they are. In the back of every stand you can see piled-up bushels of potatoes, skin still on. You can watch them being swiftly peeled, cut, and fried in clean oil, and the lines to get them are always so long that the instant they emerge from the oil, they are scooped into a cardboard container, ready to be salted (or spritzed with malt vinegar) and eaten while still dangerously hot. Each serving contains a few savory bits and tips of potato cooked to a dark gold crunch; the majority of pieces are thin-cut square logs that are crisp on their skin but sensuously creamy just underneath the burnished crust.

Naturally, Iowa's midway abounds with ways to sample pork on the stroll — as a barbecue or ham sandwich or sausage-on-a-stick — for dining while walking is what state fairs are all about. But the legendary Pork Tent is designed for more advanced porcine appreciation. It features tables and chairs and food on plates with utensils. No longer the simple canvas canopy it was when the Iowa Pork Producers first set up at the fair some twenty years ago, it has become a large, concrete-floored, open-sided dining hall known among shoat cognoscenti as the Chop Tent, in honor of its most popular item and the unofficial state dish, the Iowa pork chop.

An Iowa pork chop is not just a pork chop from an Iowa pig. It is a *huge* pork chop from an Iowa pig — well over an inch thick and approximately one pound. If skinny supermarket flaps of meat are your idea of a pork chop, this glistening Gargantua, hot off the grate, is a revelation — like eating filet mignon after a lifetime of nothing but cube steaks. It is sweet and juicy, fine-grained and dense, but supple enough to slice with the flimsy plastic knife provided, and satisfying beyond measure. The men who cook the chops on grills outside the tent wear aprons that boast of "the other white meat," but no other meat we know, white or red, has such fathomless succulence.

The most satisfying place to eat at any heartland state fair is in a church-sponsored dining room. Church suppers are a state-fair tradition going back more than a century. They allow rural traditionalists who come to the city to partake of familiar family-style meals. In these places you do not have snacks or sandwiches; you have a meal at a table. Your dining companions aren't fun-seekers in T-shirts but rather citizens of the solid sort, couples mostly, the gents outfitted in brand-new, still-creased Big Smith overalls, ladies fair in flowery go-to-meeting dresses. The menu is a farmland selection of meat and potatoes with corn niblets or green beans, bread and butter. And of course there are salads — not spartan leafy things but bowls full of sugar and carbs that are sweet enough to pass as dessert anywhere else: a sunny yellow mélange of bananas, marshmallows, and whipped topping, or perhaps a pistachio-green concoction of pineapple chunks, marshmallows, and whipped topping. Pie costs extra; icewater is free.

Two of the Iowa fair's stalwarts are the Tri-Met (Trinity United Methodist Church Dining Hall), emblazoned with the motto "Where a Good Meal Is a Pleasant Memory," and the Chesterfield Christian Church Dining Hall next door, which has been a fixture on the fairgrounds since 1912. The entrée choices in the Chesterfield cafeteria line are fried chicken, roast beef, and meat loaf. Four farm wives ahead of us approach the serving area full of distrust. They already have learned to be skeptical of Des Moines cuisine, having encountered an outrageous one-dollar cup of coffee earlier today, and now it's the meat loaf that has them worried. "I like a piece of *meat*, not filler!" one declares.

Her pal eyes a large slab of moist loaf being placed on a Styrofoam plate. "But do you see the size of it?" she counters. "It looks good."

"Mmm, it does," the skeptic allows. "But I won't eat anybody else's meat loaf." She gets roast beef instead, as do two of her companions. Only one of the ladies is adventurous enough to choose meat loaf.

At the table, when the brave one permits each of her friends to take a forkful of the loaf, the quartet agree: this is fine meat loaf, very wholesome. Not as good as what they make back home, but for city food, mighty good.

# Honey Gingered Pork Tenderloin

Each year some fifteen thousand citizens enter nearly fifty thousand things in competition at the Iowa State Fair. Categories range from draft horses and monster trucks to quilts and sculptures made of corn cobs. The variety of recipes is astounding. Of course there are pies and cakes, breads and biscuits, jellies and preserves, plus contests for the ugliest cake, most creative dough sculpture, and things you can do with breakfast cereal. In 1994, Emma Whitlock of Indianola took first prize in the "Let's Cook Healthy! Iowa Pork" category with this simple way to give pork tenderloins a sweet twist on the grill.

2  ¾-pound pork tenderloins
¼  cup honey
¼  cup soy sauce
¼  cup oyster sauce
2  tablespoons light brown sugar
1  tablespoon plus 1 teaspoon minced fresh gingerroot
1  tablespoon minced garlic
1  tablespoon ketchup
¼  teaspoon onion powder
¼  teaspoon cayenne pepper
¼  teaspoon ground cinnamon
   Fresh parsley sprigs

Place the tenderloins in a 11-x-7-inch baking dish. Combine all the other ingredients except the parsley in a small bowl, stirring well. Pour over the tenderloins. Cover and marinate in the refrigerator for 8 hours, turning occasionally.

Prepare a charcoal or gas grill.

Remove the tenderloins from the marinade; reserve the marinade. Grill the tenderloins over medium-hot coals or a gas grill for 25 to 35 minutes, turning often and basting with the reserved marinade. The pork is done when a meat thermometer inserted into the thickest part registers 155 to 160 degrees.

To serve, slice the tenderloins thin and arrange on a serving platter garnished with the fresh parsley.

4 SERVINGS

# Fried Dough with Maple Butter

Our idea of proper eating at a fair is a wanton binge, and pursuant to that goal, New England delivers the goods. Every county fair and flea market has at least one wagon selling fried dough. Granted, the name is not poetic, and there is no getting around its nutritional incorrectness, but good hot fried dough can be unbelievably delicious: flaky textured, with a puffy buoyancy. It is generally available two ways, sweet and savory, the latter usually meaning with a spicy Italianate tomato sauce. For the sweet kind, the disk of dough, hot from the fry kettle, is brushed with butter, then sprinkled with cinnamon sugar. Years ago, in a moment of regional pride, we decided to serve sweet fried dough with a slightly fancier topping: maple butter. If you are going to do it this way, make the maple butter in advance. Otherwise, regular butter and cinnamon sugar do the trick.

1   cup all-purpose flour
1   teaspoon baking powder
½   teaspoon salt
1   tablespoon vegetable shortening or lard
⅓   cup warm water
    Oil for frying

Mix together the flour, baking powder, and salt in a medium bowl. Cut in the shortening with two knives or your fingers until the mixture is mealy. Slowly stir in the water to form a ragged dough.

Turn the dough out on a floured board and knead it for 2 minutes, or until smooth. Cover and let it rest for 15 minutes.

Heat about 2 inches of oil in a deep skillet to 375 degrees. Divide the dough into 4 equal balls and roll each one out into a circle 5 inches in diameter. To keep it from puffing up, use a sharp knife to cut four or five 1-inch-long slits through it. Ease 1 circle of dough into the hot oil. Cook for 30 seconds, until it is brown, then turn it over and cook the other side for 30 seconds. Remove the cooked pastry and drain it on paper towels. Cook the other circles and serve immediately.

MAKES 4 FRIED DOUGH ROUNDS

## MAPLE BUTTER

6 tablespoons (¾ stick) unsalted butter, softened
2 tablespoons maple syrup

Beat the butter and syrup together with an electric mixer. Refrigerate. Remove from the refrigerator 30 minutes before serving so it is easily spreadable.

# The Cow on the Roof and the Living Pig

We live with a house full of animals, and as much as we love to hit the road, we hate leaving them behind. We are animal saps. Jane has always believed that if she could give birth to a litter of puppies or had a marsupial pouch, she would be mother of the year. As for Michael, his other significant other for the past twenty years has been a 600-gram yellow-nape Amazon parrot hen who quite literally flies into a jealous rage if she sees Michael pay attention to any other female, including Jane.

From the get-go, when we were students at Yale, we lived with critters. The first two were Earl and Sinclair, tomcats whom we never neutered, who fought like mad, and who sprayed on the walls. We bought Richard the bulldog before we were married, although it was necessary to pretend to the breeder that we had already tied the knot, because she was a stuffy old Yankee and did not want one of her dogs living in sin. Since then we have shared quarters with a dozen dogs, the parrot, and two Appaloosa horses, and we have been godparents to a menagerie of snakes, hamsters, and gerbils. We never go anywhere without sheaves of pictures of this extended animal family, so we can gaze longingly at our beloveds several times a day.

Animals play an important part in roadfood radar. One of the most compelling signs that causes us to hit the brakes and explore an eatery by the side of the road is a cow on the roof. A statue of a cow, that is. We have been eating at big-animal-on-the-roof places for so long that we can't quite remember exactly when this strategy for finding good meals crystallized. At some point early in our career, we came to believe that a looming bull above a steakhouse, a crowing 3-D rooster on a fried chicken joint, or a jolly plaster pig atop a barbecue parlor was a near guarantee that good meals could be had inside.

Needless to say, the animal on the roof reflects the specialty of the restaurant's kitchen. We have no interest in dining under a jumbo fiberglass aardvark or an oversized kangaroo by the roadside up ahead unless (God forbid) those animals are actually on the menu. No, basically, the menagerie in our restaurant-spotting guide is pretty well limited to chickens, cows, lobsters, crabs, and pigs.

The more homemade the statuary, the better. A totally prefabricated sculpture, while it may catch the driver's attention, simply does not have the charisma of a one-of-a-kind colossus that looks like something a precocious third-grader made from papier-mâché in art class. We are especially drawn to depictions of familiar animals with shockingly human features, such as the pig effigy we saw in Alabama with big soulful eyes and flirty Mod eyelashes, the macho Tom of Finland–style rooster in Kansas who was outfitted in jumbo army boots and a fatigue jacket rolled up to expose bulging biceps, and one big, beautiful hard-shell crab beside the Chesapeake Bay who sported bright red lipstick and resembled Joan Crawford.

Big-animal-on-the-roof restaurants almost always have terrific food. For years we have advised readers always to stop and eat whenever they see a giant cow or pig on the roof, especially if the animal is wearing a chef's toque. We can't quite explain our unreserved confidence in this restaurant-spotting technique. Perhaps our belief in dining beneath big animals is an extrapolation from the effort it takes to have an outrageous effigy manufactured, hoist it up onto the roof and batten it down, maintain it through the seasons, and keep it bright and graffiti-free. Any restaurateur willing to care so diligently for a symbol of his cuisine might logically be expected to put similar effort into the cuisine itself.

The goofier the animal, the better the food. If the bull on the steakhouse gazes down at the parking lot with a big, toothy smile, or if the pig is dressed in a natty tuxedo and carries a walking stick, or if the lobster is wearing spectacles, all the better to see the view from the roof, then we know for certain we are in good hands. If the animal has a dialogue balloon painted or sculpted over its head or a title between its hooves or claws, so much the better! Who can resist a jumbo crab that is labeled "Admiral Crustaceous" and manages to be saluting with one claw? Perhaps it's a little perverse, but we have a soft spot for animals that invite us to eat them: the plump pig that appears ready to dive into a big painted rendition of a smoky hickory pit, boasting "I'm goo-ood!" or the old knickers-wearing Chicken in the Rough bird who used to announce, "I'll gladly be fried for Chicken in the Rough!" Great chefs and restaurateurs are frequently known for their whimsy and originality, and in the world of roadside eateries, this attitude is signaled by a rooftop animal with personality to spare.

Not all animals who beckon from the roadside are made of plaster and wire mesh. Some are real. Don't let's start in about health regulations and all that. The truth is that there are probably more animals than people whose company we would enjoy at the dinner table. And for all you sophisticates reading this, may we remind you that in France, dogs are always given a seat in a restaurant next to their owners? As dog lovers, we were completely won over a few years ago when we went shopping at the very snooty Hermès in Paris. Although the salespeople were stiff and formal, they allowed an old flea-bitten mutt that had come in off the street to run happily hither and yon between counters with $5,000 Birkin bags.

One of our very favorite places to dine with animals is the Dorset Inn in Dorset, Vermont. This is a picture-perfect hostelry (New England's oldest) on the green in a pristine New England village, and the chef and owner, Sissy Hicks, cooks spectacular meals that fall into a category best called elegant comfort food. We were swooning over corned beef hash and buttermilk pancakes with maple syrup one morning, thinking that this was a breakfast impossible to improve, when we heard the shuffle of eight geriatric paws. We looked to the doorway of the dining room and saw what appeared to be the world's oldest basset hound schlepping toward us, followed by the world's oldest black Lab. These were Fergie and Whitman, both of whom had been adopted by Sissy at a ripe old age and who were obviously relishing their dotage here at the inn. With her long hound ears trailing on the old floor planks, Fergie hobbled toward us on her stumpy legs, Whitman tottering behind. We sneaked each of them a small piece of pancake, after which they hobbled to a nearby table, where the diners offered them little bits of French toast. The thump of happy tails against white linen tablecloths was some of the nicest music-to-dine-by we've ever heard. Before we finished eating, both dogs retired to the parlor to find comfortable spots on hooked rugs, where they no doubt planned to snooze until lunchtime.

Another restaurant we love because of its animals is Blue Heaven in Key West, Florida. In the al fresco, banyan tree–shaded dining area, chickens and roosters roam around the dirt floor pecking for bugs or the occasional scrap of pancake offered by a diner. While most of these birds cackle gently, often with a clutch of chicks nestled under their breast, there is often an outspoken rooster or two hanging about, and these bold cocks have been known to hop onto the back of an unoccupied chair at a customer's table and greet the morning with crowing loud enough to wake up half the neighborhood. In a former incarnation Blue Heaven was a cock-fighting den, one that Ernest Hemingway used to frequent. Happily, the blood sport has been turned around to breakfast with the flock, and believe us when we say that having a huge rooster staring at you from the back of a chair will make you think about the provenance of your omelets and give thanks for all that poultry has provided us.

Not all live poultry is as brash as the flock at Blue Heaven. Buddy, the maitre d' at the San Marcos Café along the Turquoise Trail in Cerrillos, New Mexico, was as dapper as William Powell. Buddy, who passed away a few years ago, was a rooster who began his life as a school project, raised by young children studying barnyard life. When the school project was over, he was taken to a coop behind the restaurant in Cerrillos, which he was to share with his peers. But instantly it became painfully apparent to the proprietor, Susan MacDonnell, that this was one miserable bird. "Buddy thought he was a human," Susan told us. "As soon as I put him in the chicken pen, you could see right away the look on his face: '*I don't belong here!*' So we brought him in and we kept him on the porch of the restaurant and he became everybody's pet. He loved to play the part of the naughty rooster with little kids. His ears just perked up — if he had ears — to see a little kid get out of the car. And he was so disappointed if they weren't afraid of him."

Although he started with a role as restaurant greeter, Buddy's rank was elevated over time and he was ultimately outfitted in a small black necktie and a white tuxedo bib. He mellowed out a bit and exchanged quiet gobbles with customers who weren't afraid of him. After Buddy went to his great reward, Mrs. MacDonnell tried in vain to train another fowl for the job. None measured up. Today when you go to the San Marcos Café, you enter past a free-ranging, taxonomically diverse flock of guinea hens, peacocks, wild turkeys, and roosters, all cackling around the front yard and porch. But inside the restaurant, no bird sounds are heard. No one can fill Buddy's shoes (if he wore shoes).

As comforting as it is to eat one's eggs to the cluck of mother hens and chicks or the suave crowing of an overachieving rooster like Buddy, we do not like to eat steak within earshot of lowing cows. Call us spineless gastronomic ostriches with our heads buried in the mashed potatoes, but as much as we love a good steak, there is something disturbing about seeing that good steak on the hoof, especially if it is chewing its cud and mooing contentedly. Similarly, Jane cannot bring herself to point the finger of death at a lobster in a tank. Yes, she will eat the cooked lobster, but she leaves the selection process to someone else.

So far we've always been able to resist bringing home animals from our travels. But we had a close call a while back while motoring along Route 66 through Navajo country in New Mexico. There we stopped for lunch at a place called the Navajo Chief Café. A talk radio station set the tone in the dining room. The talk was indecipherable Navajo, interspersed on occasion with the English avowal, "All Navajo, All the Time." That pretty much described the menu, too, which listed slices of deliciously peppery roast mutton served on fry bread, an aboriginal mutton stew that was shockingly bland but hearty, and servings of blue corn mush reminiscent of lavender-tinted cream of wheat. As we paid our tab at the counter, chef and proprietor Phil Padilla reminded us to write our name and address on the back of the receipt and put it in the barrel to make ourselves eligible for the upcoming lottery, whose lucky winner would take home a whole sheep. We never win contests or lotteries, but there was something so appealing about bidding on a sheep that we dropped in our receipt and, with Phil's encouragement, put in a few business cards, too. "We don't live around here," we said. "What if we win?"

"No problem," said he. "We will send it to you." He then told us about other prize animals that had been won in previous drawings by people living several towns away.

"But we live in Connecticut," we said.

"Is that in New Mexico?" asked an eavesdropper standing nearby.

"Uhhh, no, not really," we said.

Phil reassured us that if we won, we'd get our prize. We smiled and let things be.

If you have ever eaten at the outdoor picnic tables of Curtis's Barbecue in Putney, Vermont, you will no doubt know Isabelle the pig. Curtis's Barbecue is lots of fun to begin with. To call this place casual is an understatement. The kitchen facilities are located in and around permanently parked school buses, one of which has an open window where you place your order for some of the most delicious pork in the otherwise barbecue-deprived Northeast. Once we had carried our plates to a picnic table and started to gnaw crusty, explosively spiced meat from the bones, we heard a plaintive cry from ground level, tableside. Looking down, we spotted Isabelle. Isabelle is a big four-legged Vietnamese potbellied porker resembling a pygmy hippo, who is the restaurant's mascot and the much-loved pet of pitmaster Curtis Tuff. Isabelle stared us square in the eyes, oinking vociferously, until one of us thought to hand her a pork rib with a few shreds of meat on it. Isabelle took the bone and gnawed away. It was a Hannibal Lechter moment; we have pondered its inter-species ethics many times, recalling satisfied grunts and pleasure moans of a great big pig who sounded almost exactly like a happy human feasting on barbecue at the tables of a Dixie smokehouse.

# Bon Ton-Style Fried Chicken

There is no printed menu at the Bon Ton Mini Mart in Henderson, Kentucky, because everyone comes to eat one thing: chicken. Set up in a former convenience store and truck stop, this out-of-the-way treasure is an unlikely place indeed to find fine food. *Fine* food, maybe not. But some of the world's best fried chicken, definitely! We found it thanks to Kentuckian Louis Hatchett, the author of *Duncan Hines: The Man Behind the Cake Mix.*

The spice mix used for Bon Ton chicken is a closely guarded secret, but cook Donna King shared its fundamental ingredients with us, as well as the length of its marination — at least twenty-four hours. During that time, she explained, blood seems to be drawn from the meat, allowing a briefer frying time, which results in the juiciest possible chicken, with flavor insinuated into every fiber. She also told us that the pieces must rest for five or ten minutes and "get doughy" after being dredged in spiced flour, and that pure vegetable shortening will ensure grease-free chicken.

Because of limited refrigeration space, the Bon Ton can keep only one case of chicken parts marinating, meaning that supplies sometimes run out. "You want to see some angry customers?" proprietor George Markham asks. "Come here one day at noon when there isn't any chicken. You've never heard such squawking!"

THE MARINADE
- 2 tablespoons salt
- 2 teaspoons cayenne pepper
- 2 teaspoons garlic powder
- 1 teaspoon Accent

1½  teaspoons white pepper

1  tablespoon soy sauce

2  teaspoons Worcestershire sauce

1  quart water

4  bone-in, skin-on chicken breasts and 4 drumsticks, washed

THE SPICED FLOUR

1  tablespoon salt

1  teaspoon garlic powder

1  teaspoon Accent

1  teaspoon cayenne pepper

1  teaspoon white pepper

3  cups all-purpose white flour

Vegetable oil for frying

TO MARINATE THE CHICKEN: Stir all the seasonings into the water, mashing the garlic powder and pepper so they don't clump. Place the chicken in a bowl just big enough to hold it and pour the marinade over it. Cover the bowl and refrigerate for 24 hours, moving the chicken parts around once or twice.

TO MAKE THE SPICED FLOUR: Stir all the seasonings into the flour.

TO FRY THE CHICKEN: Heat about 2 inches of vegetable oil to 365 to 375 degrees in a large, deep cast-iron skillet.

Pull the chicken from the marinade one piece at a time and dredge it in the seasoned flour. Set it on a baking sheet or aluminum foil for about 5 minutes.

Cook the chicken in the hot oil for 20 to 25 minutes, turning each piece a few times so it cooks evenly and turns golden brown. Don't crowd the pieces in the pan. Cook in batches if necessary.

Drain on a wire rack and serve hot.

4 SERVINGS

# Cornell Chicken

Roll down the car windows when you drive north from Endicott, New York, and inhale. Route 96B through Owego is an olfactory thrill ride. On any nice day from April into November, but especially on weekends, the air is laced with currents of hardwood smoke spiked by the smell of sizzling chicken. The birds' perfume is unique, for its smoky essence is haloed by a bouquet that is simultaneously vinaigrette-tangy and egg-rich. It is cooked under tents outside firehouses, on portable rotisseries by the side of the road, at ad hoc backyard cafés on town side streets, and on the grills of chicken-focused restaurants.

Grilling meat is huge in this part of the world. If you think Memphisians or Carolinians are the only cooks who fuss over smoldering wood, stroll down the condiment aisle at the Giant supermarket in West Corners on Route 26. In this otherwise ordinary grocery store, we counted more than six dozen different kinds of barbecue sauce and marinade — for beef, pork, and chicken and for Binghamton's beloved spiedies (skewered barbecued meats). We found sixty-four-ounce jugs of Salamida's State Fair Chicken Bar-B-Que Sauce, a row of Dinosaur Habanero Wango Tango sauce from Syracuse, Olde Cape Cod grilling sauces in various flavors, Stubb's sauce from Texas, and Theo's Southern Style Sweet-N-Sassy Sauce (bottled in nearby Johnson City) . . . plus Anchor Bar wing sauce from Buffalo in both original and hotter recipes, Nance's Chicken Wing Sauce, Lemon Garlicious ("Rhymes with Delicious") Marinade, even celebrity chef Emeril's marinades, on a low shelf in the corner next to the two-gallon jars of kosher dill pickles. In the store's vestibule, one wall is piled high with charcoal and firewood; a bulletin board is posted with a notice of a church chicken bar-b-q and pie sale.

Across the road from the Giant market is Phil's Chicken House, opened some forty-eight years ago by Phil Card, who learned his skills at Endicott's Chicken Inn. The folksy wood-paneled restaurant is decorated to the hilt with country-crafty knickknacks (souvenir plates, angel statuettes, lighthouse miniatures) and attracts customers including local families and well-armed state police SWAT teams (who practice marksmanship nearby). There is a full menu, but Phil tells us that 95 percent of his customers come for one thing: barbecued chicken.

It is extraordinary chicken, glazed gold and with the nose-tickling aroma of a sauce with which it has been basted for up to two hours on the rotisserie. The skin's glaze is a salty punch in a plush glove, its potency a dramatic contrast to velvety breast meat and basso harmony for thighs and drumsticks. The wings, with maximum marinade and moistest meat, reverberate with exclamatory gusto.

How Phil's chicken gets so good is no secret at all; in fact, Mr. Card relies on a recipe that is well known throughout the southern Finger Lakes. "It's your basic Cornell chicken," he tells us, referring to a formula developed by a Professor Robert Baker in the 1940s. How it came to be was explained to us by a roadfood follower from upstate New York, who said that in 1946, when Dr. Baker was a young professor at the University of Pennsylvania, it was up to him to concoct something special to serve at a barbecue to which Governor Edward Martin had been invited. Considering that at the time people ate more eggs than chickens, Baker devised a marinade and basting sauce that he was certain would encourage more chicken-eating. It was a big hit at the governor's dinner, and when Baker joined Cornell University in the Department of Animal Sciences in 1949, he brought it with him. Two years after that his recipe appeared in a university publication and became known as Cornell chicken. It gained tremendous local popularity — and the nickname State Fair Chicken — when it was featured at a restaurant Baker ran at the New York State Fair called the Chicken Coop. Baker's descendants still open the Chicken Coop every summer in Syracuse.

| | |
|---|---|
| 1 | large egg |
| 1 | cup vegetable oil |
| 2 | cups cider vinegar |
| 3 | tablespoons kosher salt or sea salt |
| 1 | tablespoon poultry seasoning |
| ½ | teaspoon freshly ground black pepper |
| 8–10 | chicken pieces: breasts, drumsticks, thighs |

Beat the egg well in a large bowl, then add the oil and beat again. Add all the other ingredients except the chicken and stir well.

Add the chicken, turning to coat, and marinate for 1 to 2 hours in the refrigerator, but no longer.

Prepare a charcoal or gas grill.

Cook the chicken over the grill for 20 to 25 minutes, using the sauce to baste it. Turn the pieces frequently, cooking until done. Serve.

4 SERVINGS

# States of Insanity

Every state in America has a personality all its own, but two share a special kinship: Kansas and Rhode Island. On the surface they don't have much in common — one is large and landbound, the other small and oceanic. Their affinity is a curious insularity that makes each dramatically different from places all around it. Our travels have taught us to think of these two states as strange sisters, because when we travel in them, strange things happen all around us.

Culinarily, Kansas couldn't be more normal. If the Sunflower State had an official meal, it would be fried chicken with mashed potatoes and gravy, as served at the Brookville Hotel in Abilene (formerly of Brookville), sided by sweet corn, cottage cheese, baking powder biscuits and preserves, cole slaw, and ice cream for dessert. Fried chicken is so big in Kansas that Highway 69 in the southeastern corner of the state has long been known to food-focused travelers as Chicken Dinner Road. That's because the small town of Pittsburg contains two immensely popular side-by-side restaurants that serve nearly identical ritual meals of crisp-fried chicken along with mashed potatoes and a slew of slaws and vegetables. If you don't like fried chicken, both places offer an alternative: chicken-fried steak. Chicken-fried steak, the comfort food of the frontier, is steak that is breaded and fried just like chicken — a sort of fried chicken for chicken-frowners.

It was after lunch one day in 1976 at a favorite old chicken house, Mrs. Peter's Chicken Dinners, in Kansas City, that a very strange and somehow very Kansan thing happened to us. We headed west on the

Kansas Turnpike. The sky was clear blue, and beyond the city, the plains stretched out ahead as flat as a corn tortilla. Then we saw it: a sign for the federal penitentiary at Leavenworth. Oh, joy!

Did we mention that one of our favorite hobbies is visiting prisons? We have been to the best: Soledad, Alcatraz, Sing Sing, the Maine State Prison, the New Mexico pen, Parchman in Mississippi, and the prison in West Virginia where Charles Manson's mother was a matron. In Texas, we have seen "Ol' Sparky," the famous hand-crafted electric chair, and we have attended the convict cowboy rodeo. Our main purpose in visiting prisons is to check out their gift shops. You'd be amazed at the treasures we have found. Prisons of the West are famous as sources of spectacular hitched-horsehair bridles that only a craftsman with plenty of time could create, and we have also discovered great examples of what is now respectfully called "outsider art," or "art brut." Give a homicidal maniac a canvas and a paintbrush, and you will be astonished at the results. Some are too sinister for us, such as the clown paintings created by the serial killer John Wayne Gacy, but much of what we have found is really very nice: nautical-themed lamps fashioned out of matchsticks, lace hankies with low-rider cars painted on them, and linoleum block prints of Jesus' hands opening the prison gates. As a fringe benefit of shopping in prisons, the trustee sales associates are always extremely polite; if they forget to be, a salesroom supervisor with a shotgun is there to remind them.

Coming upon Leavenworth was for us as it must have been for the archaeologist Howard Carter to uncover King Tut's tomb. We dared not even imagine the riches that awaited in the gift shop. We had grown accustomed to having to surrender our wallets and drivers' licenses before entering and even to signing a legal paper saying that neither we nor our heirs would hold the prison responsible if we were taken hostage during a prison riot and killed.

We followed the signs off the highway onto smaller roads and finally wound up at a big brick-and-mortar gatehouse. Curiously, there was no one inside and the gate was up. We waited a while, tooted our car horn a couple of times, and when no one appeared, we drove through the raised gate. One hundred yards ahead, at a break in the tall, razor wire–topped wall that surrounded the facility, was a second security checkpoint. We stopped again, tooted the horn again, sat, and waited. When nobody showed up, we drove through and arrived at what was quite obviously a maximum-security prison building. Seeing a large parking lot with a few cars in it and a smaller parking lot next to the building where no cars were parked, we chose the empty one, imagining that it would be a shorter walk to the car from the gift shop when we came out with our purchases.

Behind us, guards' towers at intervals in the prison walls were unoccupied. When we came to a set of metal double doors in the side of the building, we did the logical thing: pressed down on the thumb latch on the door handle, pulled the door open, and walked in. We found ourselves in an exercise yard occupied by about two hundred men — big guys — in blue workshirts and matching pants. They appeared to be as stunned to see us as we were to see them. Jane walked up to a group of African-American prisoners standing around one muscleman lying on his back bench-pressing a barbell and asked, "Excuse me, could you tell us where the gift shop is?"

A long moment passed. Finally one of the spotters answered, "There ain't no gift shop, lady."

Politely, Jane thanked the man. Then we turned, went to the door, pushed the bar that opened it, and left the yard. We walked very fast back to our car, jumped in, and drove out past the two empty gatehouses, past the signs that said LEAVENWORTH FEDERAL PENITENTIARY, and back onto the Kansas Turnpike.

Not long after our Leavenworth adventure, we pulled into a café in Topeka called Ira Price. Mr. Price's place had been around a long time, and a sign outside on the roof quoted the owner: "I don't want a million dollars. I just want a million friends." We had a wonderful meal of — what else? — pan-fried chicken with whipped potatoes and cream gravy, followed by an amazing three-layer white cake with peppermint-pink frosting. Fluffy and gay, the cake looked as though it came straight out of the pages of a 1920s baking brochure, and in fact much of Ira Price's place appeared out of the past. Gag postcards on a revolving stand were so old that their punch lines had faded away; color photos of cattle and haystacks on the wall had become monochromatic sepia.

After dinner we thought it might be fun to talk to the man in search of so many friends. We found Ira Price in the kitchen, rearranging jars of mayonnaise on a shelf, and asked if we could talk to him about the café. He looked surprised and, without a word, headed down a flight of stairs into the basement. We followed, and found ourselves in a dank, windowless cellar lit only by a single bulb hanging on a wire from the ceiling. Mr. Price didn't tell us to go away, but neither did he address us directly. We ventured a couple of questions, but he turned his back and became engrossed in what appeared to be a complicated task of pulling shoeboxes off a shelf and sorting and rearranging their contents, which looked like meal receipts from the café, then putting the boxes back on the shelf in a very precise order. From the large number of receipts, we concluded that we were customers 1,000,001 and 1,000,002. The friend roster had apparently been filled. We tiptoed back up the stairs, leaving him to his shoeboxes.

Early on, we assumed that Kansas, and more than a few Kansans, are odd because the state is smack in the middle of the country, far from the restorative power of fresh sea air in all directions. That theory was proven wrong as we came to know Rhode Island, the Ocean State. Here too things are different. Why, we cannot say. Perhaps it's a Napoleonic complex. Everyone knows that you are more likely to be bitten by a chihuahua than a great Dane and that all Hollywood movie agents are under five foot seven. But overcompensation doesn't explain why this little state has such a large personality. It is like an ignored child in the New England family, and whereas neighboring Connecticut and Massachusetts are part of mainstream culture, this forgotten corner of New England developed an independent language and culinary mannerisms in no way normal.

Let's start with Haven Brothers in Providence. We were eating doughnuts next to a bunch of cops at Allie's doughnut shop in North Kingstown and happened to mention to them that we had been told Haven Brothers was our kind of place and we intended to go there for dinner.

"Are you strapped?" one of the officers asked.

We knew enough to realize that he wasn't asking if we were broke. In cop lingo, being strapped is the same as *going heavy* and *packing heat:* carrying a concealed weapon.

We were not strapped, but the fact that the cop thought we ought to be if we were going to have dinner at Haven Brothers was a little worrisome. "Is it safe to go there?" we asked.

He shrugged. "I wouldn't, but if you do go, the thing to have is a murderburger."

How could we not eat at a restaurant where the specialty is a murderburger — even if it was to be our last meal?

We arrived at the corner of Fulton and Dorrance by City Hall late in the afternoon, and Haven Brothers was nowhere in sight. We poked around the neighborhood in vain, but just after 5 P.M., Haven Brothers arrived. It turned out to be a complete small diner pulled along on a trailer chassis by a tractor-trailer cab. The inside is shadowy, the stainless steel walls of the cramped dining room so dim that they appear to be lit by gas lamps. At the front is a galley kitchen with a grill and milk-shake mixers, the power for which comes via a long extension cord that the proprietor plugs into the top of a streetlamp.

Old-timers perch on stools inside, dining on hot dogs, hamburgers, fried eggs, and a choice from among three kinds of beans: baked beans, kidney beans, and chili beans. The famous murderburger is not listed by that term on the posted menu. It is a "double cheeseburger with everything," meaning two glistening patties topped with bright orange cheese and all condiments, plus bacon and chili. Most customers get their grub from the sidewalk at a tiny knee-high window where the order taker, inside, has to crouch down low in order to peek out. Outdoor dining facilities are the steps of City Hall.

To say that the crowd of customers is eclectic is the understatement of all time. For every lowlife there is a cop, for every drunken tramp an even drunker socialite, for every hooker a John, and for every Stern a murderburger, with coffee milk shakes alongside.

Haven Brothers is one of a kind, but New York System restaurants are all over urban Rhode Island. Elsewhere in New England and the rest of the United States, the language and customs of this anomalous branch of wienerdom might seem as exotic as the cuisine of the island of Yap in Micronesia, but in the separate world of Ocean State foodways, New York System is a fundamental. It revolves around a fingerling frankfurter nestled in an untoasted bun, topped with yellow mustard, chopped raw onions, and a dark sauce of finely ground beef. It's the sauce that makes the dog — spicy but not hot, vaguely sweet, reminiscent of the kaleidoscopic flavors that give Greek-ancestored Cincinnati five-way chili its soul. How the term *New York System* came about can only be surmised (the evolutionary track must parallel the Coney Island hot dogs of the Midwest), nor is it absolutely clear exactly what the words refer to: the kind of restaurant, the presentation of the hot dog, or the distinctive method used to construct each New York System weenie.

Dog-savvy Rhode Islanders know the method as "wieners up the arm," referring to the counterman's trick of lining up a dozen dogs in buns from wrist to shoulder to be dressed. At John's New York System, across from the old Cranston Armory in Providence, Viola Degaitas, John's widow and the mother of Henry, who now runs the place, was proud to tell us that while her husband used to do wieners up the arm, Henry lines them up on a plate for dressing.

Despite the sign above John's New York System's door — WHERE THE ELITE MEET TO EAT — you will not be likely to encounter too many glitterati hobnobbing at the seven low stools in the short-order café, but you can be sure of rubbing elbows with discriminating hot dog connoisseurs. And what an amazement it is to watch Henry behind the counter, dressing dogs at warp speed, working the griddle with his spatula, taking to-go orders on his headset telephone, and sliding unbreakable plates of food along the counter to their intended. "My father called this 'New York System' because 'New York' meant stylish in the 1940s, when he opened," Henry says. "But you know something funny? They never had weenies like this in New York."

*Wieners up the arm* is one of countless unusual food terms in Rhode Island, where even common dishes have names that are elsewhere unknown. You want a milk shake? In the other forty-nine states, those words mean milk, ice cream, and flavoring. In Rhode Island, that combo is known as a cabinet or, northeast of Providence, a frappe or velvet, whereas *milk shake* is the name for milk mixed with flavoring (hold the ice cream) — unless the flavoring is coffee, in which case it is known (and bottled) as coffee milk. Seafood meals here have a jargon all their own. Stuffies are quahog clams chopped up and mixed with stuffing, then repacked in the shell. Clam cakes are balls of cornmeal dough laced with minced clams and deep-fried, whereas doughboys are fried and rolled in sugar. Clam cakes are frequently served with chowder, the terminology of which is a minefield.

Forget New England–style chowder (the creamy kind), which is seldom found in this New England state. More typical is a clear-broth quahog chowder containing nuggets of clam and potato. The usual chowder in shore dinner halls is a mongrel mix that is not New England–style or Manhattan–style or clear broth. It is more a bisque, a salmon-pink tomato-clam soup poured into a bowl on top of a short stack of saltine crackers and garnished with salt-pork cracklings.

No odd food is more distinctly Rhode Island than the jonnycake, which the spell-check on our computers insists on changing to *johnnycake*. But correct spelling is the least controversial aspect of these flapjacks made from finely ground flint corn, served at breakfast with syrup and at lunch and supper as a side dish. Jonnycakes are such a hot topic that we were once the inadvertent catalyst for a near assault at a pleasant little town lunchroom called Commons Lunch in Little Compton. Being on the eastern side of Narragansett Bay, Commons's jonnycakes were plate-wide, dime-thin, and lace-edged. We were swooning out loud over their delicacy when a scrawny young geek in a club blazer and bow tie leaned toward us and advised, "These are *not* jonnycakes. They are pancakes." He was from Wakefield, across the bay, where proper jonnycakes are silver dollar–sized, a half inch thick, moist, and plump.

From a table on the other side of the pencil-necked geek came a woman's voice. "Sir, your jonnycakes are not jonnycakes but dough-boys on a griddle." The woman was feeding little bits of skinny jonnycake to a small child in a highchair next to her.

The man from Wakefield shot straight up so fast that his chair fell backward as he whirled, whipped off his glasses, and lunged toward the woman who had dared to question his jonnycake belief system. He looked ready to reach out and strangle her when two men from another table stepped between them, hoisted him off the ground, and briskly dragged him out the front door like bouncers in a bar. They walked back in smiling and returned to their own plates of jonnycakes.

The strangest thing about eating in Rhode Island is the scale of its meals. The smallest state is home to the biggest meals served in the biggest restaurants. There was none bigger and better than the old Archie's Tavern of Pawtucket (now superseded by Archie's Mill Town Tavern in East Douglas). Best known for its sixty-ounce "Neanderthal caveman cut" prime rib, Archie's did everything large. An order of pork chops was three. Hot cinnamon rolls arrived in containers that resembled laundry baskets. The surreal size of everything was abetted by the presence of the host, a tall, slim, suave man who glided through the vast reaches of the dining room like a moonwalking Michael Jackson, outfitted in a pink prom jacket with a white carnation. Not for him the universal "Is everything all right?" Instead Mr. Slick glided up to our table for four and bent, his head hovering over the kerosene lamp in the middle like an illuminated centerpiece. Somehow he managed to swivel his head entirely around, making sincere eye contact with everyone, not speaking a word.

Our first meal at Archie's was a revelation. We ordered prime rib as well as the seafood and Italian fare one expects to be great in Rhode Island. But all around us customers were plowing into a different meal, which we soon learned was another, little-known (to outsiders) local passion: chicken dinner. Chicken is as popular here as in Kansas, but it is skillet-cooked in butter, not fried in lard, and it is always dished out with plenty of warm cinnamon rolls. And you can forget ordinary cole slaw. The palate refresher of choice in Rhode Island, and only in Rhode Island, is snail salad: cool, thin slices of chewy conch in a garlic marinade. Like we said, no two states are exactly the same.

# Rhode Island Clam Chowder

This is the kind of clam chowder that is traditionally served toward the beginning of a shore dinner, or as a smaller meal with clam cakes on the side. It is the least known of northeastern chowders, and its tomato content makes it criminal according to hidebound New England chefs, who see it as creeping New Yorkism. In fact its creamy-smooth nature is nothing like the hodgepodge vegetable soup with clams known as Manhattan chowder.

| | |
|---|---|
| ¼ | pound salt pork, diced |
| 1 | large onion, diced |
| 2 | cups diced potatoes |
| 1–2 | cups boiling water |
| 2 | cups chopped quahog clams |
| ½ | cup pulverized stewed tomatoes |
| ⅛ | teaspoon baking soda |
| 1 | cup whole milk |
| | Salt and pepper to taste |
| 4 | tablespoons (½ stick) butter |
| | Saltine crackers |

Fry the pork in a skillet until it is crisp. Remove the pork and set it aside (or discard, if you don't want to use the cracklings as a garnish), leaving the fat in the skillet. Fry the onion in the fat until it is soft, about 3 minutes. Pour the fat and onion into a stockpot. Add the potatoes and enough boiling water to cover them. Simmer until the potatoes begin to soften, about 20 minutes.

Add the chopped clams. Mix together the tomatoes and baking soda and add them to the stockpot. Simmer for 5 minutes. Stir in the milk and bring the soup back to a simmer just long enough to heat it through (but do not boil). Season with salt and pepper. Swirl the butter into the soup just before serving.

Place 2 or 3 saltine crackers in the bottom of four to six soup bowls. Pour in the chowder. Top with the salt-pork cracklings if desired.

4 TO 6 SERVINGS

# Princess Pretty Flower's Jonnycakes

Historians believe the name jonnycake comes from *journey cake*, which meant either that the small pancakes could be carried easily once they were made or that a person could stop during a journey and make some if he had cornmeal, water, and a fire. While any cornmeal will do in a pinch, the best stuff is ground about ten miles inland from Block Island Sound by Kenyon's Grist Mill, in Usquepaugh (www.kenyonsgristmill.com). The mill sells a regular stone-ground "Johnny cake corn meal" and, when flint corn from a local farmer is available, flint corn meal, which is what the Indians used. Flint corn meal has a richer flavor and is the color of top cream. This recipe is from the fondly remembered Dovecrest restaurant, a place run by a Narragansett couple who called themselves Chief Roaring Bull and Princess Pretty Flower. Made near Exeter, on the western side of the bay, Pretty Flower's jonnycakes are the smaller, thicker kind.

1    cup white cornmeal, plus more if needed
1    teaspoon sugar
¼   teaspoon salt
¾   cup boiling water, plus more if needed
1    tablespoon butter, melted
2    tablespoons milk
     Vegetable shortening to grease griddle

Combine the cornmeal, sugar, and salt in a mixing bowl. Stir in the boiling water. Add the melted butter and milk, stirring to form a batter. It should be thicker than pancake batter but thinner than mashed potatoes; stir in additional water or cornmeal to adjust.

Grease a griddle with the shortening and turn the heat to

medium. (Because these cook a long time, we highly recommend a nonstick cooking surface. If you are not using one, be prepared to use more grease as the jonnycakes cook to keep them from sticking.) Drop the batter onto the griddle in heaping tablespoonfuls. Smooth the top of each patty with a knife, leaving each about $1/2$ inch high. Cook for 15 minutes, or until the bottoms are golden and crisp. Turn and cook for 15 minutes more, until crisp.

MAKES 8 TO 10 JONNYCAKES, 4 TO 5 SERVINGS

# A Place Where
# Nobody Knows Our Name

A few years after the first edition of *Roadfood* was published, we were offered a job reviewing restaurants for the *Hartford Courant*. It sounded like fun, and for a while it was. Nothing feeds an ego like being a big-city restaurant reviewer, even if the city isn't a culinary hot spot. If we gave a place the thumbs-up, it was mobbed with customers the day the review appeared. If we consigned it to purgatory, business slumped. One week after an especially unfavorable review was published in the paper, we received a lawyer's letter threatening a suit. His client, the proprietor of the restaurant we had denounced, had gotten married the day the review appeared in print. The man was so upset that he had been rendered impotent on his wedding night.

We never set out to be mean. Our job as we understood it was to be consumer reporters — to clue readers in to excellent places and to save them from wasting their money on unworthy ones. Many of the restaurants we deemed unworthy had extremely loyal clientele who came to loathe us, because in speaking badly of their favorite eatery, we were in a way speaking badly of them, or at least of their taste in food. We started getting hate mail. Some was well reasoned, but occasionally we would receive a postcard with no return address that said something like "Die, Jews, Die!" At one point during our four-year tenure we actually got on the Christmas card list of the Connecticut Ku Klux Klan, and long after we had quit the *Courant* and the Klan's card writer had forgotten why we should die, we received a happy little card each year with a tree or Santa on the front and the Klan cross-and-blood logo inside.

The strangest thing about being newspaper reviewers was that we needed to remain anonymous when we ate in a restaurant that we intended to write about. Although we never resorted to full-blown disguises, we made all kinds of efforts not to look like ourselves, including visiting restaurants in tandem with other partners of the opposite sex. And of course restaurateurs posted our pictures in the kitchen and did what they could to ID us.

Writing about roadfood is completely different.

We are anonymous in most places we eat, but not because we've gone to any length to conceal our identity. We are anonymous because the people who run the restaurants never heard of us and don't care what we're doing. We could walk into their establishments with placards around our necks saying, "Here come the writers from *Gourmet* magazine," and nobody would be the least bit impressed.

We went to Memphis to write a story about plate-lunch destinations. We found a place that was new to us: Alcenia's, a soul-food café on the northern edge of the urban core. We ate pork chops and fried chicken and collard greens and hot-water corn bread, and they were stupendously good. We knew we had to include these meals in our story, and in fact we decided that this was one instance when it would make sense to talk to the cook. We don't often do that; generally we sit down, eat, and pay the bill just the way anybody else does. But Alcenia's fare demanded further investigation.

We wandered back toward the kitchen, where we encountered a beaming African-American woman who rushed forward to give us each a hug. She was B.J. Lester-Tamayo, cook and proprietor, who named the restaurant after her mother and granddaughter and whose trademark as a hostess is to hug everyone who walks through her front door. We assumed her affection was based on our sterling work as food journalists.

"Are you the owner?" we inquired.

"Yes, I am," she said with a smile.

"We are Jane and Michael Stern," we told her, expecting to hear "I know, I know . . ." "We write a column about restaurants for *Gourmet* magazine and would like to ask you some questions." B.J. was still smiling sweetly, patiently listening as we continued. We pulled some *Gourmet* business cards from our wallets and held them out for her to take. "Do you know *Gourmet* magazine?"

B.J. shook her head.

We started dropping impressive phrases: "huge circulation . . . published since 1941 . . . Condé Nast publication . . . Times Square, New York City . . . James Beard Awards."

No response. We may as well have been speaking Esperanto. It was clear that our mile-a-minute explanation of who we are was keeping B.J. from her duties in the kitchen, so we told her that we would return at the end of lunch hour and talk to her then. Our idea was to go out and buy a copy of the big, shiny, gorgeous magazine and bring it to her, thus impressing her with our purpose.

Memphis is cosmopolitan, but like so many cities in the heartland, most of its big bookstores are on the outskirts of town, in the malls. Circling around town, we tried Walgreen's and a couple of supermarkets. We found *Southern Living, Guns & Ammo, Field and*

*Stream, Monster Trucks, Modern Bride, Southern Bride,* and *Your Prom,* but no *Gourmet.* Finally we drove out to Bookstar, and sure enough, there was the latest *Gourmet* — a whole issue devoted to great places to eat in London. We bought a copy and headed back to Alcenia's for our interview.

The lunch crowd had cleared out, and when we entered, B.J. rushed toward us once more with big, welcoming hugs. We plopped our prize issue of *Gourmet* onto a table in front of her. B.J. acted as though we had given her a Christmas gift too fancy to open. She stared at the cover and smiled with genuine admiration. We opened it up and showed her the masthead with our names on it.

"I was written up in the *Memphis Commercial Appeal,*" she said, pointing to a framed clipping on the wall that declares her bread pudding one of the ten best desserts in town. B.J. thought *Gourmet* was lovely, but it really didn't matter to her the way the mention in her local paper did.

While our total unimportance in the world of roadfood restaurateurs has given us the kind of perspective about our station in life that an eminent critic of haute cuisine seldom achieves, it has also caused us to obsess about who does merit the fuss. These restaurants have their own hierarchy of people who matter. We know this for a fact, because we have spent years sitting under eight-by-ten photographs of such luminaries.

Frank Sinatra is one who is nearly universal, a star who seems to have spent almost as much time signing glossies of himself as he did performing. He could not possibly have eaten in every Italian restaurant on the eastern seaboard, where his image is inescapable. And if he did, why was he so skinny? And yet there are countless places between Philly and Boston (not to mention some in Vegas and Palm Springs) where, if you judged by the pictures on the wall, you'd have to say that Frank was the management's best friend. At Sally's pizzeria in New Haven, the black-and-white shots of the Chairman of the Board play second fiddle to a beautiful oil portrait of Frank overlooking the dining room like the family godfather. Likewise, at Patsy's Pizzeria in Harlem, an Old Master canvas of Mr. Sinatra hangs on the wall. Both places claim to have been his favorite.

While the most common form of celebrity icon is a signed picture donated by the celebrity (or the celebrity's press agent), a few famous people didn't autograph many pictures but get the hagiographic treatment anyway. Dale Earnhardt's image is big throughout barbecues of the mid-South, even if the late Intimidator's personal signature is fairly uncommon. And while Elvis seems rarely to have bequeathed personalized photos to favorite hamburger-flippers, that doesn't stop devoted restaurant owners from creating monuments to his memory. Memphis is replete with Elvis-themed eateries, despite the fact that for most of his career he was simply too famous to eat out. At the Barksdale Restaurant north of Graceland, the celebrity-spotting imagery is Elvis once removed. Here you dine on country ham and red-eye gravy under publicity photos not of Elvis himself but of multitudes of Elvis impersonators, as well as one unknown (to us) country singer who signed his portrait, "Thanks for the gravy fix!"

Images of famous people are an especially common decorating motif in hoagie shops of the Delaware Valley. Perhaps the overstuffed sandwich lends itself so well to celebrity support because it is a *hero* sandwich, and the faces on the wall are those of people's heroes. We have yet to see galleries of glitterati on the walls of a tea parlor, a juice bar, or a vegan café. Maybe there's a relationship between the implicit machismo of a foodstuff and the desire of big shots to associate themselves with it.

There's no more manly eatery than a Philadelphia cheese steak shop, where customers gobble big, messy bread tubes loaded with oily beef, smelly onions, salty cheese, and maybe hot peppers, too. And virtually every place that serves Philly's favorite junk food is plastered on all available surfaces with rows of pictures of its prominent fans. Sports stars seem particularly well represented: ballplayers, hockey players, prizefighters, and famous broadcast-booth personalities are all much in evidence.

We are particularly fond of the celebrity salute at Pat's King of Steaks, where it is said that Pat Olivieri invented the cheese steak in 1930, for here not only are there photos, there is a memorial of sorts to a great moment in celebrity-spotting. On the sidewalk just outside the window where your cheese steak is delivered to you (and where most customers stand, tearing away at it and letting the juices hit the ground), a plaque is embedded in the concrete. The plaque, splattered with dripped Cheese Whiz and onions, reads, ON THIS SPOT STOOD SYLVESTER STALLONE FILMING THE GREAT MOTION PICTURE ROCKY, NOV. 21, 1976.

It is not uncommon to see faces on the wall that belong to local idols unknown to passersby. For example, few people outside Connecticut know Dr. Mel Goldstein, the delightfully nerdy TV weatherman, but we viewers adore him, and you'll see pictures of Dr. Mel, pointer in hand, standing in front of a weather map, in restaurants throughout the state. Elsewhere in our neck of the woods, we have pondered images of Boo Boo the Clown, the Hattertown Triplets with their matching accordions, and Professor Pincus and his Dancing Poodles. In certain parts of the Northeast, Professor Pincus is right up there with Leo DiCaprio and David Letterman on the A list of important customers.

Throughout western Pennsylvania and West Virginia, pizzerias display photos of native son Bruno Sammartino. Pictures of the celebrated pro wrestling pioneer show him flexing his extra-large muscles in a pair of trunks or shaking hands with a restaurateur, whose hand looks like a cherrystone clam in the grappler's meaty mitt. One of the most colorful of such places is Colasessano's, located in the blue-collar Belleview neighborhood of the old coal-mining town of Fairmont, West Virginia. The Colasessano family's business has been a popular meeting place for decades, and although there are no tables or chairs in the front room and all foods are sold to go, the old bar still has a foot rest that makes for comfy waiting and easy conversation after you place your order with Joe or his mother, Josephine. As you stand and kibbitz, you face a wall on which is hung a portrait gallery of beloved family members and admired politicians, the latter category featuring John F. Kennedy, who swung through Fairmont on the presidential campaign trail in 1960. Joe Colasessano likes to remember that Ted Kennedy was about to sample the house specialty, a pepperoni roll, that day, but was reminded that it was Friday and therefore was advised by his staff to choose meatless pizza instead.

One of the great things about getting your picture on a celebrity wall of fame is that even when your star fades, your image remains. Vast numbers of framed faces at whom we have stared while dining are complete mysteries, or at best long-lost luminaries who inspire the question "Whatever happened to . . . ?" Rock groups with names such as Watts Happening or the Five Pulsators are forever resplendent in yard-wide Afros and polyester bell-bottoms. Actresses with 1970s Farrah Fawcett hair appear forever young and hopeful. Like a fossil preserved in amber, celebrity photos capture one instant of fame.

Someday, maybe a customer will look at a restaurant wall and see a picture of Jane and Michael Stern taken during the early twenty-first century and wonder who those odd birds are. Like Professor Pincus and his Dancing Poodles, we will have attained a certain immortality.

# Alcenia's Fried Corn

B.J. Lester-Tamayo of Alcenia's in Memphis, Tennessee, told us that it is possible to use either butter or margarine in her fried corn. The decision will tell whether or not you are a cultural purist. Sticklers for *cuisine verité* will choose margarine, the preference of traditional southern vegetable cooks. We admit that we like butter better. It is even feasible to abjure canned corn and slice kernels off a fresh-picked cob, reserving the milky liquid that the process yields and using that instead of the liquid from a can. The farm-fresh method sounds swell but is too precious to be used by any café cook we've ever met.

| | |
|---|---|
| 4 | tablespoons (½ stick) margarine or butter |
| ½ | green bell pepper, chopped |
| ½ | cup chopped celery |
| 1 | 16-ounce can whole kernel corn, liquid drained and reserved |
| 2 | tablespoons all-purpose flour |
| 2 | tablespoons dry Lipton's Onion Soup Mix |
| | Dash of sugar |
| ¼ | cup water |
| 2 | tablespoons jarred pimientos |

In a large skillet, melt 2 tablespoons of the margarine or butter and sauté the pepper and celery in it until they are softened.

Put the reserved liquid from the corn in a mixing bowl and whisk in the flour until the mixture is smooth and milky. Set aside.

Add the corn to the skillet along with the soup mix, sugar, and the remaining 2 tablespoons margarine or butter. Let the corn simmer over very low heat for 10 minutes. Stir in the corn liquid along with the water. Simmer for another 5 minutes, stirring frequently, to blend the flavors, then keep warm until ready to serve.

Stir in the pimientos for color just before serving.

4 TO 6 SERVINGS

# Italian Beef

Just like the hero and hoagie shops of the Delaware Valley, the Italian beef stands of Chicago display pictures of celebrities who love them. At the original Al's #1 Italian Beef in Chicago, the wall holds an eight-by-ten of Jimmy Durante standing with his arm around Al Ferreri, inscribed by the Schnozzola, "To Al's and Baba [Al's nickname]: Jink-a-dink-a-doo. What a beef sandwich!" Surrounding that are a picture of prizefighter Michael Spinks grinning with a gleaming set of dentures and a glamour shot donated by a local beauty queen. Several proprietors of beef stands have told us about celebrities who like the razor-thin, garlic-sopped beef so much that they have it FedExed to them overnight. An alternative is to make your own, thus:

- 6   garlic cloves, cut into slivers
- 1   3- to 4-pound boneless chuck roast, well marbled
- 1   cup water
- 2   bay leaves
- 1   tablespoon crushed red pepper flakes
- 1   tablespoon dried oregano
- 1   tablespoon salt
- 1   tablespoon coarsely ground black pepper
- 8   hero rolls or 4 lengths of Italian bread

Preheat the oven to 325 degrees.

Use a small knife to insert the garlic slivers into the roast all over. Put the water in a deep baking pan not much larger than the roast. Add the roast and top it with the seasonings. Cover tightly with foil and bake for 2 hours, basting 3 or 4 times and adding water, if necessary, to keep plenty of juice in the pan.

Remove the beef from the pan and let it sit. With an extremely sharp knife, slice it into razor-thin pieces.

Degrease the pan and taste the gravy. It should be highly seasoned with a peppery bite. Adjust the seasonings to taste and place the sliced beef in the gravy. Allow it to wallow at least 15 to 20 minutes before serving. Serve on lengths of Italian bread with roasted peppers or store-bought giardiniera (a spicy mélange of pickled vegetables).

8 SERVINGS

# In the Bondage of a Chef

It's great to eat for a living, but not all days of chowing down from dawn to dark are peaches and cream. On those occasions when you can't find a decent meal anywhere, you yearn to be at your own nicely stocked refrigerator at home, contemplating what to cook for supper. Some days contain both the joy of eating enormously well and the depths of culinary despair.

It was Memphis, Tennessee, the summer of 1993. As the capital of the delta and the heart of the mid-South, Memphis is a stirringly spiritual place. There are churches everywhere, and the unlikely but unequivocal connection between gospel and rock 'n' roll was forged right here. People often refer to it as the buckle on the Bible Belt, but in this distinction, Memphis is not alone. Oklahoma City also claims the title, as do Atlanta, St. Louis, Little Rock, and Indianapolis. We don't know if there ever was an actual contest to decide who would win this coveted buckle, like perhaps a pro wrestling match between evangelical preachers wearing masks and capes, or whether the Bible Belt allows for multiple buckles, like a safari jacket, but either way, Memphis definitely gets our vote as the true buckle-on-the-Bible-Belt city, if for no other reason than the restaurant called Buntyn.

We went to Buntyn many times during our travels across America, and we fell in love with it every time. We adored it not only for its amazing southern cooking but for the fact that nothing about it ever changed. In 1993, Buntyn looked pretty much the same as it must have looked the day it opened its doors in the 1930s. Like a prehistoric fossil perfectly preserved, its linoleum floor and laminate tabletops were worn smooth by time, and the aromas from the kitchen had given the place a permanent savory perfume.

Every morning at eleven o'clock, before the lunchtime rush, the staff gathered in a circle to pray together. The black dishwasher held the hand of the blond waitress, who grasped the hand of the teenage Mexican busboy, who held the middle-aged white owner's hand, who held the bony hand of the old cashier lady. A few decades earlier in Memphis these people might never have touched each other, but they had come to pray together out loud, thanking God for giving them jobs and food to eat.

Our waitress appeared and gave us two "big-gulp" tankards of ice water and then poured us even bigger glasses of ice-cold sweet tea. As we sipped the tea, she serenaded us with a short list of what was available. Her recitation sounded like plate-lunch haiku:

> We've got corned beef and cabbage
> Gizzards and rice.
> The okra's boiled
> And corn's on the cob.

It was the second week in August, probably the worst time to be in Memphis, because it's always at least 100 degrees and humid. Also, this is the week that all the Elvis fans in the world pour into the city to celebrate the anniversary of their man's death on the sixteenth. On the Elvis World calendar, the death date is the highest of holy days, far more compelling than his January birthday. After all, Elvis was born just another poor boy, but he died a King. During the week before, so many people mill around Graceland that it is virtually impossible to drive past or even find a piece of sidewalk on which to stand.

Back before the Denny's on Union Avenue became the Cupboard (which, by the way, is the best place in town to eat southern-style vegetables), it used to have a breakfast buffet that attracted Elvis fans on their way to visit Graceland. It was a nice big morning spread not unlike most others at chain restaurants, with one exception. As a salute to the King, whose favorite thing to eat was well-done bacon, this Denny's kept two extra-large trays piled high with bacon that was perfectly cooked . . . for Elvis — that is, nearly black. Legions of his fans came away from the buffet table with plates stacked with pounds of crisp bacon arranged in great tall pyres.

Amazingly, Buntyn was scarcely affected by the tumult of Elvis week. That day not a single tourist was eating lunch there, except for us. One reason no out-of-towners went to Buntyn is that it was hard to find, quite literally on the wrong side of the tracks. You parked your car a short distance from the restaurant on one side of the railroad tracks, then peered to see if a train was coming. If not, or if it was a long, slow train loaded with bales of cotton or soybeans from the delta, you could hightail it across the tracks to get to the restaurant.

From the outside, Buntyn didn't look like much of a place to eat: a big plain storefront, not exactly shabby, but certainly not landscaped or fluffed up in any way. The name of the place was painted on a plate-glass window that looked as melancholy as any rendered by Edward Hopper.

"May we please see some menus?" we asked the waitress as she walked by. Most people who ate at Buntyn didn't need menus. They knew what they wanted.

The list of vegetables at Buntyn was the edible equivalent of a Burpee seed catalogue. On an average day, you would find:

buttered hominy
English peas
field peas
black-eyed peas
butter beans
fried corn
corn on the cob
candied yams
cole slaw
mashed potatoes and gravy
rice with gravy
candied apples
stewed raisins
snap peas with ham
collard greens with ham bone
turnip greens
eggplant soufflé
dirty rice
squash and cheese casserole
perfection salad
macaroni and cheese
watermelon chunks
carrot and raisin slaw

No one ever asked the waitress for a veggie plate. Southern vegetables are not *veggies,* a word that implies undercooked health food.
Southern vegetables have had all the raw cooked out of them. String
beans are simmered with a hunk of ham bone for enough hours to be
as soft as velvet. Eggplants, squashes, and the like are cooked until
they are no longer stiff, then bathed in butter and sugar and sorghum

and flecked with jewels of crisp lardons and flakes of hot vinegary peppers. An all-vegetable plate lunch is magnificent to behold: rivers of sorghum-sweet syrup and tidal pools of butter float around hills and drifts of garden-fresh vegetables cooked into a gentle stupor.

"Whatchy'all want?" asked our waitress, notepad in hand.

"Everything," Michael said, and then offered his usual preamble, designed to disarm any waitress who might be shocked when confronted with two ravenous strangers apparently intent on devouring whatever they can spear with a fork. "We are from out of town," he proclaimed in a soothing voice, as though he hadn't already taken half a dozen pictures of the dining room's décor and the napkin-wrapped silverware. "So don't worry if we order more than we eat. We just want to taste everything."

"That's fine," she said.

With a burst of energy, Michael began to order. "I would like the fried chicken *and* the smothered pork chop, and for my vegetables I would like the squash, the yams, the collards, the turnip greens, the watermelon, and the cole slaw. Can we get a bottle of hot vinegar pepper for the greens? And also yeast rolls as well as corn bread, and could you put aside a piece of lemon icebox pie in case they run out, and also a dish of banana pudding, and, oh yeah, a Mr. Pibb." Michael is big on drinking the soda pop *ordinaire* of the region.

The waitress was scribbling fast but unfazed. "An' you, ma'am?"

Jane ordered just about everything else on the menu.

"Thank you," she said. We could hear the juicy soles of her orthopedic white waitress shoes creaking as she headed to the kitchen.

The Mr. Pibb arrived with a wrapped drinking straw stuck to the outside of its moist glass. Along with the soda came a basket of fresh yeast rolls.

Yeast rolls are a nearly lost art, but occupying a booth at Buntyn at lunchtime was a reminder of just how good this simple bread can taste. Buntyn's rolls were huge and hot, and the smell of the yeast was heavy in the air. They divided neatly in half at the first tug, and the veil of flour over the top lingered on your hands after the roll was eaten. Snuggled next to the rolls in the bread basket were squares of cracklin' corn bread: yellow cornmeal swirled with buttermilk and butter and eggs into a batter laced with cracklin's. As the corn bread bakes, their unctuous flavor permeates it. No butter was needed.

Michael began to moan. He took his index finger and gently prodded the plump yeast roll just for the pleasure of its touch, then shoveled half a square of corn bread into his mouth.

"Mmmph," he said to Jane, who understood precisely what he meant.

We were deep in roll reverie when we spotted someone we knew sitting only a few tables away: Todd Morgan, whom we had met ten years before while writing *Elvis World*.

Todd had been fresh out of Arkansas: blond, pink-cheeked, newly arrived at Graceland to become a publicist for the Elvis estate. At that time, in the mid-1980s, Graceland went from being a minor curiosity known mostly to devout Elvis followers to a tourist attraction right up there with Disney World. Todd, who was six foot four, came to town crammed into an eye-jolting green plaid suit. But this boy was no yokel: he had plans. At the top of the list was to marry Lisa Marie Presley and to have their honeymoon in Elvis's fake fur–covered bed on the second floor of the mansion.

Clearly, the person sitting near us at Buntyn was a new Todd. Just as Graceland had become corporately spit-polished since Elvis had left the building, so had our old friend. This person at the next table was an Exec-U-Todd, substantially slimmed down, outfitted in an expensive pinstriped suit, his hair razor-cut to surgical precision. He had taken off his jacket to eat, and we could see the French cuffs of his shirt embroidered with his initials.

We began to compute how much we wanted to rekindle our friendship, at the expense of losing focus on the feast that was about to be served. One of the joys of traveling together is not seeing anyone we know. But we had no decision to make. Todd had seen us, too. Whether he wanted to or not, his inbred southern politeness made him stand up, walk over to our booth, and hug us with a warm country welcome.

He indicated to the waitress to bring his food to our table. It was he who had introduced us to the pleasures of Buntyn.

"Todd, you're so trim," Jane said.

"I work out. I eat yogurt for lunch at my desk." He grinned.

We hoped we wouldn't make him uncomfortable with the vast amount of food we had ordered, due to arrive from the kitchen at any moment.

"So what are you doing at Buntyn?" we asked.

"I'm hiding from the mobs of Elvis fans," Todd said. "And I am eating! I mean, I am *eating!* This is my pig-out. I figure that it's the only way I can get through this week and stay sane."

The waitress approached with two fully loaded trays. Behind her was another waitress, and behind her a busboy, all heading our way, balancing trays of food.

In short time we realized that even though we had ordered so much, Todd had ordered an equal amount. It was a big booth with a big table, but there was no space left uncovered by the time the waitresses walked away.

Todd reached for a bottle of Red Devil hot sauce and unscrewed the little red cap. "Every August sixteenth, I go food-crazy. It's like I am channeling Elvis, and he is saying, 'Eat, son, eat!'"

There were years of history to catch up on between the three of us. But at this moment, none of us wanted to talk. Our eyes were fixed on the food. Platters of it, bowls of it, side dishes, and little salad plates. Succulent fried chicken breasts abutted kaleidoscopic congealed salads of jewel-yellow Jell-O layered with shredded carrots and bits of cabbage. Bowls of long-simmered rich brown gravy knocked against a dish of freshly mashed potatoes, stationed next to buttered orange yams with lightly singed marshmallows melting down their sides.

Todd had ordered country ham. An oval plate held a sheaf of thin cinnabar slices rimmed with translucent amber fat. They were awash in a puddle of red-eye gravy, salty ham juice mingled with a splash of black coffee. He dabbed at the gravy with torn shreds of yeast roll, then cut a small triangle of meat and forked it up along with the softened bread.

Jane slid her fork into the eggplant soufflé, a custard as light as whipped meringue but with the slightly bitter crunch of aubergine.

Michael gnawed on fried chicken, its crust clinging tenaciously to the pan-fried meat as clear juices ran down his chin. "Oh, my God, did you taste the okra?" he asked no one in particular as he popped tiny crisp-fried nuggets of that indigenous, strangely sticky vegetable into his mouth.

A platter of corn on the cob that tasted as if it had been harvested that morning came alongside a plate of plain, thick-sliced tomatoes from the Buntyn garden. Near that was a bowl full of flamingo-pink watermelon chunks, which Todd referred to by their proper Arkansas name, saline melon. We watched him sprinkle the melon with salt before he ate it. "There is absolutely nothing better than this," he declared as he took a breather and scanned the table of good food like a sultan admiring his harem. We needed no convincing.

Time passes fast when you eat well, and as we began to slow our pace and glance up from the meal, we noticed that most of the lunch crowd was gone. Our table looked like a combat zone, littered with crumpled napkins and abandoned forks stuck into piles of food like battle flags claiming a hill.

Todd reached down, opened his belt, and unfastened the top button of his suit pants. "Oh, mercy!" he said.

As the waitress began to clear the table, he filled us in on some of our favorite eateries in town. He rhapsodized about the Cozy Corner and its hickory-smoked Cornish hens; he assured us that the famous you-peel-'em shrimp and lemon icebox pie at Gridley's hadn't changed at all; he said they still served pot likker and corn sticks at the Little Tea Shop down by Cotton Row.

We asked him what he knew about the restaurant at which we had made reservations for dinner that night. We will call it Dyvina — not its real name.

He made a face that was hard to read but looked like disappointed surprise. "Remember the pork chops at the Four Way Grill?" he asked, referring to a glorious meal we had shared with him long ago in one of the city's venerable soul-food cafés. "They're still the best."

"Isn't Dyvina any good?" we asked again. "It wins every culinary award."

Todd was too busy trying to get his pants to rebutton to respond. "It was great to see y'all, but I've got to get back. I would say to stop by Graceland later on, but it's a madhouse. Best you wait until things clear out."

We said goodbye and watched through the front window as he hopped across the railroad tracks to where his car was parked.

We were stuffed, but it was our duty to sample Buntyn's banana pudding before we called it quits. The meringue that covered the nursery-soft pudding was crisp-edged and cloud-light, a miracle in the Memphis humidity, which permeates everything in town. The pudding was snuggled into a bed of half-crushed vanilla wafers. We spooned into the soft stuff like happy babies, and when it was gone we finally knew that it was time to return to our room at the Peabody Hotel for a rest. We paid the bill, including Todd's share, which we'd insisted on picking up for old time's sake. The total for all three of us was $28, plus tip.

We slowly drove our way toward downtown Memphis, marveling at the hordes of Elvis fans from all over the globe who spilled into the streets like a vast free-form parade. The Elvis Club of Tasmania marched down Beale Street in matching pink nylon jackets. Watching them, we nearly ran over a couple of Asian El-fans wearing spandex body suits covered with silk-screened images of the King.

When we arrived back at the Peabody Hotel, we made our way through the human obstacle course in the lobby. The place was mobbed with Elvis fans and conventioneers come to town for other passions and jobs. There were old black ladies in gold lamé turbans, whose plastic badges identified them as members of the Mt. Pisgah Baptist Church, knots of red-faced Shriners in their grand poobah fezzes, and slender, perfume-drenched socialites attending a rehearsal dinner in the grand ballroom. We pushed into the crowded elevator, hit our floor button, hurried to our room, ripped off our clothes, cranked the air conditioner as high as possible, swaddled ourselves in terrycloth hotel robes, and fell on the bed. It was two in the afternoon. We had until seven to get our appetites back.

No problem.

By six, we were showered and dressed and ready to go. We had eaten so much barbecue and banana pudding in the past few days that we thought it might be a nice shock to the system to eat something that wasn't smothered in hot sauce or deep-fried. Dyvina specialized in fusion cuisine.

We had made reservations under our real names. It was a serious miscalculation.

The problem was that Dyvina, like just about every other chef we've ever met, was a supremely generous person. A chef's job, after all, is to give sustenance. Chefs delight in other people's pleasure, offering special dishes to friends and strangers who show interest in their work.

We knew we were in trouble when Dyvina herself, decked out in chef's whites, greeted us at the door. She asked if we would please place ourselves in her hands and allow her to prepare a special feast. We thanked her but explained that we would prefer to order from her standard menu.

Clearly disappointed, Dyvina reluctantly agreed. The waiter handed us menus. He picked up the large linen napkins on the table and with a theatrical gesture snapped them open and placed them on our laps.

The menu wasn't as much fun to read as Buntyn's, but it was interesting. There was lots of ghee and lemongrass along with foie gras and feuilliettés. On the wall were paintings of European landscapes.

The waiter returned. We ordered. And we waited. As we waited, we discussed the fact that we were the only diners in the place.

We were inordinately happy to see the waiter arrive with two large dinner plates, which he set before us with an impressive flourish.

We looked down to see nothing we had ordered. Instead, on each broad circle of china was positioned a naked pink hunk of undercooked fish surrounded by a puddle of bright orange and red sauces. The half-cooked fish sat in the center of a masterpiece of the saucier's squeeze-bottle artwork. Jane remarked that it vaguely resembled a large canvas she had submitted for her MFA thesis.

"Dyvina would like you to try this. It is one of her signature dishes," the waiter said with pride.

"Oy," Jane said with a groan.

Shrimp and lobsters notwithstanding, Jane hates fish. She can scarf down the occasional Mrs. Paul's fishstick, or something deep-fried and served in a basket covered with lots of French fries and cole slaw, but fish that tastes like fish, especially half-cooked fish *moderne*, is the stuff of nightmares.

Fortunately, Michael likes fish. "This is good," he said merrily, forking up Dyvina's little treasure from the plate. "I think the sauce is some sort of mango thing."

"Have mine," Jane offered.

"Ah, you liked it!" said the waiter as he returned to whisk away the plates. From a tray he had parked on a nearby stand, he swirled another course down in front of us. "Enjoy!"

More fish. This one had blue flesh instead of pink, and its sauce was an ominous mauve.

"Shit," Michael said when we were alone. But he dutifully ate it and then, without being asked, reached over and plucked Jane's portion off her plate.

"What's in the sauce? Blueberries? Plums?" Jane asked.

"All I know is that we didn't order it," Michael said.

The waiter appeared again. He had a bounce to his step. "And this . . . ," he said, taking a dramatic pause, "is a special gravlax that we serve only twice a year."

"Lucky us," Jane said.

"What do we do now?" Michael said when we were once again alone with the unwanted dish.

"Leave it to me," Jane said, upending her large, elegant plate and sliding the gravlax into the napkin on her lap. "Give me your plate," she commanded. She dumped the other serving of gravlax in her lap, twirled the ends of the napkin together, and walked to the ladies' room.

She soon reappeared and sat down with a smug look on her face, but not before grabbing a fresh napkin from a nearby empty table and spreading it on her lap.

The waiter appeared again, and again, both times with fish, then with a helping of very rare duck breast fanned out on an enormous platter with sliced figs.

Like a jungle cat lying in wait for its prey, Jane followed the waiter's entry into the dining room, her eyes locked on the two plates he carried. As soon as he disappeared behind the swinging door, she snatched another napkin from an adjacent table, plopped the fish into it, and walked briskly to the bathroom.

"That was fast," the waiter commented to Michael as he glanced at the empty plates.

Alone in the ladies' room, Jane whipped open the big linen napkin and dumped the oversized fillets into the bowl. She hit the flush lever, but instead of disappearing, the pieces of fish stuck. Water began to back up toward the rim. Jane flushed again, and for a moment the water seemed to swirl downward. Then, with a great gurgle, the fish formed a massive bolus and the water surged up, over, and onto the marble-tiled floor.

Jane peeled off her silk blouse, stuck her bare arm deep into the toilet bowl, and began pulling hunks out, flushing and reflushing until, with a mighty gulp, the toilet emptied itself. Using every paper towel in the ladies' room, she did her best to wipe the overflow from the floor, washed her hands, put her blouse back on, and returned to the table looking damp and pale.

"Could we have the check?" Michael asked. "My wife is not feeling well."

"Dyvina will be so disappointed. She has many more dishes for you to try."

"I'm sorry, but we really have to go," Jane piped up, with desperation in her voice. "Let's get out of here before someone goes in the bathroom," she then whispered to Michael.

As a farewell gift, Dyvina handed us a big shopping bag. *More fish!* we thought simultaneously, wondering if the toilets at the Peabody Hotel had more substantial plumbing than Dyvina's.

But it was not food. It was a binder filled with a lifetime's supply of Dyvina's press clippings and promotional material, as thick as a vintage Sears catalogue. "For you to read later," she said.

Safe again in our terrycloth robes, we mixed two double Alka-Seltzers, burped in unison, and felt slightly better.

As Michael lay on the bed, Jane began rummaging through the shopping bag, looking at the clippings.

"Michael," she said in a small voice, after a long silence. "There really is something wrong with us. Look at all these famous people who love the stuff she cooks."

"Good. Then they can eat it," Michael said, reaching for the remote control and finding a rerun of *Bob Newhart.*

From the street outside the room we could hear the muffled sounds of Beale Street blues, and from the rooftop dance club of the Peabody an Elvis ballad floating downward.

"Wasn't Buntyn great?" Jane said sleepily. "Let's try to visit Graceland tomorrow. I want to see if the Jungle Room still has the green shag carpeting."

"Sure," Michael said, "but we have to go there early, because we need to drive down Route 61 in the afternoon. I want to find that grocery store that serves shrimp and grits in the back room at supper. The place where every table is in a private curtained room."

"Yeah." Jane sighed. "Remember how they pronounce shrimp *swimp?*"

"Maybe we can find that old guy near Mound Bayou who carves walking sticks."

"And what about Yazoo City? Didn't someone send us a postcard about a drugstore that still has a soda jerk who serves drinks like Green Rivers? And Michael, you really need a haircut. Let's see if we can find a barbershop."

"Yes!" Michael agreed. "We'll ask the barber where to eat."

"And this time we've got to get to the Crystal Grill in Greenwood for coconut meringue pie."

". . . and pompano at Lusco's . . ."

". . . and T-bones with garlic salad and cast-iron-skillet French fries over at Doe's Eat Place . . ."

"Do we need a wake-up call?"

"Naw."

At dawn we were on our way again, following the long white line.

# Whipping Cream Pound Cake

The recipe for this oh-so-southern pound cake was given to us by Janelle McComb, who was Elvis Presley's friend from the time he was a boy in Tupelo, Mississippi. This buttery cream cake was one of Elvis's favorites. Janelle used to bake two loaves of it every Christmas and take them to Graceland. On a good day, Elvis could eat one all by himself, sharing the other with his entourage.

3 cups sugar

16 tablespoons (2 sticks) unsalted butter, softened

7 large eggs, at room temperature

3 cups cake flour, sifted twice before measuring (do not use self-rising flour)

1 cup heavy cream (not whipped)

2 teaspoons vanilla extract

Thoroughly butter and flour a 10-inch tube pan.

Cream together the sugar and butter in a large bowl with an electric mixer until fluffy.

Add the eggs one at a time, beating well after each addition. Mix in half the flour, then the cream, then the other half of the flour. Beat for 5 minutes. Add the vanilla.

Pour the batter into the prepared pan. Set the pan in a cold oven and turn the heat to 350 degrees. Bake for 1 to 1½ hours, until a sharp knife inserted in the cake comes out clean. Cool the cake in the pan for 5 minutes. Remove it from the pan and cool it thoroughly. Wrapped well in aluminum foil, this cake keeps for several days.

10 TO 12 SERVINGS

# 'Naner Pudding

Banana pudding was another Elvis favorite, which he called 'naner pudding because he liked talking baby talk, especially about food. Elvis was not unique. Banana pudding is a nearly universal comfort food for adults who need to feel nurtured. It's especially popular in the mid-South, in homes as well as on café menus. It is *always* made using Nabisco Nilla Wafers, except at the Loveless Café of Nashville, where pastry chef Alyssa Hunt makes her own cookies. As delicious as that special version is, here is the classic café way to do it, a recipe we were given many years ago by a cook in Arkansas.

⅓  cup sugar
   Pinch of salt
3  tablespoons cornstarch
1  12-ounce can evaporated milk
1½ cups whole milk
4  egg yolks
1  teaspoon vanilla extract
16–20  vanilla wafers
2  large ripe bananas, sliced
⅔  cup dark brown sugar, packed
4–5  teaspoons hot water
1  cup heavy cream (not whipped)

Mix together the sugar, salt, and cornstarch in a medium bowl. Add the evaporated milk and whole milk. Cook in the top of a double boiler or in a small saucepan set in a larger one filled with several inches of water, stirring frequently, until the mixture coats the back of a spoon.

Beat the egg yolks in a medium bowl and add about ½ cup of the warm pudding, stirring, then add the yolks to the pudding, whisking it vigorously. Cook for 3 minutes longer, continuing to stir. Mix in the vanilla. Cool to room temperature, stirring occasionally.

Layer the vanilla wafers and bananas in an 8-inch square baking dish.

Melt the brown sugar in the hot water, creating a thick paste. Stir the paste into the pudding just enough to create streaks. Pour this over the wafers and bananas. Refrigerate.

When the pudding is well chilled, whip the cream, spread it gently across the top, and serve.

6 TO 8 SERVINGS

# Featured Restaurants by State

ALABAMA
Mary's Place
5075 Highway 188
Coden, AL 36523
251-873-4514

ARIZONA
El Charro
311 N. Court Ave.
Tucson, AZ 85701
520-622-1922

ARKANSAS
Coursey's
Highway 65
St. Joe, AR 72675
870-439-2503

Rhoda's Famous Hot Tamales
714 Saint Mary St.
Lake Village, AR 71653
870-265-3108

CALIFORNIA
Jocko's
125 N. Thompson Ave.
Nipomo, CA 93444
805-929-3686

CONNECTICUT
Blackie's
2200 Waterbury Rd.
Cheshire, CT 06410
203-699-1819

Frank Pepe Pizzeria Napoletana
157 Wooster St.
New Haven, CT 06511
203-865-5762

Louis' Lunch
261–263 Crown St.
New Haven, CT 06510
203-562-5507

Olive Market
19 Main St.
Georgetown, CT 06829
203-544-8134

O'Rourke's Diner
728 Main St.
Middletown, CT 06457
860-346-6101

Phillip's Diner
740 Main St. South
Woodbury, CT 06798
203-263-2516

Rawley's
1886 Post Rd.
Fairfield, CT 06824
203-259-9023

Ridgefield Ice Cream Shop
680 Danbury Rd.
Ridgefield, CT 06877
203-438-3094

Sally's Apizza
237 Wooster St.
New Haven, CT 06511
203-624-5271

Shady Glen Dairy Stores
840 Middle Tpk. East
Manchester, CT 06050
860-649-4245

Super Duper Weenie
306 Black Rock Tpk.
Fairfield, CT 06825
203-334-DOGS

Ted's
1046 Broad St.
Meriden, CT 06450
203-237-6660

DELAWARE
Helen's Sausage House
4866 N. Dupont Hwy.
Smyrna, DE 19977
302-653-4200

FLORIDA
Blue Heaven Restaurant
729 Thomas St.
Key West, FL 33040
305-296-8666

GEORGIA

Blue Willow Inn
294 N. Cherokee Rd.
Social Circle, GA 30025
770-464-2131
800-552-8813

Harold's Barbecue
171 McDonough Blvd. SE
Atlanta, GA 30315
404-627-9268

Mamie's Kitchen
1294 S. Main St. NE
Conyers, GA 30012
770-922-0131

Mary Mac's Tea Room
224 Ponce de Leon Ave. NE
Atlanta, GA 30308
404-876-1800

ILLINOIS

Al's #1 Italian Beef
1079 W. Taylor St.
Chicago, IL 60607
312-226-4017
630-858-9121
800-618-0666

Carson's
8617 Niles Center Rd.
Skokie, IL 60077
847-675-6800

Garrett Popcorn Shop
670 N. Michigan Ave.
Chicago, IL 60611
312-944-4730
888-4-POPCORN

Gene & Georgetti
500 Franklin St.
Chicago, IL 60610-4169
312-527-3718

Walker Brothers Pancake
House
153 Green Bay Rd.
Wilmette, IL 60091
847-251-6000

INDIANA

Nick's Kitchen
506 N. Jefferson St.
Huntington, IN 46750
260-356-6618

IOWA
Bill Zuber's Dugout
Homestead, IA
319-622-3911
800-522-8883

Ronneburg Restaurant
4408 220th Trail
Amana, IA 52203
319-622-3641
888-348-4686

White Way Café
718 5th Ave.
Durant, IA 52747
563-785-6202

KANSAS
Brookville Hotel
105 E. Lafayette Ave.
Abilene, KS 67410
785-263-2244

Chicken Annie's Original
1143 E. 600th Ave.
Pittsburg, KS 66762
620-231-9460

Chicken Mary's
1133 E. 600th Ave.

Pittsburg, KS 66762
620-231-9510

Doc's Steak House
1515 N. Broadway
Wichita, KS 67214
316-264-4735

Ira Price
3102 N. Kansas Ave.
Topeka, KS 66617
785-286-2187

KENTUCKY
Bon Ton Mini Mart
2036 Madison St.
Henderson, KY 42420
270-826-1207

MAINE
Moody's Diner
Route 1
Waldoboro, ME 04572
207-832-7785

MARYLAND
Copsey's
28976 Three Notch Rd.
Mechanicsville, MD 20659
301-884-4235

Leonard Copsey's
29084 Three Notch Rd.
Mechanicsville, MD 20659
301-884-9529

St. Mary's Landing
29935 Three Notch Rd.
Charlotte Hall, MD 20622
301-884-3287

MASSACHUSETTS
Durgin-Park
340 Faneuil Hall Marketplace
Boston, MA 02109
617-227-2038

MICHIGAN
Cherry Hut
246 Michigan Ave.
Beulah, MI 49617
231-882-4431

MISSISSIPPI
Crystal Grill
423 Carrollton Ave.
Greenwood, MS 38930
662-453-6530

Doe's Eat Place
502 Nelson St.

Greenville, MS 38701
662-334-3315

Hick's Tamales
305 S. State St.
Clarksdale, MS 38614
662-624-9887
888-404-4257

Lusco's
722 Carrollton Ave.
Greenwood, MS 38930
601-453-5365

MISSOURI
C&K Barbecue
4390 Jennings Station Rd.
St. Louis, MO 63121
314-385-8100

MONTANA
Eddie's Supper Club
3725 2nd Ave. North
Great Falls, MT 59405
406-453-1616

Pekin Noodle Parlor
117 S. Main St.
Butte, MT 59701
406-782-2217

Pork Chop John's
8 Mercury St.
Butte, MT 59701
406-782-0812
800-782-0812

NEW MEXICO
El Norteño Restaurant
6416 Zuni Rd. SE
Albuquerque, NM 87108
505-256-1431

Navajo Chief Café
815 E. Route 66
Gallup, NM 87301
505-722-4020

San Marcos Café
Highway 14
Cerrillos, NM 87010
505-471-9298

NEW YORK
Anchor Bar
1047 Main St.
Buffalo, NY 14209
716-886-8920

Patsy's Pizzeria
2287 First Ave.

New York, NY 10035
212-534-9783

Phil's Chicken House
1208 Maine Rd.
Endicott, NY 13760
607-748-7574
800-523-8863

Sharkey's
56 Glenwood Ave.
Binghamton, NY 13905
607-729-9201

NORTH CAROLINA
Hannah's Bar-B-Q
137 Blowing Rock Rd.
Lenoir, NC 28645
828-754-7032

NORTH DAKOTA
Carol Widman's Candy Com-
pany
4325 13th Ave. SW
Fargo, ND 58103
701-281-8664

Farmers' Inn
102 3rd Ave. North
Havana, ND 58043
701-724-3849

OHIO

Balaton Restaurant
13133 Shaker Square
Cleveland, OH 44120
216-921-9691

Flat Iron Café
1114 Center St.
Cleveland, OH 44113
216-696-6968

Henry's Restaurant
6275 Route 40 SE
West Jefferson, OH 43162
614-879-9321

Liberty Gathering Place
111 North Detroit St.
West Liberty, OH 43357
937-465-3081

Pine Club
1926 Brown St.
Dayton, OH 45409
937-228-7463

Putz's Creamy Whip
Putz Place and West Fork Rd.
Cincinnati, OH 45211
513-681-8668

Rick's Café
86 North Main St.
Chagrin Falls, OH 44022
440-247-7666

OKLAHOMA

Cattlemen's Steakhouse
1309 S. Agnew
Oklahoma City, OK 73108
405-236-0416

OREGON

Bar M Ranch
58840 Bar M Lane
Adams, OR 97810
541-566-3381
888-824-3381

Cimmiyotti's
137 S. Main St.
Pendleton, OR 97801
541-276-4314

PENNSYLVANIA

Dutch Kitchen Restaurant
Route 61
Frackville, PA 17931
570-874-3265

Pat's King of Steaks
1237 E. Passyunk Ave.
Philadelphia, PA 19147
215-468-1546

RHODE ISLAND
Allie's Donuts
3661 Quaker Lane
North Kingstown, RI 02852
401-295-8036

Haven Brothers Diner
72 Spruce St.
Corner of Fulton and Dor-
rance
Providence, RI 02903
401-861-7777

John's New York System
326 Cranston St.
Providence, RI 02907
401-861-7090

SOUTH CAROLINA
Beacon Drive-In
255 John B. White, Sr. Blvd.
Spartanburg, SC 29306
864-585-9387

Carl Duke's
789 Chestnut St.
Orangeburg, SC 29915
803-534-9418

Fishnet Seafoods
3832 Savannah Highway
Johns Island, SC 29455
843-571-2423

TENNESSEE
Alcenia's
317 N. Main St.
Memphis, TN 38103
901-523-0200

Barksdale Restaurant
237 South Cooper St.
Memphis, TN 38104
901-722-2193

Belle Meade Buffet Cafeteria
4534 Harding Rd.
Nashville, TN 37205
615-298-5572

Cozy Corner Restaurant
745 North Parkway
Memphis, TN 38105
901-527-9158

The Cupboard
1400 Union Ave.
Memphis, TN 38104
901-276-8015

Dyer's Burgers
205 Beale St.
Memphis, TN 38103
901-527-3937

Gridley's Bar-B-Q
6430 Winchester Rd.
Memphis, TN 38815
901-794-5997

Little Tea Shop
69 Monroe Ave.
Memphis, TN 38103
901-525-6000

Loveless Café
8400 Highway 100
Nashville, TN 37221
615-646-9700

Ridgewood Barbecue
900 Elizabethtown Highway
Bluff City, TN 37618
423-538-7543

Satsuma
417 Union St.
Nashville, TN 37219
615-256-0760

TEXAS
City Market
633 E. Davis St.
Luling, TX 78648
830-875-9019

VERMONT
Curtis's Barbecue
Route 5
Putney, VT 05346
802-387-5474

The Dorset Inn
8 Church St.
Dorset, VT 05251
802-867-5500
877-367-7389

WASHINGTON
Oasis Steak and Seafood
Restaurant
85698 Highway 339
Milton-Freewater, OR 97862
541-938-4776

WEST VIRGINIA

Colasessano's
506 Pennsylvania Ave.
Fairmont, WV 26554
304-363-9713

Southern Kitchen
MacCorkle Ave. and 53rd
Charleston, WV 25301
304-925-3154

WISCONSIN

Benjamin's Delicatessen (now
  Benji's)
4165 N. Oakland Ave.
Milwaukee, WI 53211
414-332-7777

# The Recipes by Category

# Index

Entries in SMALL CAPITALS refer to recipes.